Hollywood

G A Y S

Hollywood
G A Y S

*Conversations
With:*

CARY GRANT

LIBERACE

TONY PERKINS

PAUL LYNDE

CESAR ROMERO

BRAD DAVIS

RANDOLPH SCOTT

JAMES COCO

WILLIAM HAINES

DAVID LEWIS

by Boze Hadleigh

BARRICADE BOOKS / NEW YORK

Published by Barricade Books Inc.
150 Fifth Avenue
New York, NY 10011

Printed in the United States of America.

Library of Congress Cataloging-in-Publication Data

Hadleigh, Boze
    Hollywood gays / by Boze Hadleigh.
        p.   cm.
    Includes index.
    ISBN 1-56980-083-9
    1. Gay actors—California—Los Angeles—Interviews.
2. Motion picture actors and actresses—California—
   Los Angeles—Interviews.
PN1995.9.H55H33 1996
791.43'028'092279494—dc20   96-20453
                                     CIP

Page layout by CompuDesign

First Printing

TO RONNIE

ACKNOWLEDGMENTS

WITH WARM THANKS to those mentioned in this book, and to: Jim Backus, Michael Cart, Carlos Clarens, Tom Connelly, Carl David, Samson DeBrier, Richard Dyer, John Erman, Lee Graham, Colin Higgins, Stan Kamen, Sheila James Kuehl, Joan Nestle, George Rose, Tom Steele, Steve Turner, and Richard Valley.

For photos from their collections, Manuel Cordova, Ken Ferguson, Dick Sargent, and Douglas Whitney.

Also Lyle and Carole Stuart, Sandra Lee Stuart, Lisa Beck, Bonnie Segall, and everyone at Barricade Books.

And of course, Linda Fresia.

CONTENTS

INTRODUCTION

Hollywood is where the truth lies . . . still.

In 1933 Clark Gable and John Huston each killed a woman in a car accident. The studio system protected the men and kept it out of the newspapers, paid the necessary hush-money and out-of-court settlements, and ensured that neither career was hampered by the tragedy, each apparently due to drunk driving.

Also in 1933 actor William Haines was spied upon and found to have another man on his cot in his room at a downtown YMCA. He and the sailor were arrested, imprisoned, and both their careers were killed. The studio system kept Haines's name out of the papers—it would have embarrassed MGM—and kept the case from ever reaching court, but Louis B. Mayer fired the former silent star and saw to it that no other studio would hire him.

In February, 1996, columnist Marilyn Beck reported that accused wife-beater Billy Dee Williams was the latest in a long, sorry line of male celebrities who have been charged with or convicted of battering their wives or girlfriends (e.g., Dudley Moore, Sean Penn, Richard Pryor, Anthony Quinn, Burt Reynolds, Jim Brown, Axl Rose, Mickey Rourke, George C. Scott, Steven Seagal, O.J. Simpson, David Soul, and James Wood). As Beck noted, none of this hurt the (heterosexual) men's careers. In fact, one of the 1996 Academy Award nominees for Best Actor was Sean Penn.

The same month saw a star-studded tribute to producer Don Simpson, who died in his early 50s of a drug overdose (the previous summer, the 44-year-old doctor treating Simpson for drug abuse died at Simpson's estate of a drug overdose). The ultra-aggressive and successful, casually homophobic producer whom Hollywood was eulogizing as a master storyteller and model moviemaker was more than a batterer—as Beck revealed, Simpson once disfigured a female prostitute, fond as he was of dominance and rough stuff.

Another 1996 Oscar nominee was Mel Gibson, whose movies are often larded with homophobia. One form of which is de-gaying a character—as Gibson did to the protagonist in his directorial bow, *The Man Without a Face* (based on a novel), and to the gay or bisexual composer Beethoven in *Immortal Beloved*, which Gibson's company produced. That tinseltown still doesn't consider homophobia an issue is obvious via *Braveheart*, nominated for ten Academy Awards, more than any other picture in 1996. (It actually won five, including "best" picture and director.)

L.A. Reader critic Andy Klein pointed out that *Braveheart*— directed, coproduced by, and starring Gibson—includes a sorry scene played for laughs: throwing a gay man out of a window to his death. And that although the film purports to be historical— had the incident occurred, its inclusion would be justifiable, though not the tone of levity and satisfaction—this episode (involving royalty) *never happened*. Therefore, the gratuitous and hate-mongering scene presents homophobia as "entertainment" at a time when gay-bashings and murders are at an all-time high.

Imagine the same scene being filmed, or viewed, with any *other* minority as victim. . . .

Back in 1933, MGM began to banish its homosexual male stars (Garbo was still a big moneymaker for them). It canceled the contracts of Ramon Novarro and Nils Asther, and, as mentioned, blacklisted Billy Haines, a fading but still viable leading man. (Ten years later, MGM saved the career of—and its future profits from—another gay actor trapped in similar circumstances; he was younger and still big box-office material.)

In August, 1933, MGM art director Cedric Gibbons was helming his first movie; the cast included Rod La Rocque, formerly a silent star, but by then a supporting actor. Three and a half weeks into production, *Tarzan and His Mate* was shut down. Weeks later, it resumed—minus the two men. No explanation was given, and memos covering the episode are missing from the studio's film file. Gibbons did receive credit and stayed on—a valuable studio asset—for decades, but he never got another chance to direct. He remained confined to the art department.

What happened? Hollywood's greatest fear, its least mentionable subject. For, apart from homophobia *on* screen—practiced from the mid-1930s through the late '50s by the exclusion of all gay, lesbian, and bi characters—*off* the screen Hollywood, then as now, lived in panic. In that summer of '33, Gibbons and La Rocque—each gay or bisexual, both contractually married to notable women (La Rocque to the reputedly sapphic Hungarian actress Vilma Banky, Gibbons to sometimes-bi star Dolores Del Rio)—began an affair, somebody found out and told, and that set Hollywood off. That the men weren't professionally destroyed had much to do with their having wives. Plus, Gibbons' already-famous, sole child was Oscar—*he* designed the coveted statuette.

The necessarily brief affair was later confirmed by Del Rio (whose first gay husband committed suicide), Johnny "Tarzan" Weissmuller, MGM director George Cukor, MGM set decorator Edwin B. Willis, and . . . William Haines.

Openly gay actor Ron Vawter explained, "In show biz, they usually go after the guy without a wife. As if to warn that if he had a wife, this wouldn't happen. It's what Christopher Isherwood called it: a heterosexual dictatorship." In *The Gay Book of Days* a list of 24 famous men arrested on gay-sex or "morals" charges includes Leonardo da Vinci, Botticelli, Oscar Wilde, Jean Genet, William Haines, Pier Paolo Pasolini, Sir John Gielgud, Montgomery Clift, and Alan Turing, "the English Einstein" and father of the modern computer. Of this group, only Oscar Wilde was married.

Today's Hollywood requires, if not a contractual mate, then a romantic, possibly live-in "love" of the opposite sex. Success on a national network or studio scale prods a player into the age-old game. While doing stand-up at San Francisco lesbian bars, comedian Margaret Cho sometimes stated that she had sex with women, according to *Deneuve* magazine. Once Cho got her own ABC-TV sitcom, the *All-American Girl*, she began referring to a boyfriend, her "partner in life," Scott Silverman. But it so happens that Silverman, a fellow comic, is openly gay. . . .

Likewise, in 1995 Jodie Foster was nominated for an Oscar for *Nell*. Columnist Arlene Walsh of *Beverly Hills (213)* reported that Foster had "taken up residence with casting director Randy Stone, but according to my sources, her love interests lie in another direction. The dish is that stories are being planted to make the perennial bachelorette more simpatico to Oscar voters." Most columnists treated the story as a romance, never questioning its motivation—nor was Jodie seemingly aware that no actress under age 60 ever won a *third* Academy Award.

Foster attended the Oscar ceremonies with Stone, smiling and holding hands with him. That evening *he* won an award, for his documentary *Trevor*, a teenage coming-out story. Later in the year, Stone came out as gay in *The Advocate*. . . .

(Barring a boyfriend or husband, lesbian performers sometimes "pass" via motherhood, typically by adopting—as was recently done by two nonfemme "comediennes," to use oldspeak.)

I'll focus briefly on one more female star—since male stars other than musical, Broadway, or British don't even allow themselves to be officially "bi." Last year, the *National Enquirer* did a cover story on Ellen DeGeneres's girlfriend moving in with her as a happy couple, one that hoped soon to adopt. The story was surprisingly subdued and nonjudgmental, probably due to *Ellen*'s popularity—the show and the star—but it avoided use of the *l*-word. On the other hand, *TV Guide* in '96 completely buried the gender and sexuality issue:

"She's in a loving relationship, and she feels too selfish right now to take on the challenge of motherhood." The second half of the conservatively crafted sentence does three things: a) it heterosexualizes the unspecified first half; b) it ignores past statements that if DeGeneres ever became a mother, it would be via adoption; and c) it attributes selfishness to a child-free woman ("childless," in oldspeak).

In the interview, Ellen—an open feminist—declares, "I'm very comfortable with who I am," and, "I'm a very liberal, very strong woman," stronger than she lets on because "I realize how much it scares them." Then she semi-acknowledges Hollywood's and the general public's discomfort with actors who are different than their roles. "Everyone thinks I have a responsibility to divulge my personal life. The more people know about me, the harder it becomes for them to accept me in different roles."

Which takes us back to 1933, when Haines was caught being other than the roles he always played. (Actually, he wasn't terminated until 1934, after the release of his final picture—its costs had to be recouped before Haines was made a pariah. Its title was *The Marines Are Coming.*)

So what's changed in Hollywood? In the music world, a handful of male Brits and Canadian and American women are openly gay. But even though it's generally understood now that actors *act*, Hollywood—never a social pioneer—still lags behind. Wide-ranging homophobia, including that of too many gay actors, publicists, agents, writers, directors, producers, and *viewers*, still allows only officially heterosexual entertainers and role models. This continues to send the message to young people that only heterosexuality is okay, regardless of whether one is born with it or not.

As producer Randy Stone's *Trevor* partner Peggy Rajski said in her Oscar acceptance speech, over one-third of all teen suicides are committed by homosexual kids—America's children, frozen out of its much-trumpeted "family values"—because of anti-gay hatred, discrimination, and exclusion.

The ten men in this book—interviewed between 1972 and 1993—in varying ways and to various degrees shed some light inside the Hollywood closet. *Hollywood Gays* is a follow-up to my ten-years-ago *Conversations With My Elders* (featuring six gay men of film, not all Hollywood), and a companion volume to my more recent and descriptively titled *Hollywood Lesbians*.

After trying seven times to obtain an interview with Raymond Burr—who lived with the same man for over 30 years, but was even posthumously closeted by the all-mainstream *TV Guide*—I gave up. I told Ron Vawter, "I guess he's just too deeply in the closet." He replied, "He *is* a closet." People eventually become their surroundings.

Somebody once said that Hollywood is a state of mind. As Vawter put it, "It may be the world of entertainment, but Hollywood's just a state of denial."

Where the truth still lies.

March 11, 1996
Beverly Hills, California

Latin Lover

CESAR ROMERO
(1907 – 1994)

Never a superstar, Cesar Romero was nonetheless a household name and had several claims to fame. His first was as a grandson of Cuban liberator José Martí. Then as the latest "new Valentino" imported by Hollywood—from back east, not Cuba (New York-born Cesar attended high school in New Jersey)—to fill *the* Latin Lover's shoes. Another claim to (whispered) fame was as Tyrone Power's on-and-off lover and lifelong friend.

Another was as a "dancing fool." He began as a dancer, dancing on screen with Betty Grable and others, and was a favorite escort of Hollywood actresses from Joan Crawford, Lucille Ball, and Carmen Miranda to, in latter days, older actresses like Jane Wyman, Ginger Rogers, and Anne Jeffreys. At nightclubs and parties, awards ceremonies, and other events, from the 1930s through the '80s, the "confirmed bachelor"—as gossip columnists usually described him—was always in demand. One source explained, "It was well known that Cesar could be counted on to be charming, to be an excellent dance partner, and to be discreet." He was, and had to be, discreet, for often he would escort an actress to a public spot, later depart with her, drop her off at some pre-arranged rendezvous with her male (or female) lover, and then drive to the arms of his own current male paramour.

On screen, the 6' 3" hunk with the flashing smile found fame neither as a professional Latin nor an acclaimed dancer, though occasionally he enacted either role, sometimes simultaneously. Rather, he became a busy character actor, essaying both villains and chums to the male lead, with or more typically without a foreign accent. He worked with most of the stars of the golden age of cinema, from Dietrich and Shirley Temple to William Powell, Henry Fonda, and "Charlie Chan." He appeared in a handful of classics and dozens of enjoyable A- and B-movies. His more reflective film titles include:

The Shadow Laughs; Cheating Cheaters; The Thin Man; The Good Fairy; Uniform Lovers (Hold 'Em Yale in the USA*); Strange Wives; The Devil Is a Woman; Nobody's Fool; Love Before Breakfast; Dangerously Yours; Always Goodbye; The Gay Caballero; Tall, Dark and Handsome; A Gentleman at Heart; Deep Waters; Love That Brute; Street of Shadows (Shadow Man* in the USA*); The Leather Saint; All's Fair in Love; The Story of Mankind; If a Man Answers; A Talent for Loving; How to Make It; Soul Soldier;* and *Now You See Him, Now You Don't.*

When television hit motion pictures in the back of the knees, Cesar Romero took to the small screen in over 40 years' worth of varied guest roles—and one brief series of his own, *Passport to Danger.* In the 1960s he won a new generation of fans as the campy, green-haired, ever-cackling Joker on *Batman.* And while his golden-era contemporaries retired or died, Cesar soldiered on, looking great. He commented in *California* magazine, "People are starting to call me Dorian Gray!

"But whatever else I may or may not have in common with Oscar Wilde, he did not create me and I was not a personal friend of his! Nor did Rudy Valentino give me my first break in pictures, as has been rumored. When he died, I was in my teens." So, Cesar's latest claim to fame became his enduring looks. In 1968 *TV Guide* dubbed him one of the most "beautiful men in the world," with "hair the color of stainless steel," an alert, "erect" posture, and charm to spare. Unsurprisingly, he launched a chain of men's clothing stores in California.

As he became elderly, his lifestyle didn't. Romero was known as Hollywood's most party-going citizen. At most any celebrity event—at the opening of an art gallery, a fashion exhibit, or a function commemorating Old Hollywood—Cesar was there, with or sometimes without a female celebrity in tow (not just glamour gals; often it was matronly Los Angeles philanthropist Sybil Brand). People joked that Cesar Romero would attend the opening of a napkin. Most nights of the week found him out on the town, away from the Brentwood condo that he shared with his sister Maria, whom he outlived.

Cesar continued going out—when he wasn't attending a function, he was likely at a dinner party—until the very end. The last time I saw him was in late autumn, 1993, in Beverly Hills at a tribute to our town's late honorary mayor, Will Rogers (killed in an airplane crash in 1935). The event tied in with the L.A. production of the Broadway hit *Will Rogers' Follies*, and Cesar was seated, grinning from time to time, on the dais. He was 86, and his one notable physical flaw was a brownish discoloration on the middle of his nose. Sometimes he covered it with makeup, but frequently let it go, explaining:

"I'm not quite that vain now. It's just how it is, no big deal. Of course when I work, the makeup man or girl covers it for me. . . . My lower teeth aren't perfect either. I've been advised I can get them changed or capped or whatever, but to me it's no big deal. And who'd want to sit still that long?"

To friends, he was known as "Butch." Certainly he acted more butch than stereotypical, though his off-camera humor was often self-mocking (e.g., after taping a TV talk show also featuring a female beauty queen, he instructed the technician removing the guests' clip-on microphones, "You can do the young lady first—the young queen before the old queen!"). His nickname was given to him by George Murphy when both were hoofers. The future Republican senator reportedly felt that as a dancer, Cesar could stand a more virile cognomen:

"I told him 'Butch' Romero would be his fast ticket to posterity, but then all the studio bosses thought it sounded peculiar for a 'Latin Lover.' I figured for a dancing man, 'Butch' would be smarter than going with an ancient Greek's [sic] name. But you can't second-guess Hollywood, and I guess that's one reason I left the place."

In 1933 the Cuban-American was transported to Hollywood, where MGM didn't know what to do with him. By then, during the depths of the Depression, male foreigners—as Romero was considered, because of his name—were fast going out of style. Louis B. Mayer's notorious homophobia may have played a part (he'd already been defied by MGM star Ramon Novarro after repeating his request that the gay Mexican take a wife). At the more Euro-oriented Paramount in 1935, "the new Valentino" was costarring with Marlene Dietrich in Joseph Von Sternberg's Spanish extravaganza *The Devil Is a Woman*. Had it been a hit, he would likely have gone on to romantic leading roles rather than Fox and such Shirley Temple vehicles as *Wee Willie Winkie* and *The Little Princess*.

Woman was probably too exotic for mid-American audiences, who in any case hardly got to sample the final Dietrich/Von Sternberg collaboration. As the director put it in his memoirs, "The film was banned by the Spanish government, which in turn was banned by Generalíssimo Franco." Spain's protestations led

Paramount to pull the picture from release and agree to destroy most of the prints. Cesar's big break was thus negated. Said Von Sternberg, "Most who saw it were Hollywood minions, before the few extant prints were shelved, to gather dust except for [being seen at] MOMA, then a screening at the 1959 Venice Film Festival, and finally a limited circulation in 1961."

But rumor had it that, pre-release, the homophobic director had already cut Cesar's part—to favor co-male lead Lionel Atwill—after learning Cesar was gay. To this writer's knowledge, Romero never acknowledged the rumor. Ironically, Elsa Lanchester, widow of closeted gay star Charles Laughton, told me, "When Charles was doing [the aborted] *I, Claudius* for Herr Von Sternberg, who was an American and *not* of aristocratic origin [*Von* indicates Teutonic nobility], he gave Charles his unsolicited opinion of Señor Romero. He said Cesar was a bit on the 'fancy' side and ought to find himself a wife if ever he expected to get anywhere in the picture business. The kraut said this with a straight and obviously naive face to our Charles. . . ."

Apparently the next time Romero's career suffered from homophobia was after he inherited the role of the Cisco Kid (including *The Gay Caballero*, 1940). The Hispanic hero was derived from a 1907 O. Henry short story and in 1929 won the second Best Actor Academy Award for Warner Baxter. Fox turned it into a popular early '40s series that didn't sit as well with moviegoers in nations to the south. James Horwitz in his book *They Went Thataway* explained:

"Romero was no cowboy, but one of those Brill-creamed Latin Lover types, and played the Kid as a smarmy dandy and fop, while Chris Pin-Martin's Pancho (the Kid's sidekick) was a gutbucket slob. Latin American sensibilities were offended by this unlikely duo. An international incident nearly occurred. Diplomatic cables flew back and forth between Latin America and the State Department. The Cisco Kid, as portrayed by

Romero, was, so to speak, queering America's south-of-the-border foreign policy. Darryl Zanuck at Fox was more or less ordered by Washington to change Cisco's style or stop making the pictures. He decided to drop the series altogether."

The series was later revived with heterosexual Mexican sex symbol Gilbert Roland. But the replacement of the "mincing Romero" with a "lecherous Roland" proved unpopular with US *and* Latin audiences. Horwitz described the new Kid as "a typical Rolandesque cigarillo-smoking, hot-sweat-of-passion, lusty, mucho macho caballero. The films bombed out." It was the allegedly Rumanian Duncan Renaldo who eventually struck the right note of asexuality and nonviolence, becoming the most famous Cisco Kid of all—with a big plug from TV.

The publication of the above explanation in my 1990 book *Hispanic Hollywood* put an almost two-year chill into Cesar's and my friendship and interviews (since 1977, usually at the fabled Château Marmont). We were to have appeared together on a local TV talk show, but Cesar canceled when he discovered it would feature not my other current book (*The Vinyl Closet*, about gays and lesbians in music) but *Hispanic Hollywood*.

Pre-publication, I'd asked Cesar if he would pen a foreword to my book about Latins in motion pictures. He politely demurred, and so Edward James Olmos wrote it. As for the Cisco Kid material from Horwitz's book, I photocopied it and sent it to him care of Morgan Maree, his business manager. No reply. Later, when we began speaking again, I asked why Cesar hadn't gotten back to me if he didn't want the factual, already printed information in my book? "I never got your letter." End of subject.

By and large, Cesar Romero was an excellent interviewee. Sadly, he was seldom sought for interviews. Almost never was he asked about his private life. True, he never officially came out of the closet, but for one of his generation he was relatively open about his sexual and affectional orientation, and he rarely took steps to disguise it. His avoiding contractual marriage, as he pointed out, was a statement in itself—one that the mass media had no desire to give voice to.

The first time we met, at the Marmont, I couldn't resist, and greeted him with "Hail, Cesar!" When I later called him Mr. Romero, he flashed a smile and insisted, "Mr. Romero was my father. Don't make me feel so old!" I asked what should I call him? "You can call me 'Butch' or Cesar." I couldn't help feeling both were too familiar, particularly on such short acquaintance, and compromised with the honorific *Don* Cesar (now and again we spoke Spanish together, especially when the waiter or nearby customers weren't meant to understand).

Cesar—as I eventually called him—was an avid and thoughtful conversationalist on most topics. On one he was unwilling and protective: "my close friend, my dear friend, Ty Power." He never stated what most of Hollywood knew at the time—that they were lovers. When he spoke of Power on TV, he would mention Tyrone's wives or girlfriends—real or imaginary—and although he admitted to me that Power was "bisexual," even that was uttered reluctantly. A closeted movie actor friend—best known for his role on a TV series about a policewoman—himself also legally (if not actually) single, declared, "I gather Ty was rather tortured about it. He was a prominent movie star and icon. He wanted to be straight, but more than that, he was terrified of being found out.

"Cesar's not a movie star, and never had the same pressure or fears. And I think he's more comfortable within himself, he's a survivor [Power died at 44]. . . . When Cesar talks about Ty, he feels he's being loyal to him, even if those same pressures and fears don't exist anymore. Or not to the same degree."

The year I met Don Cesar, he turned 70. He still flirted and had a zestful gleam in his eye. But whether in his 70s and 80s he had affairs with anyone, I have no idea. A few times, in the 1980s, we video-watched some porno flicks together. In 1991, after Paul Rubens (né Rubenfeld), aka Pee-Wee Herman, was arrested at an "adult theatre" in Sarasota, Florida, Cesar joked on the phone, "Think how much grief he could have saved himself if he'd stayed home or in his motel and played with his *toy* in front of a video machine!" I wondered aloud why Rubens had bothered to go out to a porno theatre.

"I guess to see other toys in action," Cesar chuckled. "Poor fellow—such hypocrisy [from the media]. I wonder if Sarasota has a *gay* adult theatre. . . ?" When in 1992 a tabloid ran the story of "Pee-Wee's Gay Wedding . . . & Jim Nabors Sang at Secret Ceremony," he clipped it and sent it to me, noting, "I knew I liked this guy. And Jim Nabors' voice!" When next we met, Cesar said that a lesbian official from the national Hispanic organization La Raza in Washington, D.C., had informed him that Rubens's sister was (reportedly) a well-known gay rights activist back east. "Young people are all right," he intoned.

Q: **Where does one begin with as colorful a life and career as yours?**

A: You mean as long (grins).

Q: **How many movies have you been in?**

A: I'm pushing 100. Oooh, I don't like the sound of that! If it isn't 100 movies, it will be soon.

Q: **But now you seem to do more TV than movies.**

A: Undeniably true.

Q: **Because of . . . age?**

A: Age and because there's more work on the small screen. What it's missing in quality it makes up for in quantity. From an actor's selfish point of view.

Q: **Speaking of quality, it varies wildly in movies too.**

You've been in classics like *The Thin Man, Springtime in the Rockies,* and *Around the World in 80 Days.* But you've—

A: The last one doesn't count. Everybody in Hollywood was in that. If you weren't, you left town and made up an excuse.

Q: **Not just everyone in Hollywood. Noel Coward was in it, and for a day's work he received an automobile, a Bonnard. A reporter visiting the set was flabbergasted and said, "Just for a day's work?" and Noel Coward replied, "Not at all, madame. For a lifetime of experience."**

A: (Laughs, claps hands together.) Classic Coward. I think a few other guest stars got paid in automobiles.

Q: **Yes. Sir Noel said that Ronald Colman got a Cadillac.**

A: Said to you or . . . ?

Q: **(Smiling.) I got to interview him. By then he was—belatedly—Sir Noel. He wasn't in 1956.**

A: And you weren't born, I'll wager.

Q: **I beg your pardon. I was a toddler.**

A: You got to meet Sir Noel Coward? I met him too. Didn't know him well. But you are lucky.

Q: **I know I am. He was not only brilliant, he was kind and down-to-earth.**

A: Sometimes that happens with celebrities. (Grinning.)

Q: **What I meant is, most people like that aren't so . . . sincere.**

A: Well, you know what they say in Hollywood—the most important thing is being sincere, even if you have to fake it. . . . They also say the camera never lies. It lies (leaning closer) every day.

Q: **Do you mean actors playing characters unlike themselves?**

A: Yes, yes. A pompous ass playing a concerned hero, a bitch playing the girl next door . . . but also tricks about aging or emotional insincerity—project a mask, and people can project onto it whatever they think you're feeling.

Q: Or want you to be feeling.

A: Yes. A good rule of thumb in acting for the camera is not to emotionalize. Keep your expressions pretty still. *You* have very expressive eyes. If an actor's face is more of a blank, he can let the audience do the acting for him.

Q: Like who?

A: . . . Spencer Tracy. Not to take anything away from him, but many a morning he came to the set hung (over), and during a line—or particularly when he had no lines—he'd present an expressionless face to the camera. People would read all kinds of reaction into it, but Tracy told me himself that half the time he was just standing very still, trying to look sober and composed. (Shrugs.) That takes nothing away from him. The fact he got away with it was a tribute to his talent.

Q: He's become known among younger actors for his advice about just saying your lines right and not bumping into the furniture.

A: Aha! That is wrong, and we can put this on record. He did say that too, but it didn't come from him. He very rarely did interviews, but in one interview long ago he said that he got that advice from Noel Coward! He gave Coward the credit.

Q: And now others give Tracy the credit.

A: There was another thing I remember Noel Coward said—I should remember more, and I have a pretty good memory. He said when he was very young, in his 20s or 30s, the critics would complain that he was "precocious." That's the word. And Coward said, "How do they think I could be clever and not know it?"

Q: Makes perfect sense. Which is worse—a critic's bad review, or not getting mentioned in a review?

A: What do you think?

Q: . . . Silence is the worst insult.

A: You said it.

Q: Getting back to the uneven quality of movies—

A: Movies I've been in?

Q: Actually, yes. But hey, it's a living. Anyway, you've more recently done films like *Sergeant Deadhead, The Computer Wore Tennis Shoes,* and *Won Ton Ton, The Dog Who Saved Hollywood.* . . .

A: (Grinning.) That last one is a classic dog.

Q: A classic dog movie?

A: No. A classic dog. (Nods.)

Q: Yet they say movies—still—have more prestige than TV.

A: It's also harder to get into them. Not that television is so easy. It's all uphill now.

Q: Mmm. But enough about TV. More about your background. Let's go back to the very beginning.

A: All right. What do you want to know about the Civil War?

Q: Funny. You were born in the USA. . . .

A: Which many people still find hard to believe. And if you can believe it, Hollywood wanted to change my birthdate. I was born after Valentine's Day, so they wanted to change it to February 14. You know why?

Q: Latin love and romance?

A: You said it. A Latin lover *should* be born on Valentine's Day. I said no.

Q: You know who else did? Elsa Lanchester. She was born around Halloween, and when she starred as *The Bride of Frankenstein* (1935), the publicists wanted to change her birthday to October 31.

A: And not being a *real* witch, she refused.

Q: Yes (both laugh). Your first movie wasn't *The Thin Man* (1934)?

A: No. I did a handful in '33 and '34, then I got the buildup in

1935. *The Thin Man* was a good break, because it was highly popular. I played a gigolo in it.

Q: **There's Latin typecasting for you.**

A: Yes. And no. His name was Chris Jorgenson. An Anglo-gigolo—but at least not a transsexual (like Danish-American Christine Jorgenson).

Q: **You were a Latin from Manhattan. So, before movies, you had to be on the stage.**

A: Oh, of course. We all came up through the theatre—or in some cases the thee-ayder. I was in a show called *Lady Do*, late '20s. My big break, my Broadway bow, was *Dinner at Eight*. I played Ricci (spelling it). That was very popular.

Q: **But you didn't get into the movie version, which was helmed by the gay George Cukor. . . ?**

A: No. And I didn't *know* about him then (nods significantly).

Q: **Could that have helped you, if you had?**

A: It's possible. I don't know at what point Cukor supposedly or actually started favoring particular young actors with roles . . . perhaps not just then (in the early 1930s). He was starting out himself. He had to be careful. By the '50s, I know, he was giving big breaks to—

Q: **Big newcomers?**

A: (Laughs.) So I often heard.

Q: **Like Valentino, you began as a dancer. How and why?**

A: Well, first—and I should only have been as lucky as Valentino, in the movies—*I* didn't have to be a gigolo. In real life.

Q: **And Valentino did?**

A: People who knew him in Italy said he engaged in male prostitution there. Could be. But in New York, he was a paid dance partner and a gigolo for older ladies of affluent means.

Q: **Would that have involved sex?**

A: More probably not. But it was widely known that those boys were either queer or went both ways.

Q: As far as it's possible to know, Valentino was apparently gay or bisexual.

A: Yes. And his two lesbian wives. But without any question, he had sex with men. From choice. So he was one or the other.

Q: **Did you ever know anybody who made love with him?**

A: I did. One heterosexual who later gave up acting. He was very young, experimenting, and quite flattered when "the Sheik" made clear his interest in him. And I knew several gay actors who . . . *knew* Rudy, including my good friend Ramon Novarro. He was almost as popular a star as Rudy was.

Q: **Novarro was stunning—they called him "Ravishing Ramon"—but he also seemed very nice.**

A: A gentle, sweet man. His murder (in 1968 at the hands of two hustler brothers) was so gruesome and bloody, it was so senseless—one of this town's greatest tragedies. (Even so, the self-avowed heterosexual brothers have long since been released from prison.) It was the biggest shock I had since Ty's death (in 1958 from a heart attack on location in Spain).

Q: **I imagine the murder scared most sensible gay men in Hollywood off of using hustlers?**

A: Anyone with any sense. . . . That and the murders of Sharon Tate and her friends helped make us all extremely wary. A lot of paranoia set in.

Q: **Stars are increasingly being targeted.**

A: All kinds of celebrities, political ones as well. In this country, with all the countless guns.

Q: **However, in Novarro's case, it had more to do with robbery and gay-bashing—that extra viciousness directed against a gay man—than his being a celebrity. Correct?**

A: Yes, I don't even think those two brutes knew who he was. He hadn't been a movie star for a very long time. His name wasn't known to young people.

Q: Except via *I Love Lucy*, where Lucy's mother still had a crush on Ray-Monn *Navarro*, as she pronounced it.

A: (Smiles; frowns.) But those two barbarians did know that he kept a lot of cash in his house, whoever he was. That's what they were after. . . . During the murder trial, it was the dead man who was put on trial, as if he'd corrupted these two barbarians.

Q: It's an ongoing travesty of justice. Victimizing the victim of anti-gay violence. The basher or murderer tries to justify the violence by saying, "But he came onto me," whether true or false.

A: Whether he did or not, nothing justifies a violent reaction. Unless it's an attempted rape, and even then.

Q: If every woman reacted the same way to sexually eager men, there'd be few heterosexual males left!

A: It's true. It's awful, the unfairness. But that's why one must stay out of trouble.

Q: And why the laws must be changed, and people elected who aren't mere conservers of traditional injustices. . . .

A: Amen. But . . . oh, it's depressing. We were talking about . . . dancing. Much less depressing! (Sighs in relief.) Several of those fellows working in the dance parlors, I forget what they called the places, they had to live down the reputations they got there, for years after . . . George Raft. He may or may not have gone both ways, but he was very sensitive to what they said about him, and it was one factor why he decided to play all those gangsters in the movies.

Q: One rumor is he had a crush on mobster Bugsy Siegel.

A: (Laughs.) The mobster with the beautiful blue eyes. I know Raft did have some genuine affairs with actresses.

Q: So he may have been bisexual. Or heterosexual.

A: In reality he may have been . . . "bi." But in . . . common parlance, in or out of our business, if a man has a marriage or an affair with a lady, he's thought of as heterosexual.

Q: **As though everyone is only hetero- or only homosexual.**

A: They go by what they can see.

Q: **And they force the sexual minority to hide what they do and feel, so that the public assumes almost everyone's heterosexual. How were you able to evade pressure to marry?**

A: I wasn't able to evade some pressure—we all had some pressures brought to bear on us—but I did evade the noose. I mean the knot! Freudian slip.

Q: **More like a Freudian slap.**

A: (Laughs.) But that brings us right back to dancing. You see, very, very often, I was out dancing with one actress or another. And that got press. Even when it didn't, the whole town knew I was a dancing fool, and since I couldn't very well dance with a man, they saw me dancing with a lady, and . . .

Q: **And they assumed the rest.**

A: That's it. What they saw was what they got in their heads. Now, as to how I started dancing. I'd learned with my sister—we learned from our cook, who was Puerto Rican. I liked dancing, it was fun and expressive, and I was good at it.

Q: **And it was socially approved.**

A: You said it. Again, it put any doubts out of most people's heads. But I'll tell you something not for public consumption in *my* lifetime. . . . All right? That's how I . . . found out. That I was different. While dancing . . . you understand?

Q: **You mean that you weren't sexually turned on to your partners?**

A: (Nods, smiling.) I enjoyed dancing, I enjoyed the girls I danced with, but . . . that was all. I wasn't distracted by them, and on the dance floor, I could see other partners I would rather have had. . . .

Q: **Males.**

A: (Nods.) So I had to keep from laughing when a male relative of mine became concerned about how often I danced.

Q: **What, he thought you should be outdoors playing sports?**

A: Mentioning sports, I was very good at tennis. Not quite championship level, but . . . No. This well-intentioned relative told me confidentially that so much dancing was bound to make me, ahem, frustrated. (Grins.) So I shouldn't do too much dancing. Or else I'd be bound to practice self-abuse. Frequently!

Q: **"Self-abuse." What a misnomer for self-pleasure.**

A: (Smiles.) Lovingly practiced the whole world over.

Q: **Indeed. If anything, it's the norm—autosexual, and part of the time heterosexual, homosexual, bisexual. . . .**

A: I think that covers it (grins). Anyway, I told the poor fellow not to worry. He thought I'd get sick or drain myself of all energy and not be able to conduct a business career. Which I would have been miserable at. But due to a big bust in Cuba, my father's business suffered badly, so I was free to choose my own career. I became a professional dancer, and I went on the road and started making real money.

Q: **I hope you don't mind this question, but why, in the movies, didn't you become another Fred Astaire or Gene Kelly?**

A: Thank you! (Mock-bows, smiling.)

Q: **"Thank you"?**

A: You're presuming I had enough talent to compete with those excellent dancers. (Shrugs.) I don't know. I may have had. But being a Latin, that wasn't what they were grooming me for. I was supposed to be a romancer, either wooing the leading lady or competing with the leading man for her.

Q: **Did male dancers of star stature have to have a more**

mainstream image?

A: That is perceptive of you, because in this country men dancers have always been viewed with suspicion. If you were an actor, a star, and a dancer, you had to be, or have a name like . . . as you said, someone "mainstream." You can name the top three (male) dancers in the movies, can't you?

Q: **Fred Astaire (born Austerlitz), Gene Kelly, and Dan Dailey. Dailey is gay.**

A: Yes. As well. . . . (A warning finger; end of subject.)

Q: **One clarifying question. When *you* say gay, do you mean homosexual or bisexual?**

A: Either.

Q: **Ah. Well, to me it means homosexual. And bi means bisexual. There can be a difference.**

A: In Hollywood, I agree. I don't know about out *there* anymore. But a Hollywood actor can genuinely enjoy sex with either.

Q: **Why?**

A: Beauty. We have the most beautiful people in the world here. Of both sexes.

Q: **Look at Tyrone Power. In his heyday, he was, I'd say, universally desirable. As were some of the goddesses.**

A: Ty was the most beautiful of all, man or woman. He was matchless. And you know, people often mistook him for Latin, from his dark hair and brows and eyelashes.

Q: **And probably because he played Latins in films like *Blood and Sand* and *Captain from Castile*.**

A: (Beams.) *Captain from Castile* . . . wonderful memories. . . . At that time, we had several beautiful, glamorous Latin American stars. They were the best fun at parties and clubs, we always got along great. There was a whole colony—the handsome Hispanics, like Ramon, Gilbert Roland, and others. (Sighs.)

Q: **Those wonderful Latin looks, eh?**

A: I'm not the only one. You know who had a crush on Gilbert? Lucille Ball. I don't know if they had an affair, but several people in this town believed they would end up married.

Q: **Instead she married another Latin—and you worked with him, didn't you? (He grins.) A renowned, or notorious, ladies' man. Did you ever have a crush on Desi Arnaz?**

A: (Nods.) Desi loved sex. He couldn't get enough.

Q: **How about that syndrome, the Casanova thing, where a man—a Don Juan—who has hundreds of female lovers, at some point along the way also has a few male ones?**

A: Well, of course! An erection's an erection. It just wants satisfaction. Wasn't it . . . was it Gertrude Stein who said a mouth is a mouth is a mouth?

Q: **Could be. There didn't used to be surveys on this topic, but now they indicate that more men enjoy oral sex— receiving it—than the standard male-female sexual position, the "missionary," for want of a better word.**

A: They may prefer it, but until not so long ago, a man, a regular married man, didn't know where to get it. Mostly, they had to do without. Wives or girlfriends wouldn't do it. Guys had to go to a professional and pay her.

Q: **Or . . . ?**

A: Or something like a highway rest stop where the truckers go. "Glory holes," they call them. Which gives a new meaning to the old expression, "gone to glory." (Smirks.) So, anonymous oral sex—no names, no faces. So that the fellow can still think of himself as . . . living a completely normal life. Right?

Q: **It helps him think of himself as just one category, instead of as simply sexual. The Greeks, for instance, didn't have words for "heterosexual" or "homosexual."**

A: Smart people, the Greeks. You mean the ancient Greeks?

Q: **Of course. Not the Greek Orthodox. So did Desi Arnaz**

ever know how you felt?

A: He'd have been rather slow if he didn't. He knew he was pretty irresistible—I mean well before *I Love Lucy*, and even then. And he knew about me, and . . . I guess he could see it in the eyes. When someone's acting for a scene, they can fool the camera. But in everyday life, unless you're watching and censoring yourself every minute, or spending all your time in the company of ladies, what you feel is bound to show in your eyes. Sooner or later.

Q: **Men *look*. Most men, any type.**

A: Yes. And to make a very pleasant story short, one day Desi said to me, "All right, we both know what you want. Let's get it over with." We did. End of story.

Q: **Just once?**

A: (Grins widely.) Men aren't potato chips. . . .

Q: **But I'll bet—**

A: Desi said "one time only." For our friendship. Neither of us made a big deal out of it, excuse the pun, and we never referred to it again.

Q: **Do you think Lucy ever knew?**

A: Of course not! It would have been the least of her worries, later on. And I know I wasn't the only one; Dorothy Kilgallen's husband (Arnaz's Broadway co-star Richard Kollmar) was another man. Desi loved pleasure. Who doesn't? He wasn't "compromised," as they say. He received the pleasure, for a change. I mean, Desi screwed women, and he never got screwed—physically; in Hollywood, *everyone* gets screwed—so how much more heterosexual than that does anyone have to be?

Besides, it didn't harm anyone or create problems. Later, when he was cheating on his wife all over the place, in addition to his problem with alcoholism, *that* led to heartaches for poor Lucille.

Q: It's certainly true that if a man with a wife goes outside—

A: The expression used to be "steps out."

Q: If he "steps out" for . . . a frolic with another man—and there's any number of things either or both can do, or not do—it should cause no problem. But if he steps out on her with another woman, he may later decide to leave his wife—and their kids—for her, or he may impregnate the girlfriend or mistress—

A: As well as spending household money on the mistress!

Q: Right, and all of that would certainly create problems and heartache.

A: When it's same-sex, no one gets pregnant. Before there was the pill, and before women made themselves so sexually available, that was a big consideration.

Q: It's still a big one in Latin America, Asia, and Africa. Heterosexual sex, because of pregnancy, must occur within legal marriage. Thus, young, unmarried men often have sex with each other as relief and an alternative.

A: You said it. But you know something? They don't think of themselves as gay. I've heard it over and over.

Q: Denial. Even though it takes two people to perform one homosexual act.

A: Yes! When they could just think of themselves as flexible. Or just plain sexual. But there's something you younger kids don't realize. In the, uh, old days (cocks an eyebrow) . . . how shall I? . . . fellatio was a big status symbol. If someone was willing to do that for you, you felt like a king. Few would have said no.

Q: *Once.*

A: Yes. Twice might be embarrassing.

Q: I think it was Voltaire who said, or wrote, "Once, a philosopher. Twice, a sodomite."

A: (Laughs and claps hands.) Very good! But I think he must have been referring to that other activity?

Q: Well, that particular biblical word is both judgmental and inaccurate.

A: And not even limited to homosexuals.

Q: Right. Getting back to the dance floor, you escorted Lucy a few times, didn't you?

A: Oh, we had several dates. She loved to dance. And she loved Latins.

Q: Do you think she'd have known you were . . . just there to dance?

A: You know, I have no idea, and I wouldn't have cared. We went out because that's what we beautiful young movie people did! We were encouraged to. We were living the high life, it was very glamorous and elegant, it was wonderful fun. And far more innocent than now. Less sex, less drink, absolutely less drugs—if someone did *that*, it was unusual, and it was private. Today, half the girls powder their noses from the inside!

    Remember, I was much younger then. It was all before the war, I was in my late 20s and then my 30s. But what did happen was if you went out together several times, those columnists—there were dozens of them then—they'd link you romantically, on paper. It meant nothing, but if it kept popping up in print, someone at the studio might suggest that you make it legal.

Q: So you didn't need publicists then?

A: They called them press agents. Today they're very, very professional . . . liars. Mostly. Back then, a press agent would be better for pressing pants. All the top columnists had leg men, and when you showed up somewhere, it automatically got covered. Most of the time.

Q: And again, what the public read about, and saw photographed, was what they took literally.

A: Yes. But there really were, in those days, several gay, carefree bachelors. In the old meaning of the word. Someone once told me "gay" now stands for "Good As You." But people weren't at all as suspicious as now.

Q: **No, because it was so suppressed and invisibilized, that average people thought somebody gay was one in a million. Worse, gay people, especially away from the big cities, were made to think so too.**

A: Or people thought they were mostly foreign. There was a lot of that thinking too.

Q: **Yes, the over-emotional Latin, the effete Englishman. . . . But you know the word "bachelor"? Originally it meant a young knight who had served under another knight's banner.**

A: That sounds interesting. So it had . . . connotations.

Q: **In days of old, when knights were bold. . . . But by the time you reached 40, people must have begun to suspect?**

A: (Nods.) By that age, almost everyone had married. Me, Ramon . . . Clifton Webb, very few of us hadn't tied the knot.

Q: **Not to contradict, but there were several others, though most of them weren't stars.**

A: Most of them worked in comedy.

Q: **Funny men.**

A: Watch it! (Laughs.) But by the time I was 40, everything was winding down. It started after the war. On the plus side, there was *more* . . . more plenty, more products and technology. But for me (shakes head), the nightlife was winding down, the glamour, the fun. The *movies*—and how! Times were getting tough.

Q: **The witch-hunts. They passed you by?**

A: *Ave Maria!* I was Latin. Communism and Latins? There was no Castro then.

Q: **Lucky Cuba. Although Batista (his predecessor) was terrible too.**

A: You said it. Unless you were terribly rich.

Q: **You know one of the worst things about communist regimes?**

A: The food?

Q: **Be serious. They're always rabidly homophobic.**

A: Ah. Yes, that's true. But in Hollywood, with the witch-hunts, most of the targets were intellectuals and Europeans.

Q: **And a huge percentage of them were Jewish or gay. Two of the extreme right's ongoing targets.**

A: Many weren't even communists. Just liberal.

Q: **Much of it was a backlash.**

A: You mean against the Iron Curtain going up?

Q: **Yes, and the Bamboo Curtain, but domestically a backlash against Democrats. After almost four terms of Franklin Roosevelt, and then Truman.**

A: It was awful. A terrible, terrible time.

Q: **As Lillian Hellman called it, "scoundrel time." Though I must add that her defense of Stalinism was terrible.**

A: I agree! But let's wash our hands of politics. I've avoided it. I always prefer to leave it alone.

Q: **It would be nice if one could. But the only type of person who can afford to ignore politics is someone who's male, white, heterosexual, and Christian— "preferably" Protestant.**

A: You've hit it on the head. It's true. But at my age, I think I can beg off politics. I try to vote, but . . . I'm too old to get involved with it. (Smiles.) The young people can do it.

Q: **Young people must do it.**

A: (Shakes head.) Yes. There *are* good things now, but there were good things then. Those nightclubs! The way we dressed up! And it was safer then. Muggings—what muggings? If you weren't in the mafia, you didn't have to worry. It was carefree, it was beautiful and glamorous. I wouldn't have missed it for anything.

Q: But *your* nightlife's never ended. You must never watch TV.

A: I don't miss it, either. I do miss the nightclubs—those wonderful spots are almost all gone.

Q: And the people.

A: Yes. . . . Those beautiful-looking people.

Q: You were at the head of the line. I'll bet most of the women you squired got crushes on you.

A: (Smiles bashfully.) Oh, I don't know. Could be. But people had very good manners then. If you were out on a date, that's just what it was. You didn't have people throwing themselves at each other or trying to do a mating dance. . . .

The 1990 book *Lucy in the Afternoon* by Jim Brochu was a fond reminiscence by a young fan who befriended and interviewed Lucille Ball toward the end and got to play backgammon with her in the afternoons. In the nonbiography, Lucy revealed her sympathy for Hedda Hopper, because the columnist's son William, best known for TV's *Perry Mason*—and a husband and father of two—was in love with another man, unnamed in the book (for Raymond Burr was alive then).

Ball also told Brochu, "Cesar's a great guy. I had a real crush on him, and he was terrific fun on a date. The best dancer in the world. One night we went to Mocambo, and we both had too much to drink. I thought that maybe he'd make a pass after all the times we went out, but he didn't. He's a real gent. The best. As we danced, he started to cry. I asked him what was the matter, and he just said, 'I'm strange.' I told him that we were all a little strange, and then he really broke down." Whether the story or reportage was exaggerated or not, its point was to indicate, but not state, Romero's sexual orientation—like Burr, Cesar was still alive at the time.

(Lucy also recounted a date with acerbic writer-actor Oscar Levant, whose oft-expressed homophobia may have been a veil for sexual insecurity or latency. Afterward, in the car, he felt compelled to explain why he wouldn't be making a pass at Ball, claiming, "I have syphilis.")

The difference between Cesar Romero and Raymond Burr was that, although Burr lived with another man for over three decades, he remained mentally closeted. He'd wed a woman once, but later fabricated—and kept doing so in interviews—two additional wives and a son. Amazingly, Burr's 1993 obituaries typically printed his lies but omitted any mention of the man with whom he spent most of his adult life. Such nonjournalism included *Variety*, also known as the show business "bible." But that's Hollywood—where the truth lies . . . still. Deadly still.

Q: **Cesar, I have a clipping from the *Hollywood Star* (1981). It asks the sartorial question, "Who's the most clothes-conscious actor in Hollywood? Cesar Romero, we've been told . . ." (he leans forward) but not by me, I've never been in your closet—**

A: Nor my bedroom, so far.

Q: **We don't want to spoil a beautiful friendship.**

A: It might spoil it for you, it would heighten it for me.

Q: **Oh, tut-tut.**

A: He was before my time. Believe it or not (frowns).

Q: **(I laugh, then we both laugh.) Back to your closet, for a moment. "Cesar Romero, we've been told, has 500 suits, 190 sports jackets, and 30 tuxedos."**

A: I wonder who counted?

Q: **I know! It goes on, "Douglas Fairbanks Sr., in his heyday, owned 454 suits, one for every day of the year plus two**

for each Sunday and holiday."

A: That's a lot of arithmetic. Well, clothes make the man. We were all expected to look our best in public. It went for everyone, star and featured player alike.

Q: **Do you prefer the term "supporting actor" or "character actor"?**

A: I prefer the paycheck! And bigger is better. Speaking of that, you're circumcised?

Q: **Yes. But—**

A: But back to the closet? (Grins sexily.)

Q: **For a moment. All those clothes! I can't imagine.**

A: I think for your generation, clothes are just what you wear after you get out of bed. . . .

Q: **With so many clothes, was that for a sound business investment or monumental vanity?**

A: (Laughs.) Couldn't it be both? I do have to say, if I hadn't been out on the dance floor so much, I probably wouldn't have bought so many clothes. But it was a good investment, and sometimes I wore my own clothes in a picture, which paid off.

Q: **I believe in the late 1950s you began promoting a line of men's suits?**

A: Yes, we all did promotions. Of course, the bigger the star, the more promotions you got to do, the actresses even more so—cosmetics, hats, all that. I pushed suits. And it even helped my social life. The company wanted me to go out and be seen in their suits. With a lady on my arm, they stipulated.

Q: **Was it in the contract?**

A: (Laughs.) No, no. But it was understood. To get more customers.

Q: **And publicity.**

A: Ah, yes. There's always more publicity in a pair, a couple— a man and a woman. So I did it. After all, it was business, to sell our suits.

Q: **But you didn't sell yourself, the way most actors did—and do.**

A: Not a lot. (Smiles.) I'm just very lucky I loved dancing. Otherwise . . . (shrugs). It was a great cover, but great fun. What wasn't any fun, later on, was when I had my own chain of men's clothing stores. All kinds of losses, and I had to bust my ass to pay them off. I was right from the start—business was never my strong suit.

Q: **Nice pun. Tyrone Power was a snappy dresser too. . . .**

A: (Posture stiffens.) We all did our best. Of course, clothes have even more of an effect, worn on someone so exceptionally handsome.

Q: **Do you think that some men—they said this was true of Robert Taylor—resent being beautiful, that is, they're embarrassed by their looks or even feel categorized as non-heterosexual by them?**

A: Bob Taylor, I know, had some deep-seated problems. Not because of who he did or didn't go to bed with; I just think he wasn't very happy. But with Ty, he was for the most part happy-go-lucky. Into *my* life, he brought a lot of sunshine, and not only mine. At Fox, he was beloved by everyone. Even Zanuck had a slight crush on him. Ty was irresistible, not just physically. But some damn biographers want to dramatize everything. They write about Ty as a personality of much light and shade. Not true!

Q: **Yet there had to be some conflict, in that he was bisexual, and as a star he had to do the expected, with three wives and three kids, and he had to hide his gay affairs and relationships. (No response.) In his early 40s, he looked closer to 50.**

A: Lots of pressure . . . professional pressures too. Becoming a star—that's tough. Staying a star—even tougher. Sometimes he overdid or drank too much. But Ty was never alcoholic, and he never burdened his friends with his problems. Which some of us would have been happy to share.

Q: It's remarkable how many male Hollywood stars—gay, hetero, or bi—died by age 50 or 60. Gable, Cooper, Flynn, Alan Ladd, Tyrone Power, of course—a long list. As opposed to nonstar males—character actors and comedic ones—and of course non-sex symbol actresses, who typically last into their 80s or even 90s. Why?

A: Why do the men, the men stars, die young? (Shrugs.) Fortunately, I'm no authority. All I can think is great pressure—on all of them, as you said. Some weren't very happy being stars, believe it or not. Ty was, for the most part. And most men stars don't have the happiest or stablest private lives. Perhaps because their lives aren't private, and all the pressures of being and staying a masculine sex symbol . . . and a role model too (nods).

Q: The women stars don't have to prove anything.

A: No, they just have to keep looking great. (Smiles.) And learn to defer.

Q: That, they're brought up with from the time they leave the cradle—I have a sister. You too (he nods). . . . I imagine you've heard that the bisexual star in Gore Vidal's novel *The Pillar and the City* (1948) was based on Power?

A: I don't believe Mr. Vidal knew Ty very well.

Q: Perhaps not, although he did write movies in Hollywood. But one doesn't have to know a public figure well to write about him in a novel. . . . You've been described as "feline." Any comment?

A: *Meow!* (Laughs.) But I never played Catwoman on *Batman*.

Q: Your Joker was very campy.

A: I loved it. Except for all the laughter—my throat. . . . At first I felt somewhat foolish, the show was rather juvenile, and the guy never stopped laughing like a hyena in heat.

You notice, if you've seen it, that they often put a young lady, some blonde, in a scene with me. Like you were supposed to think she was the Joker's girlfriend.

Q: **To, uh, butch you up? To make the character seem heterosexual?**

A: Yes! But I doubt it worked. . . . But once I saw how juvenile TV was getting, and what a popular hit *Batman* was—*twice* a week, and a feature film from it—I relaxed into it. I just laughed and made more money than I had in some time.

Q: **You laughed all the way to the bank. To re-coin Liberace's pet phrase.**

A: (Shudders.) "Pet". . . . Now, *he's* the kind Ty or Bob Taylor wouldn't have wanted to be grouped with. (Shakes head.) But do not print this, or he'd sue, and I'd have to deny saying it. (Leans forward.) Here. Rewind that part. (I do.) Again, you understand that anything I say about anyone . . . like *that*, it's not for public consumption in my lifetime.

Q: **(Leaning into the mike.) Yes, I do.**

A: Good. I now pronounce us man and husband. (Both laugh.)

Q: **But Liberace, who regardless of selfish or self-loathing denials, is gay—**

A: Careful!

Q: **Well, he is. A blind man can see he's gay. He's the stereotype, so he stands out. Unlike Tab and Rock and Cary or Sal or . . . on and on. The point is, he sued more than once for being described as what he was. Would you?**

A: . . . Probably not. I would if someone described what I do in bed; I would think a heterosexual would too. I would sue if the person saying or writing it was being vicious, if he was—what's the word?

Q: **Homophobic.**

A: Yes. But in this day and age, if it's just written in passing, and they don't dwell on it . . . (shrugs). Why fuss over it?

Q: In fact, most gay celebrities would avoid the publicity of a lawsuit. And the possible scrutiny. I doubt Liberace could so effortlessly win his cases today.

A: The law is still biased.

Q: But not as blind. That's why it's usually settled out of court, with token damages. Stars have much to lose.

A: Yes. They've often made fortunes out of fooling the public. But this whole business is based on make-believe. (Shrugs.)

Q: There's make-believe, and there's make-believe. Fiction is one thing. But pretending nobody rich or famous or admired is ever non-heterosexual is appalling, especially for young people.

A: You mean role models? That's true. It would have been much easier for all of us.

Q: On TV recently, I saw a clip of a 1930s movie premiere, and there you were. (He smiles.) That gaze and that smile! (Beams.)

A: Who was I with?

Q: That's just it. You were actually with Tyrone Power. But one of you was arm in arm with Sonja Henie and the other with Ann Sothern. I believe you all got out of the same limousine. Did you and Ty go home together, afterward?

A: (Grins.) It was a studio arrangement. You were paired up with someone by the publicity department, usually another contract player.

Q: Playing the hide the sexual minority game.

A: Yes. Arranged dates. They called them dates. But usually you just showed up at the premiere together. Sometimes you didn't stay for the whole movie. It wasn't like nightclubs, where you were obligated to arrive and leave with the same . . . "date." The crowds and photographers and announcers didn't usually stick around very long after the movie was underway.

Q: Who was "paired" with Henie and who with Sothern?

A: . . . I don't remember. It might have been . . . could it be *Ali Baba Goes to Town*? I don't remember seeing it, but I went to the premiere with Ty. That would have been the late '30s (1937).

Q: I know people in Argentina and Mexico, in the 1940s, who read in the papers there that you and Power were lovers, when you traveled there together. . . .

A: *"Amantes"?* (Spanish for "lovers.")

Q: I don't know what it said in Buenos Aires, but in one of the Mexican articles I read, the word was *"novios"* (meaning "sweethearts," "fiancés," or "bridegrooms"). Such coverage—not that Latin America is so socially enlightened—would *not* have occurred in US papers.

A: You said it!

Q: And such coverage didn't hurt either career. Can you explain?

A: Well, Mexico . . . we were there shooting *Captain from Castile* (1947). We were there about three months, we shared a house, and it was a wonderful experience, I think an excellent movie (about Spaniard Hernan Cortez's conquest of Mexico and the destruction of its Aztec empire).

Q: Did you like it so much because it was a bigger role than usual for you?

A: . . . Yes. But, um, before that, during the war (WWII), we were sent on a goodwill tour of South America, to promote the Good Neighbor Policy. One of the places we visited was Argentina. It was a great trip, lots of fun, and of course my Spanish was very helpful and practical, for both of us.

Q: Did you know about such newspaper stories?

A: I don't think I remember. I may have heard about it. But not at the time.

Q: Who would have been more upset about it, you or Ty?

A: Ooh! *He* would have. He was more of a worrier.

Q: ***Your* reaction would have been what?**

A: Well, in those days . . . but as long as they didn't get personal. (Shrugs.) I wouldn't feel it was any kind of an insult to be paired with Ty, in any way.

Q: **(Gently.) You're devoted to him.**

A: Yes (nods several times). I am. I always will be.

Q: **This quote sounds rather modern, but did Ty ever advise you, "People who live in glass houses shouldn't"?**

A: (Laughs.) Probably something of that nature. About not getting married. He was more Latin than me, in that regard. Many Latin men carry on their gay affairs after getting married, but to protect themselves—from suspicions, you know—they have these relationships with other married men. Which no one ever suspects.

Q: **Oscar Wilde said, "Nothing looks so innocent as an indiscretion."**

A: I think he went to a lot of dinner parties, that one. (Smiles.)

Q: **Cesar, you said earlier that in show biz it's all make-believe, so where's the harm? But the thing is, people like you and Ty—due to the one-sidedness and invisibility—had to distort your lives, hide your natural inclinations, and undertake an entire lifestyle to continue that make-believe after hours. . . .**

A: Well, *he* did. In a way. But it was to placate the public.

Q: **Not all of the public—the heterosexual public.**

A: Yes, well, I went my own way. I wasn't going to compromise myself that much. Just enough to earn my living and stay in the business. Ty may have urged me to get married, but I also had my own ideas on what he should do. Everyone does. Still, you do what you want, and he does what he wants.

Q: **Or feels he has to do. Would you have advised him to**

marry less?

A: . . . What's the difference? It's done and over with now.

Q: **In his place, as a star of his . . . box office, would you have undertaken all those marriages and offspring?**

A: I can't say for sure, but I don't think so. (Shakes head.) I certainly hope not. Though I'd probably have married once.

Q: **As Rock Hudson did.**

A: A good example. But remember another thing, Boze. When there's a mutual motive, things can be . . . properly arranged. I won't name names, or say which ones we're already discussing. But more than one star of gay persuasion—whatever, homosexual or bisexual—has married a lady, famous or not famous at all, who had little or no interest in the male sex.

Q   **Wasn't Ty's first—**

A: End of story. (Puts finger to lips.)

Predictably, during and after Tyrone Power's lifetime, the media dwelled far more often and speculatively on Cesar's more visible socializing with actresses. One of his closest pals was Joan Crawford, whom he met in 1932 while on Broadway in *Dinner at Eight*. They began dancing right away; like Romero, Crawford started out as a hoofer and later admitted that she never minded if her dancing partners were gay, since she even preferred dancing to sex. The friends danced almost weekly for years, and Cesar said, "It was the best therapy. Dancing together helped Joan get over her second and third divorces."

In between her marital liaisons, while conducting her ongoing but hidden affair with the oft-married Clark Gable, Crawford would be seen and photographed nights dancing with "eligible bachelor" Cesar Romero. Their mothers were also friends; Madames Romero, LeSueur, and, yes, Power, were members of the Motion Picture Mothers Association, a social group that met frequently, mostly to verbally bask in their famous children's successes. "Joan got her mother Anna to join, primarily to get her off her back. Joan never had much luck with her relatives," including her alcoholic (and bisexual) brother. By contrast, Cesar was close to his mother, Maria Mantilla, as was Ty to Patia Power.

Another good friend was sexy blonde Carole Landis, who later took her life after Rex Harrison—"a pompous cad and an ambitious creep," felt Cesar—jilted her. In the press, Romero was sometimes hinted to be romancing his actress dance partners. He was even announced to be "engaged" to Sally Blane—"We were just good friends," she later allowed—and, separately, to Landis. He told me, "I might have considered marrying Carole. We were the best of friends, and she'd had lots of problems with abusive or two-timing men—a rather sorry lot of husbands. . . . We had plenty in common." Landis was bisexual. Reportedly, one of her female lovers was co-star Martha Raye (whose final, far younger husband is now openly "bisexual"). Another was future novelist Jacqueline Susann, who based one of her three *Valley of the Dolls* heroines on Landis (played in the movie by Sharon Tate).

Yet another terpsichorean date and fellow spirit was Carmen Miranda, "The Lady in the Tutti Frutti Hat." Ironically, the most famous photograph Cesar ever appeared in focused on his fellow player at Fox. The "Brazilian Bombshell" favored a no-panties feel; one could scarcely call it a *look*, though it was captured on film once. Hollywood's most celebrated suppressed photo—until the one mentioned but not *in Hollywood Babylon II* of Marlon Brando allegedly performing fellatio—was of Carmen doing a dance turn with her costar in *Springtime in the Rockies* (1942). Photographer Frank Powolny recalled:

"It was a hot July day, and Miss Miranda knew the photographs would call for her to be quite active. . . . At one point in the action, Cesar swooped her up and twirled her about. . . .

The entire session was very gay, with two such animated performers from south of the border. But nothing, or so I thought, out of the ordinary." Powolny returned from his summer vacation after the roll of film had been developed. He found Fox in an uproar, for one of his shots revealed all—in one thoughtfree moment of *cuanto le gusta*, Carmen, suspended in midair, was on total display through the slit of her full-length skirt! The still was clandestinely circulated around Hollywood for decades.

Much later, Cesar said, "I believe Carmen was lesbian or a latent lesbian. . . . I do know that she was very close to her lady friends, who weren't actresses and weren't necessarily all Latinas." Miranda didn't wed until toward the end of her life—a producer who reportedly beat her. Cesar felt the brief marriage "was a business thing, for mutual benefit. I doubt he was anything but straight. . . . I think she married, after the war, because her career was in a serious downturn.

"We'll never know the exact truth about Carmen. But I know she could take or leave men, and was much more passionate about her lady friends, one of whom was a socialite known to be lesbian, even though long since married. . . . But above all, Carmen's career came first."

Q: **I'll bet if you'd had to marry an actress, it would have been almost anyone but Carmen Miranda. Am I right?**

A: Yes. And you know why, don't you? A Latin was expected to marry a non-Latin.

Q: **As happened with Gilbert Roland, Dolores Del Rio— two gay husbands—Lupe Velez (the "Mexican Spitfire") with Johnny Weissmuller—**

A: What a beauty!

Q: **Her or him?**

A: (Grins.) Both, but I meant him. Lupe knew how to pick them.

Q: **Cesar, you're one of very few Hispanic gays—and I mean mostly *off*-camera—who hasn't been a husband and a father.**

A: I think there should be a compliment in there.

Q: **There is. You've been true to your nature. I know several Mexicans and other Latin men who are gay, but all have been married and have kids, and they're still in the closet—in their 30s or 40s, 50s, 70s. . . .**

A: Well, in Latin cultures, only a screaming drag queen doesn't get married.

Q: **All that invisibility probably convinces them that every man is basically hetero, don't you think?**

A: In some ways, it's a very . . . backward culture. I can say that. Half the men in those macho cultures despise femininity, and the rest of them fear it.

Q: **Which spills over into how they treat women.**

A: Also how they treat gays, because it's mistaken, but they connect gay men with that. You know the thinking: If women are attracted to men, then other people who are attracted to men must be like women.

Q: **When does such stupidity cease? And what's so supposedly awful about women?**

A: (Shrugs.) Nothing. But it won't cease in my lifetime. I guess it stops when we stop going along with them.

Q: **You didn't go along. You didn't wed, and you've shown that obviously most gay men are not "women-haters."**

A: (Beams.) I always had a feeling, or . . . resistance. I remember one fellow, a family friend, a Cuban, when I was about 30 he told me, "You *have* to marry!" He was so vehement. Hostile, as if I'd personally injured him. I said nothing, but then he almost shouted, "You have to marry a *woman*!" And before I walked away, I thought, that makes no more sense than if I told him, "You have to marry a man!" But, of course, I said nothing.

Q: **Yet you didn't give in to his ill-founded advice.**

A: You said it! He might have thought he was well-meaning, and back then I might have thought he was against me—me, personally—but later I realized that it came from neither good or bad, it was just conformity. . . uniformity.

Q: **Ignoring individuality and diversity.**

A: Yes. He didn't mean bad, or badly, but if I'd have followed his advice—or even Ty's—that would have been bad for me.

Q: **And the woman lured into the relationship.**

A: Oh, I agree. (Pause.) After all, there's more to a wedding than the coming of the bride and the swelling of the organ. . . .

Q: **You said it!**

A: But now you tell me something. When I got that letter from George Hadley-Garcia, about *Hispanic Hollywood*, I didn't connect him with you. Of course, I knew you speak Spanish, and your *abuelito* (mother's father) was a Mexican general and diplomat. . . .

Q: **And author of over 40 books—my father's also an author. Well, of course in the USA only one surname is used—the father's—so you didn't know my *Garcia*. While "George" is my father's first name; I went by that, mostly, growing up—to my mother I was *Jorjito*. We had a maid who mispronounced it "Hirohito"! And my given first name is ancient Egyptian; I never use it, though it means "the well-protected one."**

A: And Hadley's the American for Hadleigh?

Q: **Yes. For that familial pseudonym I shortened it, otherwise, three names and a hyphen, it would be too long. But I wanted Hispanic readers to know the book was by somebody who shared the culture. I found in my research that over 95 percent of all Hollywood films with Latin**

themes or characters were written by non-Hispanics. So
no wonder there's not much reality in those depictions.

A: True. It's an excellent book—for the most part (half-frowns).
As you say in it, one should encourage the young Latinos—

Q: **And Latinas.**

A: That's why "Hispanic" is a better word. It's not . . . sexist. And
none of us speak Latin, most of us speak some Spanish. . . .
Anyway, as you said, encourage the young Hispanics to become
writers and producers (and directors), not just actors. So
they can shape the material and bring some truth in.

Q: **As with gay and lesbian writers, producers, etc.**

A: Yes. But now, *Hadleigh* . . . that grandmother was English?

Q: **My father's mother. Her father's surname was Alexander;
her mother's surname was Hadleigh—from Hadleigh, a
town with a ruined castle, Castle Hadleigh. It's near
Ipswich, England. And Boze Hadleigh is my legal name.**

A: Hmm. And you're of the Jewish religion?

Q: **Buddhist religion. Since age 11. But yes, part-Jewish—
my father's father, from Syria. My father was teaching at
the university in Damascus when I was born there, in the
British hospital. Delivered by Dr. Helen Thomas.**

A: Circumcised?

Q: **Me? I think you once asked that.**

A: Oh, anyone can *say* he is. You'd have to *prove* it. . . . (Grins.)
Anyway. Damascus is the oldest among cities, isn't it?

Q: **It's actually the oldest *existing* city in the world. I was on
a talk show once, and I said "the oldest," and somebody
irate—maybe from Iraq, I dunno—called in to correct me.**

A: Well, who would care about some ancient pile of bricks that
used to *be* someplace? You should have told him to screw off.

Q: **It was a woman.**

A: Oh, a lady. That's different. To "piss off."

Q: **Now, now. What did you think of Liberace's death? Not** so much that it was AIDS—at 67—but all the coverups?

A: Yes, rather old for that. But very sad. About him, and for him. He said he lost weight on a watermelon diet, all right, it's understandable. He knew how they'd react if he'd said AIDS.

Q: **But when it became known that Rock Hudson had AIDS, much of the reaction was compassion. And who cares about the bigots' reactions? They couldn't hurt him by then, and being honest would be a good example and a support to nonfamous people with AIDS.**

A: I guess he just wanted to stay socially respectable.

Q: **You mean socially approved. What's respectable about bigots? Instead, Liberace became even more of a joke, with his denials about AIDS *and* being gay.**

A: Mmm. A lot of people liked him, and a lot of people didn't.

Q: **Which is true of most public figures.**

A: . . . What was awful was the death certificate being faked, then the authorities digging up the body to prove it was AIDS. I felt sad for him, such an indignity. Of course, I know—if he and his doctor hadn't lied, they wouldn't have exhumed . . . him. But awful, such an indignity.

Q: **It was. But dignity begins at home. With being oneself.**

A: Openly. I agree. But you know, people like Liberace or this exercise person—the one who's overweight. . . ?

Q: **Richard Simmons?**

A: The one and only. Perhaps I shouldn't say it, but they're the sort of people you wish weren't gay. (Grins.) Or at least not famous.

Q: **It wouldn't matter, if the majority knew there are all kinds of gay people.**

A: Yes, . . . the diversity. One hears "the gay community," but the only thing we have in common is a same-sex preference. Nothing else.

Q: And oppression.

A: Of course. But otherwise, it's like left-handed human beings. And not only human beings, but animals—apes, and dogs and cats. . . .

Q: **Gay sex has been observed in over 60 species of mammals.**

A: Apes are basically bisexual.

Q: **But back to *homo sapiens*. Your comparison to left-handed people is the most apt, because both groups encompass every gender and nationality and color and religion and personality type.**

A: Every culture. Like in your book, just seeing the photos, *there's* the diversity of Hispanics, past and present. If anything, I'm surprised you didn't say who else was gay besides Ramon Novarro.

Q: **As you know, an even bigger percentage of Hispanic stars were gay, because of the macho attitude against becoming an actor.**

A: Tell me about it! I know. . . . Not just gay, but all the ones who go both ways—Fernando (Lamas) went both ways. He was a beautiful man. Very much in love with himself (laughs). I just thought you didn't name some of us because we're still alive. . . .

Q: **I did note Novarro and Antonio Moreno, both from the silent era. I didn't name today's stars . . . (Cesar then mentions a young gay movie actor, E.M., on whom he has "a passionate crush") . . . nor for instance Cantinflas, who was alive but did only two Hollywood movies.**

A: You damn near gave *me* away! (Frowns, then half-grins.) You didn't mention Arturo De Cordova, and he's been gone a long time. He was beautiful. I think all the most handsome Mexicans, the gay ones and Gilbert Roland, got into the movies.

Q: **From early talkies, I touched upon José Mojica. A gay**

Mexican singing star who worked in Hollywood and supposedly promised his mother on her deathbed that he'd become a priest. Later he gave it all up—the material world—and joined a monastery in Peru.

A: Where he didn't have to kiss any leading ladies! (Grins.) I heard him sing. He was very good. As the kids say nowadays, "He gives good throat." (Rolls eyes.) No finesse! The story I heard, from a friend in Mexico City, was that José's mother *knew*, and under duress he promised to join a brotherhood—he was already *in* the brotherhood, but . . . and I wondered what kind of fanatical mother he had? Thank heavens my mother wasn't like that. Maybe because she was a singer, that had something to do with it.

Q: **With relatives, it's a matter of luck. But what sort of "duress" would obligate Mojica to honor such a needless promise? Unless he genuinely wanted to be a priest. Or he felt guilty. . . .**

A: In which case his mother did her work well. Or, perhaps he was washed up in the movies.

Q: **Who knows—*quién sabe?***

A: You know what bugs the hell out of me? You should've put this in your book. When you have to fill out some application or government document, and it asks are you Hispanic or white? "*Or* white"! They have no idea. Can't they see? Haven't they ever seen a Cuban, a Puerto Rican, Columbian, Argentinian, etc., etc.?

Q: **I think they assume from the average Mexican immigrant, who's typically of Indian blood—"Indian," meaning pre-Columbian.**

A: But even with Mexicans, they're not all brown.

Q: **Most are *mestizo* (a mixture of Native and Spanish). And obviously the more wealthy or powerful Mexicans don't usually emigrate.**

A: And they're white. So what's this "Hispanic or white" business? It pisses me off. Not because I'm any kind of racist, but because it's stupid and incorrect.

Q: **I know what you mean. But at least they're recognizing Latins and Hispanics. Gays and lesbians aren't included in any census or application. Whenever it says "single or married," that doesn't signify. I, for one, have not been "single" since October 5, 1975.**

A: So what do you put on an application?

Q: **Depends on what it's for, but usually I mark "doesn't apply" or leave it blank. I seldom fill in what they legally pretend is "single." Or contractually "married." The one I never fill in is "divorced," which will never apply.**

A: You're lucky to know your own mind.

Q: **Who else's?**

A: What else surprises me is there hasn't been any book on Ramon Novarro. They come out with all these books on everybody. I even saw one on Audie Murphy a few weeks ago! And Ramon was a big star . . . if anything, I would think the story of his murder would make a book about him more commercial.

Q: **You know what happens? Because of his death, he winds up as a chapter in books about Hollywood murders or stars who died young. Usually written from a biased, judgmental point of view. You know, like his "lifestyle" helped end his life, or maybe he "provoked" his own death.**

A: You think because Ramon was gay there won't be a biography? A whole book?

Q: **Eventually. Maybe from a smaller press. But being gay is part of it. There's been no biography of Sal Mineo, who was murdered not because he picked up hustlers, but because there happened to be a robber, an ex-con, in his carport, who stabbed him to death. Sal's also featured in** those "true crime" books, mostly by male rednecks.

A: You knew Sal. Couldn't you do a book on him?

Q: I was interested, and my agent proposed it. But the responses from most editors, including the gay ones, were, yes, there's a cult, or yes, he was a star in his day, but there's never been a book about him.

A: What an excuse! I can see there's no hope for a book on me.

Q: There was only a trashy, biased *novel* about Sal—about his death. . . . When they publish biographies of gay or bisexual actors, they prefer them to have had a wife or wives. Like Cary Grant or Valentino.

A: I once heard Cary Grant, at a party, say he was Jewish on his mother's side. Then someone who knew him well said Cary would say he was Jewish on his father's side. And in one interview he said he wasn't Jewish at all! Strange man.

Q: In various ways, he couldn't decide who he was, or "should" be.

A: Very confused. But I repeat: *Audie Murphy?*

Q: He was bi, you know.

A: Yes, I heard often enough.

Q: But not in the book. . . . It's by some military buddy. Again, all a celebrity needs is one contractual marriage and/or child, and they're officially heterosexual.

A: Not even that, Boze. All they have to say is, "I'm not gay," and they're officially heterosexual.

Q: Biographers can and do leave out a subject's bisexuality very easily. Which makes the book incomplete and mis-representative.

A: Some people say that it's just one aspect of a person and not the most important one.

Q: In men, sexuality is certainly very important. And yes, sexuality—and *love*—are just aspects of a person. *But . . .* how come biographers never leave out a subject's sexuality

when the person is heterosexual?

A: *Touché*.

Q: **Likewise.**

A: It's true, though. One of the stars who's had a lot of books pinning him to the page is Marlon Brando. And as we know, he's admitted to being bisexual—they used to say "double-gaited." I haven't looked inside the books about him to see if they mention it, but I didn't imagine they'd leave it out. After all, *he* said it—and good for him. But I was at a friend's house, and there was some new book about him, by that (Charles) Higham guy—I almost read his book on Errol Flynn. Now, don't hold me to this, but I've heard he *might* be gay. I don't know. But this book, I looked all through it—the index too—there was lots of time, and it had *nothing* about Brando being bi. Not even his own statement. . . .

Q: **Quite an omission.**

A: So I guess they don't always put that in. But it seems to me, if a fellow voluntarily says he's gay or bisexual, and someone else is doing a whole book describing the fellow and his life, they should put it in. For the truth, and so it could even help. . . .

Q: **Exactly—the terrible statistic that more than three times as many gay and lesbian teens commit suicide because of the homophobia they face at every level. The distortions that make gay kids feel freakish, and the omissions that make them feel lonely.**

A: That's important. It should have gotten more publicity, when they found that out.

Q: **Hah! It almost had to be leaked. That statistic was the unexpected result of a study during the Bush administration, and then the Republicans tried to suppress it. They don't give a damn about reality or suffering.**

A: And yet some of them have gay kids.

Q: As many as anyone else does. What people often forget is that gays and lesbians are America's kids too.

A: It's depressing . . . the cruelty. And indifference.

Q: And the indifference to cruelty.

A: A young associate was telling me how most of the gay-bashings and murders don't even make the news.

Q: Or the homophobia that caused them is omitted from the reporting. Which does nothing to make such bigotry less acceptable.

A: And yet they talk so much about "family values." (Shakes head.)

Q: Code words; it usually means "heterosexuals only." Actually, a friend of mine came up with an excellent slogan for a bumper sticker; she's also urging people to write it on those postpaid postcards one finds in magazines. It says, *"Family Valued: We Love Our Gay Son Too."*

A: (Beams.) Tell her to get me a bumper sticker like that. Tell her I'll order some from her. . . .

Cesar Romero died peacefully at 86 on January 1, 1994.

Funny Men

PAUL LYNDE

(1926 – 1982)

First I met Richard Deacon, a nonrival comedian and grudging fan of Paul Lynde.

Then Deacon helped me to meet Paul Lynde,
once I got an editor interested in a profile of "the
new Paul Lynde"—as if the old one weren't up to
snuff!

Years after Paul Lynde's passing, in the final
months of his own life, I met Wayland Flowers, of
Wayland and Madame fame. Flowers had been
Lynde's colleague, friend, and confidant.

Richard Deacon was always the straight man,
comedically speaking. He appeared in hundreds
of TV shows and films and is best remembered as
the dour, bespectacled Mel Cooley of *The Dick Van
Dyke Show*. But let him describe himself:

"I was born in Philadelphia, a good place to
begin a career in comedy, don't ask me why. I
acted in college and began in Hollywood in the

67

early 1950s. I did a lot of uncredited appearances, my roles have been small, and nearly everything I've done reflects the physical me. I'm tall, I'm bald, I wear glasses, I'm seen as either dignified or pompous. But I'm not threatening enough to be a villain, so I often get cast as supercilious types. Like on *Dick Van Dyke*.

"I've done over 50 movies. *The Solid Gold Cadillac* with Judy Holliday, *Lover, Come Back* with Rock Hudson, *Touch of Mink* with Cary Grant, Hitchcock's *The Birds*, *Critics' Choice* with Lucille Ball—I also did her program; I was Tallulah Bankhead's butler in one of them—and Walt Disney things like *That Darn Cat*, movies with Shirley MacLaine, and so on.

"Loads of television, to the point where I couldn't count it all. I've done everything from *Leave It to Beaver* to *The Mothers-in-Law*, which Desi Arnaz produced. I replaced Roger C. Carmel on that, as Kaye Ballard's husband. Roger wanted more money, Arnaz wouldn't pay it, so I came aboard when Roger left. On Broadway, I was in *Hello, Dolly* with Phyllis Diller.

"I'm a great cook, cooking's my hobby and the only thing I'm allowed to brag about. I'm a cookbook author, I also collect rocks, and love art, mostly painting and sculpture. I'm pretty private, but not a hermit. I have a few friends, mostly women. Don't talk about my personal life, even if I'm asked. They never do. Same with Mel on *Dick Van Dyke*—people guessed his personal life was as dull as he was, so no one inquired. It was stated he had a wife, and that was that."

Unlike Cooley, Deacon hadn't a wife.

I met him at Pioneer Chicken one night on Sunset Boulevard in Hollywood, in the late '70s. I was in town on business, and after a movie stopped off for some drumsticks. I recognized Deacon as soon as he stepped out of his old white Cadillac. An elderly man was also staring at him, probably trying to assign the familiar face a sitcom's name.

We placed our orders, Deacon, then me, and as we waited, I

sidled up to him. He looked glum, and might have been intimi-
dating, if one didn't know that's how he always appeared. I told
him how much I'd enjoyed his work, and that a month or so ago
I'd seen him (in a fleeting performance) in *John Goldfarb, Please
Come Home*.

"Did you like it?" he asked with little enthusiasm and no
smile as yet.

"You were good in it." He stared. "It's a funny movie." I
paused. "Shirley MacLaine's great in it."

A semi-smile. "I liked her too." He was that *rara avis*, a performer who declined praise under false circumstances. Sadly,
Deacon rarely got a chance to shine. As Paul Lynde put it,
"Richard has the kind of career nobody plans on. It just turned
out that way."

It was a balmy night. We ate on an outdoor table. "You can
call me Richard" eventually thawed, from frostily polite to
politely chummy, smiles occasionally indicated at the corners of
his thin mouth or in his beady eyes.

It struck me as funny-odd that this man, associated solely
with comedy, had so little funny-ha-ha about him. Rather, he
existed on big and little screens only to contrast with funnier
personalities, e.g., Lucy, Tallulah, Dick, Carl Reiner. . . .

"As a straight man," he later explained, "I'm hired for my but-
toned-down quality. I'm nearly always an executive of some sort,
in suit and tie, and somebody always pricks my bubble of dignity. I've been called every adjective—smug, lugubrious, unctuous, bland, you name it.

"My character always represents the Establishment. I'm
never an individualist. Not at all flamboyant . . . ," the only time
I ever heard anyone say it with regret. It was a key to his personality. Paul Lynde later said, "Richard's a *nice* enough person.
Bit on the dry side, not overly exciting as a performer. Or anything else."

One got the impression he was somewhat uncomfortable among heterosexual men, yet not quite at home—because of his stolid rigidity?—among gay men. Particularly among gay comedians of a certain age, like Lynde—or Flowers or Billy De Wolfe, etc.—given to camping it up on screen and especially off.

That first night, it was Deacon who made the comparison: "I'm nearly the exact opposite of a Paul Lynde."

When I noted I was a fan of Lynde and hoped to meet him, Richard offered, "*I* know him. I can introduce you, if it's a matter of an interview. We're not close, socially—he's very private." In an atypical tone mixing envy and disapproval, he added, "Of course, he has a lot to be private about. . . ."

I imagined he referred to Lynde's well-known drinking and possibly his reported penchant for young Orientals and Mexicans. I wondered what Richard's private life was like. "Do you live with someone?" He answered readily, "No, I'm a loner. But I do like company." At last, a smile. "Would you care to be my guest for bruncheon tomorrow?"

I hesitated because I was surprised and pleased but didn't want to say yes too quickly. During my silence, his eyes went from hopeful to hurt, and he stated in a compensatory way which embarrassed me and probably him, "I'm quite good in the kitchen."

I invented a white lie. "To have brunch with Richard Deacon, I'll gladly cancel my prior engagement. You're on!" The seldom-smile returned. He had nice teeth—large and pearly, like Paul Lynde's—but rarely seen.

I drove the few miles to Richard's modest but cozy and artistic apartment. He prepared wondrously light and zesty eggs Florentine, "in case you're sick of eggs Benedict."

At his glass table, I asked what he really thought of Paul Lynde. "I'm jealous of his gift for being funny, regardless. He doesn't even have to try. In comedy, if you try, you're dead.

When I was young, I tried. I fell flat on my face—that's how it got this way." He said this minus the grin that would have looked alien on his face during a funny moment; Deacon during a laugh was always dead-serious.

"Then I learned the only way I could get laughs was through a situation. *I* do nothing. The star or other character does it. For instance, if a female character finds me sexy and chases me, it's funny because I'm no sex symbol at all. If I get spray-painted, like on *Lucy*, it's funny as long as *I* don't act as if I think it's funny.

"But Paul only has to *look* at someone, and he's funny. He can ridicule somebody just by looking at them. His body language is funny. It's a gift few have. Jack Benny had it. Also Danny Kaye, and certainly Franklin Pangborn."

I interjected, "Do you realize all the men you've named are either gay or rumored?"

He half-smiled. "It's a sound theory. Gay is funny. It just is. If a man is innately funny, he can't be a sex symbol. Don't ask me why I'm neither. But any man *that* funny is bound to cause rumors. Like Benny. Of course, he was married. . . ."

"So are most Hollywood gays. Tell me, do you think Lynde didn't get as far as Benny or Kaye because his image is less hetero? Because he's not married?"

"The only way Paul could have gotten further would be in a hit series, which is a matter of luck. I think people suppose Paul's a regular bachelor, don't you?"

"At *least*. Do you think people suppose that of you?"

"With minor actors, it doesn't even enter their heads. As far as they're concerned, we're sexless."

"Or vaguely 'straight'? Do you imagine any segment of the public guesses Richard Deacon is gay?"

He shook his head. "Not even gays. Most would be surprised. Only because what you see on TV—a serious guy in a suit, unsmiling—isn't how anyone thinks of gay males."

"Are gay comedians more outrageous than hetero ones?"

"I think so. With a few exceptions. Like [Milton] Berle—and he got his biggest laughs in drag, which is considered gay humor, though I wouldn't do it, unless ordered. But gay comedians are less boring, as a group. Danny Thomas, for one, just standing around joking, isn't very humorous."

I asked, "What's Paul Lynde like as a private person?"

"Not the most sincere man on earth. Come into the kitchen, and I'll tell you. Before the egg stains stick to the plates. . . ."

"Several years ago, Paul convinced me he'd taken a sincere interest in my work. 'I want to take your career to a new level,' he said. He said he hadn't done any writing since his early days in nightclubs in New York, but for me he was going to write a 'hilarious' nightclub act. He'd use his connections and see about getting me a gig in Vegas, and he planned to be at a ringside table each night and coach me afterwards.

"The idea appealed to me, although stand-up is something I fear, something I don't think I've done well, when I've ventured to do it at all. At any rate, Paul convinced me of his sincerity, and one evening, here, in front of me and his associate Wayland Flowers, he did a nightclub routine—short but very funny. Sort of what *I* was supposed to do, and he was so good at it, he convinced me.

"Then, for several months, we lost touch—separate ways, separate gigs—and when I saw him again at a party over at Rock Hudson's house, I asked him—in an undemanding way, of course—how the written act was coming along. He looked at me like he had no idea what I was talking about, and at first I thought he'd been drinking. Which he had, but everyone knows *that* . . . and when I inquired further, Paul said, 'Oh, Richard! Ya don't mean you took me *seriously?* It was an *act.*' For Paul Lynde, my act was an act. An acting exercise for him."

"That pretty much killed the relationship?"

"No, it only soured it. Anyone in a relationship with Paul has to be prepared for the worst. It's the down side of his ability to entertain."

"What about the saying that inside every comedian is a tragedian crying to get out?"

"Not me. I've done a couple of dramatic things. Always with a light touch, of course. But I don't see myself invading Shakespeare's domain. Nor that of Buddy Hackett—who *looks* funny, so right there he has a head start."

"Professionally, who if anyone do you think you resemble?"

"I've been asked that before. Once. The interviewer wasn't happy with my answer. It was in the '60s, during *Dick Van Dyke*, when I *got* interviews . . . I told him I sympathized with Bud Abbott, who was forever the straight man to Lou Costello. Of course, Abbott spoke much more than I ever get to, but he was always there to show off the funny man, and that means being personally underrated.

"By another token, he was half of an incredibly popular comedy team, so Abbott probably didn't complain as much as I did to that interviewer."

"Is the fat person, like the evidently gay man, always funny?"

"Again, our society perceives gay to be funny, and fat also. Look at Abbott's Costello, or Laurel and Hardy. Except, with Laurel and Hardy—who were the best of them all—both were funny. Sublimely funny and in my opinion geniuses.

"But there's one other comedian, or comic actor, I've drawn a parallel with. Do you know Richard Haydn?"

Haydn, a spinsterish British "bachelor," played supporting roles in films like *Ball of Fire*, *And Then There Were None*, *Please Don't Eat the Daisies*, and *The Sound of Music*. He essayed priggish professors, officious clerks, and generally waspish types. In *Sitting Pretty*, he was the mama's boy and town snoop who made (fellow gay) Clifton Webb's Mr. Lynn Belvedere— a genius "bachelor"—look macho by comparison. In later years, Haydn, whose fondest pursuit was gardening, became a recluse, seldom leaving his Pacific Palisades home.

"Haydn was known in the old days as a fish mimic. He imitated fish. A critic once compared me to him, and I can see a similarity, but not much. Haydn's more prissy."

"Have you ever been cast as gay?"

"No. Asexual, often. Heterosexual, now and then—if the part's bigger than usual."

"Do you think within the industry it's known you're gay?"

Deacon shrugged minimally. "No idea."

I glanced about in his living room. In the shadier side of the room, on a triangular wood table, sat a bust of Michelangelo's David. Unusual, since the David is usually full-bodied, nudity and all. This was just the beautiful—chaste—head. Had Richard become his own character?

He continued, "On the debit side, where *my* brand of deadpan is concerned, Paul's branch of outrageousness is very 'in' now. It's more acceptable than ever, and he works steadier than me—much. *He* can get away with playing it very nearly gay. That's all he does anymore."

"Do you think most people perceive him as gay or not?"

"Straight civilians have to be hit over the head with a mallet to recognize that even Paul Lynde is gay. His character would have to have a boyfriend, before it occurred to them."

"Have you ever at all wanted to be Paul Lynde?"

He took no offense. "Yes, as a performer. I admire what he does and the results he gets. I admire his wit and comedy. He still has several good years, which isn't true of most men our age. For instance, the TV people think I'm overexposed. . . . And I'm sure Paul has fun with what he does.

"But on a personal level, no. I feel sorry for him. He's special, and he knows it. But in show biz, if you're too special, it can lock you out of the success you deserve or think you deserve. Paul is a bitter man, and I can't blame him. He never found that one special vehicle to take him to the top. *Hollywood Squares* is probably his pinnacle." Richard paused, maybe searching my eyes for prurient interest, before continuing. "He covers it with drink, and he's very difficult to get along with. A prima donna. No wonder he's lonely.

"I'm alone but not lonely. He's alone and frequently drunk. Paul's big enough to swank, but not big enough to command or buy the cuties he craves. A little Paul goes a long way—in life or on the tube. He's fun in a program, but if he's the star, it's too much Paul Lynde. Like Ethel Merman in movies; she was too big for them and put the men off.

"I think Paul gets on straight men's nerves. . . . So I don't envy him too much, because if I was as funny as he is, and that effortlessly, I'd be somebody else. Or *him*. And being me isn't a barrel of monkeys, but from where I sit, it's a lot easier than being Paul Lynde."

I concluded with questions about gay comedy, a subject first broached by Richard.

Q: **How do you differentiate gay and hetero comedy?**
A: . . . We can laugh at ourselves. Straights—straight men— usually can't. In a nutshell.
Q: **How would you compare Paul Lynde with, say, Franklin Pangborn?**
A: They're similar, as you say. Both have nervous-Nellie images. Pangborn was always an official or a harassed desk jockey, and Paul, when he does get to act, is the same sort. With one difference—now and then, Paul plays fathers. I

don't think Pangborn ever played anything except a single man. That's odd, isn't it?—about Paul, I mean.

Q: **How do you react to critics who feel the Pangborn or Lynde stereotype demeans gay men?**

A: Some entertainers *are* stereotypes. Gertrude Berg was very successful, radio and TV. She was a stereotype—the Jewish mother, or as she was then called, the Yiddishe mama. Chico Marx played an Italian stereotype and wasn't even Italian. Jerry Lewis plays an idiot, but I doubt he is one. And Liberace's a stereotype, although he's not intentionally funny.

Q: **What sort of person or comedian makes you laugh?**

A: . . . People who aren't too confident. If you have enormous self-assurance, I don't think you can be that funny.

Q: **Paul Lynde isn't the most confident character, is he?**

A: Are you kidding? That's what made him. He always seems on the verge of a nervous breakdown. Or at least a major snit. *Snit*—with an "n." (Deadpan; fadeout.)

Paul Lynde became a household word on the original *The Hollywood Squares*. He starred in and dominated via his central square and un-square wit some dozen years of the 16-year series, considered by many TV's all-time favorite game show. Lynde was described by Alice Ghostley as "amiably crotchety." *Squares* host Peter Marshall called him "the funniest man I've ever known, and in this business, I've known thousands."

Lynde was discovered in *New Faces of 1952*. He stood out in a show that introduced the likes of Eartha Kitt, Mel Brooks, Ronnie Graham, and Alice Ghostley. In *Bye Bye Birdie* Lynde wowed Broadway, then got to reprise his role in the hit movie version. However, his film career languished, though he did two films with Doris Day—one less than Rock Hudson did. Lynde also turned up in the camp classic *Beach Blanket Bingo*, opposite the 60's ideal hetero couple, Frankie and Annette.

But it was Paul, not Frankie, who went into *Hollywood Squares* and found that his subsequent stage appearances were sell-outs due to the game show. To his utter amazement. Elsewhere on TV, Lynde was less successful, with numerous failed pilots. He finally played a paterfamilias in his own but short-lived *The Paul Lynde Show*.

In 1978 *Talk* magazine asked me to interview Lynde, who was instantly ready, willing, and agreeable. The resultant piece was titled "Now I *Love* Me!" Like all pieces at the time, it briefly circumvented Paul's "bachelorhood" by noting that, like Mae West, he felt, "I'm single because I was born that way" (West, however, had contractually wed).

The first thing I noticed in Lynde's home above Sunset Boulevard was his taste. We sat on a Recamier chaise longue, the tape recorder between us. The living room of the Mediterranean-style home was blue and white. Sunshine flooded the place, lending what Paul called "a Doris Day ambiance." He waggled his head at his campiness, but in repose his tanned face was actually handsome. It was difficult to picture him as the fat, unhappy youth he said he'd had to grow to love.

After the *Talk* questions and topics were covered, I asked some questions of personal interest. Both sides of the tape had been used up, and then came the campier and more honest Paul Lynde. He allowed me ample time for notes, in between head-wagglings. If he was unusually candid, it was partly because he knew that his statements, and the individuals mentioned, would not find their way into pages edited by women and men afraid of lawsuits and of the truth that *well* over 10 percent of Hollywood's performers are homosexual.

Q: **When I first saw you, in the movie *Bye Bye Birdie*, you were definitely middle-aged. Now you have a far more youthful image.**

A: My image has gotten younger, even though all these years have gone by.

Q: **I was fascinated by that movie. It was the first one I ever saw—the whole family—at a drive-in. We'd just moved to California from Michigan.**

A: I'm from Ohio, myself. People are nicer in the Midwest. In general (waggles head).

Q: **You were in the play and film of *Bye Bye Birdie*. What did you think of the film?**

A: Well, Dick (Van Dyke) was also in both versions. We loved that show. It really made us. And Chita Rivera, who was in the musical, was marvelous. But they signed Janet Leigh for the movie, and she worked like a trouper, so we had no bones to pick. But I *hated* the movie version! They should've called it *Hello Ann-Margret*. They went and built it around her and ruined the rest of it.

Q: **You brought the house down—or the car down—with your song "Kids."**

A: And ya know, that wasn't even in the show, originally. Well, not for me. Another character sang it. Then they gave it to me, because I was the one character older people could relate to. So I had to have one song, to put the kids in their place. But the teenagers loved it! They loved me—I always communicate with teenagers.

Q: **At the time I saw it, I was in elementary school. The references to Elvis Presley completely escaped me.**

A: Oh, that's funny. Because Birdie was Elvis. The whole thing was about this Elvis Presley character, only we called him Conrad Birdie. And it was such a hot potato, at the time. Parents, when we were on Broadway, they were afraid to let their kids go see it. They thought it would be this wild, Elvis kind of thing. My character, Harry MacAfee, helped reassure them.

Q: **One of the funniest things in the movie is when you and your wife and kids, as a heavenly choir, sing a hymn to Ed Sullivan.**

A: Yes. Well, little Miss Ann-Margret didn't quite steal *that* scene from the rest of us.

Q: **You are thinner now than then. . . .**

A: Well, thank God! You name a diet, I've tried it. Oh, don't even *talk* about it! Yes, I'm thinner, all right. But another reason I seem younger today is that I'm freer. Less conservative in my dress and my outlook. I'm *with it*, sonny! (Snickers.)

Q: **Do you also work less often, now that you can pick and choose?**

A: Yes! I used to work so hard it was ridiculous. Maybe I was trying to prove something to myself, I don't know. I worked myself into a stupor, until I was ready to drop. Now I concentrate on *Hollywood Squares*, which I enjoy.

Q: **You're just as funny now, but you seem less nervous.**

A: I also like myself more, which I think comes with age. When you're young and tend to be twitchy, you see the negative and risky side of everything. As you grow, you become comfortable with yourself and learn from your mistakes. You also take more time to enjoy life and to focus in on quality in relationships and experiences.

Q: **Do you have a special relationship in your life today?**

A: Well, I'm always looking. And you never know who might be just around the corner!

Q: **Such a beautiful home you have. Do you ever get lonely?**

A: There's a difference between being alone and being lonely. I guess it's an old cliché, but when you're young, you always want to be on the go, around someone all the time. I'm not saying I prefer to be alone, but now I can enjoy it. And if I were involved with someone, I'd want time and space to myself, which might sound selfish, but would be essential.

Q: **Do you have hobbies? Or time for them?**

A: Telling little jokes—that's a kind of hobby. For instance: I have a very, very rich friend. He even has a roll of one-dollar bills. . . .

Q: **What's unusual about having a roll of one-dollar bills?**

A: In his *bathroom*?

Q: **Very good! Speaking of rooms, do you spend much time in the second-smallest room in the house?**

A: My closet? (Titters.) No, strike that. *Please!* Oh, you mean the kitchen! *Yes.* I'm a lifelong dieter, but I feel very secure in a kitchen with a big refrigerator and very little in it. Cupboards are nice, when you're seeing them from the outside.

Q: **As for relationships, do you think being a busy performer discourages long relationships?**

A: Oh, absolutely. I worked 24 hours a day to make sure that the loves of my life *didn't* work. Maybe I should keep my big ole mouth shut, but hate is very close to love, and many people do live in hate, in so-called loving relationships—legal, respectable, and everything—but they can't stand the sight of each other. I couldn't live that way.

Q: **Your dog is named Harry MacAfee, isn't he?**

A: Yes. He's adorable. He's a Dandie Dinmont. If he ever has a little girl-dog, a bitch, I can always call her *Kim.* Or Ann-Margret! (Ann-Margret. played Harry's daughter Kim.)

Q: **I'm supposed to ask your feelings about divorce. (Both laugh.)**

A: This must be a magazine run by ladies, right? Divorce? Isn't that a rather tacky song by Tammy Wynette? "D-I-V-O-R-C-E"? Let's see. What can I say about that? Well, love can exist outside of marriage. And I just look at marriage as not being that important today. If that's too revolutionary for the *Talk* ladies, feel free to censor it out.

Q: **Don't worry.**

A: So enough about divorce and marriage. Let me say more about that not liking yourself. I guess that's the theme of this—unless you want a picture of me and Harry (waggles). Anyway, that's very important. Some people in Hollywood are terrific, but they just don't seem to *like* themselves. That's sad, yet at some point it seems to happen to all of us. And I think it's stronger when you're young. That's why so many young people choose suicide, just ending it all, which is heartbreaking.

And I could list you the names of some very sexy and attractive young performers who have just everything in the world, yet they're awfully self-destructive. They're trying to put a stop to themselves, because they don't like themselves.

Q: **Do you mean via drugs?**

A: Not just that. Bad relationships, or going for the big buck—taking the money and running. Which ruins a career—it means you do shoddy work, shoddy, shitty projects. I mean you have to look at the long run. But if you don't like yourself, you don't even want to see a long run.

Q: **Why should these young people hate themselves?**

A: Most of them feel replaceable. They know there's plenty more where they came from. It's this whole population explosion, only if you mention *that*, then it seems like you're totally pro-birth control, and the religious groups say that's anti-family. I hardly dare open my mouth for the public on any serious subject—it's so easy to become an *issue*! Most stars are frightened to death to say anything.

Q: **Do you have a motto or something that you live by?**

A: Not really. But I do have a favorite saying: "And this, too, shall pass." It's comforting. Don't get me wrong, I was never extreme or anything, but I was often dissatisfied with myself. From time to time I just didn't like me. Well, I must be doing something right, because now I *love* me, faults and all! And that's the most wonderful, healthy feeling in the world.

Q: In your career, is there anything you've never done that you'd love to do?

A: Yes! To be an opera singer. Imagine the kind of release that must be, getting up in front of the whole world and *screaming* your little heart out for two hours! I'd love to do it, and I am going to. Maybe on TV someday. I always say, if you want something bad enough, you'll get it.

Q: But didn't someone once say, beware what you wish for, for your dream might come true?

A: Oh, he was probably just some tired old wet blanket!

Q: Anything else you'd like to tell the women at *Talk*?

A: I wouldn't *dare*! I'd like to ask *Talk* something, in all honesty. How come, with such a big readership, I've never heard of it? I mean, I've heard of *McCall's* and those other ladies' magazines.

Q: *Talk* is in every beauty parlor in America. Only. It used to be called *Girl Talk*, but they had to license that title from a TV network, since it was also the name of a talk show hosted by Virginia Graham.

A: So now it's just *Talk*. No *Girl*, huh? Do they figure *boys* are gonna read it in them there beauty parlors? Say, does the editor listen to this tape, or do you just send the finished article?

Q: Usually they request the tape, for a listen-through, if the subject is "controversial."

A: Oh, *well*, then. I'm anything but *that*. At least on tape. . . .

Q: You worked with Eartha Kitt. Was she fun or fury?

A: Eartha Kitt the cat, fun? Lemme tell you, sonny, she gave ego a bad name. . . .

Q: **Are female stars harder to work with than male ones?**

A: All stars have hard-ons about themselves. . . . Now, then.

Q: **Alice Ghostley is so funny; she has many of your mannerisms. I've always thought of her as a female Paul Lynde. I remember her best from *Bewitched* and Julie Andrews's variety series.**

A: Oh, Alice is a pearl. A real gem. And the stories she could tell you about Miss Julie Andrews! (Covers mouth with hand.)

Q: **Julie isn't Mary Poppins, is she?**

A: Well, you know what (Hollywood columnist) Joyce Haber says about her—she makes General Patton look like Pollyanna.

Q: **You know what was *so* funny? Your drag scene in *The Glass Bottom Boat*, one of my favorite comedies. You looked so uncomfortable and antsy in that gown and red wig!**

A: Not *that* uncomfortable, dear. (Winks.) Actually, my dress was more expensive than any of the ones Doris (Day) had to wear. That day that I came in fully dressed and coiffed, I was the belle of the set! Everybody went wild! Doris came over and looked me up and down and told me, "Oh, I'd never wear anything *that* feminine."

Q: **You were also hilarious as the funeral director in *Send Me No Flowers*, with Doris Day and Rock Hudson.**

A: Wasn't that fabulous?! Those were some of my best lines in any movie.

Q: **Was Rock Hudson any fun to work with?**

A: Not on the set. The guy was—maybe I shouldn't say this—he was mentally constipated. Real tight-ass. I suppose anyone in his shoes would have to be, but he didn't seem a very happy man.

Q: You mean because he had to repress his own sexuality all the time?

A: Well, *yes*. What a pain in the ass! It's a tremendous price to pay, but apparently it suits Rock.

Q: Wasn't Tony Randall in all three of those Rock Hudson/Doris Day movies? He was funny, too, but in a much more low-key way. I think it took television to bring him really out.

A: Oh, honey, it would take a miracle to bring that man really *out*. . . . His thing is to act one way, like everybody's nellie uncle, then mention his wife in every other sentence. He was closer to Rock than I was.

Q: Let's see: you were also in a movie with Debbie Reynolds . . . ?

A: Yes (sourly). *How Sweet It Is*. Her and James Garner. They were nice enough; the movie stank. We did make it on an ocean liner, on the way to Acapulco. Jerry Paris, the director, wrote it on-board, each day. We all had fun, but no wonder it stank.

At night, we'd sit around and dish. Jerry told me those rumors that everybody's heard about Debbie and her *close friend* Agnes Moorehead. Well, the whole world knows Agnes was a lesbian—I mean classy as hell, but one of the all-time Hollywood dykes. I'd heard those rumors, but Jerry filled in some details that . . . Oh, I'd better not; I'm not even sure if the story's really true. (Eddie Fisher, Debbie's first husband, had announced his intention to include the story in his memoirs, until Reynolds threatened a lawsuit.)

Q: You know, I vaguely remember *The Paul Lynde Show*, mostly because it was set in my hometown, Santa Barbara.

A: Yes (waggles). It was kind of based on *All in the Family*, only we had someone who looked like a human being for my son-

in-law. I was no Archie Bunker, though—the guy didn't have
a mean bone; just cranky. The actor who played my son-in-
law was real nice too. I had a wife, two daughters, the whole
bit. Oh, well, that's TV for you!

Q: **Before that show, you had numerous failed pilots, didn't
you?**

A: *Thank* you for reminding me. Oh, God, yes. Five of 'em. I
did them with Bill Asher (a producer-director), who did *I
Love Lucy* and *Bewitched*. Oh, well.

Q: **Did you have hopes of moving up from smaller parts in
movies to comic leads?**

A: For a while there. I mean if Don Knotts could star in
movies, *anyone* could. I think comedy is pretty dead, for
right now, except in television.

Q: **I once read that Desi Arnaz almost cast you as a husband
in *The Mothers-In-Law*. Whose—Eve Arden's or Kaye
Ballard's?**

A: I don't know. There were preliminary negotiations. They
stayed preliminary. But I'd have loved to do that show—oh,
it's a riot! It's the only worthwhile thing poor Eve has done
since *Our Miss Brooks*.

Q: **Have you ever noticed how the Eve Arden character in
all those movies is always treated as butch and unattractive and almost referred to as a man?**

A: I don't know much about Eve's private life, but they *did* call
her a man in one or two of those movies. Wasn't it *Mildred
Pierce*? Some guy tells her, "Too bad you're not a woman. . . ."
Something like that. And Lucy has certainly made some
disparaging remarks around town; *she'd* never play such a
"masculine role."

Q: **Why would she do that?**

A: I think it was jealousy. Or rivalry. For a time there, *Our
Miss Brooks* was a real rival for Lucy. But let's not get *too*

negative, dear. *Kaye Ballard.* She discovered me, you know.

Q: She doesn't seem old enough.

A: Oh, she's been around. Kaye's a man of the world. Anyway, she was touring with Ray Bolger in *Three To Make Ready*, and I was nuts about Kaye. I thought she was the funniest woman I'd ever seen. Then she came to see me, and eventually she took me back to New York with her. I got to meet the important people. Which is, unfortunately, important.

Q: Tell me a bit about your background. Ohio, right?

A: Yes, Ohio—Mount Vernon. I was one of six—kids. In the middle, so I didn't get spoiled as the eldest or coddled as the youngest. My father was a butcher. Of meat. Didn't take to me much—the old buzzard!—and when I announced my intention to act, he hit the roof. I hit the road.

I was very fat. I was a teenage Edward Arnold, whom you probably don't remember. My mom thought food was love, and it was a pretty good substitute, I'll admit. But I weighed 260 pounds during high school and college. Obviously, I could either become a monk, a lunatic, or become a comedian. I chose a combination of all three (snickers).

Q: So you really don't have someone special in your life?

A: Oh, of *course* I do! You think I'm gonna tell the girls at *Girl Talk*? Yes. Yes, there is someone special.

Q: I've heard you have a preference for Orientals. . . .

A: Now where on earth did you hear that? Outer Mongolia? Yes, well, Orientals are nice. When they're handsome, they're really handsome, and they tend to be gentle and introspective. I don't really like shallow people. The worst thing of it is, nobody shallow *knows* they're shallow. Somebody ought to *tell* them! So they could work on it.

Q: Do you know John Gielgud?

A: He's a fan of mine, believe it or not! Anyway, he loved *Bye*

Bye Birdie. He saw it ten times or something, and then he said, "It's so delightful, so uplifting. Why they would send *My Fair Lady* to Moscow representing the American musical is beyond me. *This* is what they should've sent." Isn't that fabulous?!

Q: **You've certainly been on everyone's show—Carol Burnett, Dean Martin. . . .**

A: Yes, yes. But I always wanted to have my own show. Oh, but you know what was marvelous? Jack Benny sent me a note once, after I did Carol Burnett—she's nice too. It was so complimentary, so lovely. . . . But ya know, we could never have worked together. It wouldn't work—too lavender, with two old queens together. It's a shame, though.

Q: **The official Benny biography is Mary Livingstone's project. . . .**

A: Yes, the truth about *that* will be a long time coming. I mean the truth always does get out, even officially. But look how long it takes—look at Cole Porter.

Q: **It takes longer when the individual was particularly popular.**

A: God, yes.

Q: **Let me throw some other comedians' names at you, for reactions. No, you don't have to brace yourself. Just say whatever you want to.**

A: That's what I'm afraid I'll do.

Q: **Bob Hope.**

A: Bobs for jokes—in vain. Makes Eartha look modest, but without any of Eartha's talent to back it up. He proves you don't need talent to make it, even as a comedian. You just have to appeal to the masses on some level.

Q: **Lenny Bruce.**

A: Important. He was important to what we do, but his style was too crass for me.

Q: **Beatrice Lillie.**

A: *So* funny. Delightful and butch and feminine. It's so awfully sad, how she became senile. God, if that ever happens to me, let them drive a stake through my heart!

Q: **Phyllis Diller.**

A: She's lots of fun, but it wears thin, doesn't it?

Q: **George Burns.**

A: He's cute. But like he's the first to say, his wife is the one who made him funny.

Q: **Now who do you think is quite funny? Comedians, I mean.**

A: Well, . . . Richard Deacon (of *The Dick Van Dyke Show*) is very amusing, in his deadpan way. He's so one-note, you'd never *guess* about *him*. Stop me if I'm shocking you, sonny! But if you've hung around Hollywood, you've *heard* who's gay—what else do they talk about at cocktail parties? Cock sizes and big deals. And who's sleeping with who and why. It all boils down to sex and deals. . . . What were we talking about?

Q: **Who you think is funny.**

A: I'm sorry, I just think the sisters *are* funnier. Outsiders develop humor as a defense, but they also think funnier. If you're on the inside, you can *afford* to be more shallow. Why do you think most of the comedians and also the composers are gay or Jewish? It's a defense, a refuge—laughter and music. So, to round off this list, I have to say another deadpan character actor, Richard Haydn. I mean he's best known as that gay old uncle in *The Sound of Music*, but he's done a million and one things. Oh, of course: and Billy De Wolfe. Now he was on Doris's TV series, and he was priceless! He's done drag and everything.

Q: **Other than your drag turn in *Glass Bottom Boat*, do you have any partiality to drag?**

A: No, no. Not really. It gets a guaranteed laugh, and I love that, but no. Women's clothes are so *tedious*. Not to mention the hair and makeup. They're crazy to put up with it. I guess men just don't like women the way they already look. Besides, the only transvestite I know is a married man—not gay—and he does it so he can make it with his wife. He can't, otherwise.

Q: On *Hollywood Squares* your quips are often quite risqué, sometimes daringly gay. Is your sexual image a big concern to you?

A: As long as I can work, I'm okay. And they like this quirky persona I've got. If they call me nellie, okay, so long as they call me. You'd have to be a moron not to guess that I'm not a heterosexual, by my age. Best of all, the young people love me. They're my biggest audience. That's extremely comforting to a young man in his early 50s.

Q: How big a concern is aging?

A: For a man, it's big. For a comic—a comedian, a droll—not so big. Not big at all, professionally. But ya know, it's the quality of life that's important, and at my age I can honestly say that. Today I'm thin, successful, I'm far more confident . . . I'm happy, as I said before, and I truly meant it. I think, regardless of whether you're a celebrity or not, if you can honestly say that the recent years you've lived through have been the best so far, then you *are* doing *some*thing right!

Before I departed, Lynde—who didn't ask me to call him Paul—volunteered, "If you want to talk more, I'm available most of this week." He said it in an eagerly social rather than a professionally perfunctory way, so that evening I called and arranged to lunch together the next day. I had more than enough material for a standard *Talk* profile and decided to take him to the Brown Derby at Hollywood and Vine.

"We'll go someplace *nice*," I hinted on the phone.

"Ya mean," his voice indicated a head-waggle, "Hamburger Hamlet instead of McDonald's?"

"*Even* nicer than that."

The following day, he was visibly surprised and pleased (as I hoped I'd been in front of Richard Deacon). "Oh, this is *ritzy*," he murmured, sliding into a booth. "And it's not even my birthday—thank *God*!"

When the waiter inquired if we cared for drinks, Paul turned to me: "What are *you* gonna do?"

"Coffee for me, please."

"Coffee for me, too," he said. Nor had we imbibed anything alcoholic at his home, so if he did have a drinking problem, he hid it well. Naturally, I wondered how much of Paul's *bonhommie* was due to my being a journalist and whether he'd act very differently if I were a coworker, an old friend, or a new beau. I would never know.

The sheltering booth provided cushioned privacy, and the guest supplied a cheery intimacy, more at ease and quicker to make eye contact than in his habitual surroundings. The aged waiter seldom came by, even to replenish the coffee, but I didn't miss him or the caffeine, for I had a more refreshing stimulant. Again, I wondered if others weren't too harsh in their judgment of Paul or whether he was an accomplished actor.

Wherever the truth lay, hopefully he had at least half as good a time as I did. I'm sure it was fun being Paul Lynde—as Richard had guessed—for it was certainly fun watching and listening to him. A transcript can only suggest the peppery performance of the funny man in the red leather booth.

Q: You have the reputation of a connoisseur of the grape. Would that be red or white wine?

A: Uh, sonny. Not to put too fine a point on it, but I don't have a big partiality to liquor.

Q: **I didn't say you did, Mr. Lynde. But I've heard you go to gay bars. . . .**

A: Oh, I don't go there to drink. Well, (waggles his head) maybe the odd Shirley Temple. I go to get an eyeful.

Q: **Would you perchance call yourself a swinger?**

A: No, perchance. I'm just a big square at heart! I like my home best. My friends. A lifelong relationship would be ducky, but (pinches self) who's dreaming?

Q: **I'm surprised you call yourself a square.**

A: Well, that's my defense against having a wild image. A gay image, yes. Wild or booze-ridden, no. Unless you've read something I should know about?

Q: **Not at all. Do you socialize much with Hollywood folk?**

A: The *A*-list? (Sarcastically.) Boo-hoo. *Those* invitations don't come my way anymore. When you're new to town, with a hit or two under your belt, they invite you to the superstar parties, but they stop as soon as they peg you as *support*. A-list means bankable stars, bankable directors, bankable writers. . . .

Q: **And bankers?**

A: Only bankable ones! No, they're stupid, those hostesses. The average actor, doesn't matter how big his b.o. is—box office— is *shy*. Little Miss Wallflower. Or he has a chip on his shoulder that it took him all of three years to reach the top. Actors are drab, petty people, most of 'em.

Comedians are funny, right? By definition! And entertaining. But instead of inviting *us* to liven up their moronic parties, they invite the box office yokels and the Method people who sit in corners. Even in *this* weirdsville town, a room can only have four corners.

Q: **Did you ever go to a party and meet one of your film idols?**

A: Ya mean (waggles) like Clara Bow?

Q: **I'm sure she was even before your time.**

A: *Well!* (Does a Jack Benny take.) . . . Since we're dishing idol gossip, I once met Cary Grant. Lust at first sight! This was the previous decade, y'understand. *Very* previous. I'd worked with him. In his movie, anyway. Being a mere comic—a *droll*—I didn't have access to his actual person, but at that party, we got to shake hands, and he complimented my work! Nearly fainted.

Q: **You or him?**

A: *Me.* I shook hands with the man and thought, "Well, this is the closest I'll ever get to sexual intercourse with you."

Q: **He really impressed you?**

A: The ones you grow up with, they impress you. They're familiar, like relatives, and like relatives, ya never get to know what makes them tick. But in *their* case, they're glamorous, so you at least want to know. . . . Someone at the party whispered in my shell-like ear that Cary Grant once tried to kill himself. I'll bet *you* didn't know that. . . .

Q: **No. *When?***

A: (Snickers.) Not long after the, uh, first *marriage.* . . .

Q: ***That* makes one stop and think doesn't it?**

A: Who's fooling who?

Q: **The reality behind the public facade.**

A: The public being the public.

Q: **Did he ever admit to the suicide attempt?**

A: They never do. They claim they cut a wrist trying to open a jammed window. But it's *true.* I have a friend who collects clippings on Grant, and it was in all the papers, way, *way* back when.

Q: **I imagine Hollywood has put that incident well out of mind. Speaking of Grant, who wed, what, five times?, do you find it curious that gay comedians, unlike gay**

actors, are usually bachelors? I mean, as far as women are concerned.

A: If you're funny, they almost expect you to *be* a little funny. . . . We don't have the same pressures at all. A comedian doesn't have to carry a movie or carry that burden of public sex fantasies, like Grant or Rock Hudson. They *have* to marry.

Q: **They're pressured to, but they don't *have* to. Many haven't, including Tab Hunter, Monty Clift, Sal Mineo, Ramon Novarro . . . a long list. And after all, Hudson married once. Why do you think Grant did it five times?**

A: Five times more insecure? I dunno. But there's different levels of integrity. There's the official bachelor, the guy with one arranged marriage—like Hudson—there's the guy who marries twice—

Q: **Like Robert Taylor, whose first (to Barbara Stanwyck) was arranged. . . .**

A: Yeah, and the guy who does it four or five times.

Q: **Then there are kids. . . .**

A: Well, even Adrian, the designer, had a kid. So that doesn't prove much.

Q: **No, I know that.**

A: I have a friend, divorced, a passel of kids. Not only is he gay, he's passive with a capital Pass. . . .

Q: **That gives one pause.**

A: Oh, it's a conspiracy of silence. They want all the homo roles played by heteros, and the gay actors or comedians only get to play straights.

Q: **Why is that, do you think?**

A: I don't think, I *know*. Publicists have *told* me, often enough. They're afraid if they have me play a gay—*if* I accepted such a role, which is iffy—when I'd get interviewed about what it's like playing gay, I'd say it was no problem. No big deal. But they *want* it to be a big deal. They want the actor to say how he had to really use his imagination to play someone like *that*, and that at the end of a day's shooting, he goes home to his wife, and she tells him what a brave thing he's doing, and when the reporter asks *why* the actor took such a part, he says, "Well, I wanted the chance to stretch. . . ."

Q: **Mostly, they stretch the truth.**

A: That's just what they do.

Q: **Mr. Lynde, have you ever had—**

A: Oh, . . . (waggles). Call me *Paul*.

Q: *Paul.* **(Semi-waggling; we both laugh.) Sorry, I couldn't resist.**

A: You do it well. A little subdued.

Q: **Like they say, imitation is the sincerest form of—**

A: The sincerest form of flattery is a blow-job.

Q: **I'm sure it's hard to beat. . . . Where was I?**

A: About seven inches away. . . .

Q: **More than that. . . . But back to the question in hand. Have you ever had a lasting love relationship?**

A: Like a marriage?

Q: **A marriage in all but the legal sense. Since bigotry chooses to "legitimize" some relationships and not others.**

A: It *is* bigoted—we all pay taxes. I don't know *how* many families *I* help support! Let's see, now. (Waggles.) How do I acquit myself? let me count the ways. I'll say this: I've been in love a few times. As for a real union—a marriage—not yet. Won't happen, either, 'cause I'm gay and famous.

Q: **What's gay got to do with it?**

A: Men are tough to live with, haven't you heard? Men won't put up with as much as women do. So if I'm looking for a chappy to keep me happy *and* stick around, that'll take some looking. But being a *star*—'cause that's what I am, let's face it—it's that much tougher, finding one who wants *me*.

Q: **Gold diggers need not apply?**

A: There ain't that much gold in these here hills! I'm *famous*, not rich. Okay, I'm "comfortable." But set for life? Not if it's a long one. And I *love* long ones. . . .

Q: **Do you. If you had a partner for life, would you acknowledge it, that is, among other gay men?**

A: In a kinder world than this, sure. It *should* be. If you can call a merger between two corporations a "marriage," and they do, then a marriage between two men, or between two gals, is a marriage too.

Q: **Besides which, that word isn't a legal term, unlike "matrimony."**

A: Or mattress-phony, in Hollywood.

Q: **Society discourages gay men from forming long-lasting relationships, then chastizes the lack of such relationships and points to this as supposed proof of promiscuity.**

A: Oh, but let's hear it for promiscuity! Nothin' wrong with *that*! Men are men, gay or what-have-you, and men are horny—with a capital Whore. It's a fact of life.

Q: **According to my lesbian friends, relationships between women last the longest.**

A: I'm sure. That's because there ain't any men involved. Men can be such pricks!

Q: **Literally.**

A: But in my humble, nonlesbian opinion, no marriage should be without one. A prick, I mean!

Q: **So you're for gay marriage? As you know, many young gays shun the whole concept.**

A: I *said* I'm a square. Promiscuity's nice, but what's wrong with a long-term relationship? What happens when you're too old to hop from bed to bed? I think marriage, period, is a sound idea. Unfortunately, the heterosexuals, they want to keep marriage a restricted club. Keep the gays out. And that will not change in this century. (It's already changed in three Scandinavian countries, with more European nations to follow. . . .)

You'll probably find out, you can't help it when you get to mixing with people, that a whole bunch of gays don't really want anything legalized or brought out into the open. For a lot of them, it's more fun and exciting, and more sexy to them, to have it be half in the dark and stay hidden and taboo.

Q: **Isn't that less and less, with younger, less closeted gays?**

A: You tell me, sonny! (Waggles.) It *is* a serious point, I know.

Q: **Anyway, "a whole bunch" isn't necessarily a big percentage, let alone most. Moving on, who's the funniest comedian ever?**

A: Myself excepted? Wouldn't it be undiplomatic for me to say?

Q: **Oh, come on. Most of this isn't going into our interview, obviously.**

A: *Ob*viously! Tell ya what: I'm not a great believer in A versus B. How do you compare, for example, Charles Nelson Reilly to Franklin Pangborn? Who's funnier? It's an opinion. And Pangborn worked in the golden age of movies, had far more opportunities to do funny roles. Were movie comedians funnier than TV ones? Now, I think Tony Randall's amusing. Not funny-funny, but amusing. I think W.C. Fields was, maybe, consistently the funniest man in motion pictures.

Laurel and Hardy were entertaining, whatever they did. Sometimes funny, sometimes hilarious, sometimes amusing, always entertaining.

Q: **Where do you rate Abbott and Costello?**

A: Well, the first one wasn't particularly gifted, and Costello was tedious, after a while, *so* repetitious.

Q: **How about the hierarchy of gay comedians and comic actors?**

A: I don't want to say A is funnier than B.

Q: **Okay, then who is funny and gay, period?**

A: First of all, some people are funny doing one kind of thing. You have your English comics, who play butlers or bureaucrats. Richard Wattis does bureaucrats. He's always funny, but of course he doesn't tell jokes. The least funny people are the ones who have to tell jokes. . . . Other people are funny in most any circumstance, because they think funny, they have a funny outlook. Billy De Wolfe. Pangborn. Jack Benny.

Ya know who else is funny, maybe funnier than even he thinks? Alan Sues. He was on *Laugh-In*, usually playing gay types, like Big Al, the poofy sportscaster. Everything he does, he's funny—those faces of his, his reactions. He's like me, very quick to get laughs.

Q: **How do gay comedians differ from heterosexual ones? Or can comedy be categorized according to sexual orientation?**

A: Oh, I think so. Don't you? At least, there's *one* big difference. The *others* specialize in put-down comedy. Straight men put down women—their nagging wives, their mothers-in-law, their moms. They also put down gay men—

Q: **Attributing to gay men the feminine characteristics they hate in women, wouldn't you agree?**

A: Yes! That kind of comedian just demonstrates his contempt for women. 'Course, in the old days, he could also put down other races and nationalities. *Put*-down humor. Gay comedians, we don't dare to put anyone else down, and nowadays we're trying not to put ourselves down, like we used to be expected to do.

Gays poke fun at pretensions, at the arrogant, and we laugh at things we *all* have in common—like dieting or foreign travel, *you* know. It's a gentler comedy.

Q: **Where do "comediennes" fit into being funny?**

A: Again, they don't do put-down comedy. Except of themselves, if they're traditionalists.

Q: **Like Joan Rivers and Phyllis Diller, you mean, always going on about how ugly they supposedly are?**

A: Yes. That's very female. Men *never* do that; we're so much more vain, we could never stand on a stage and ridicule our looks or desirability.

Q: **Yet women are stereotyped as being more vain.**

A: That's why stereotypes are dangerous—they can be used to spread lies.

Q: **And keep people down—and make them *believe* the lies. As was the case with black film stereotypes.**

A: You oughta write a book, sonny! You could be the male Margaret Mead (waggles).

Q: **Come now. My hair's not curly enough. Do you think if a Franklin Pangborn were alive today, he'd be on *Hollywood Squares*?**

A: Oh, yes, he'd have beat me to it! I'm *sure* he'd be doing all sorts of things.

Q: **Do you envy his career in movies?**

A: Movies is *it*. It's what I'd like to star in, so long as I could control my own. Ya see, at *my* level, I may as well not do a movie role if it's in a crummy movie. It hurts me. I don't need the money—there's television for money. . . . But in the golden era, someone like Pangborn could do movie after movie after movie, and some wouldn't be that good, but it didn't hurt him.

Q: **Because of sheer quantity.**

A: That's it, plus he didn't hang around long enough to share the blame if the movie bombed! I'm in a trickier position because I won't take most roles that are too small, but if I take a sizeable one, I like to think the movie has a fighting chance at the box office. Otherwise, you get associated with clunkers, and so far, I'm associated mostly with this long-running hit quiz show, so people think of me as a winner.

Q: **Your comic type is very specific, and you've made a success of it. But hasn't it also limited you?**

A: You mean the prissy-Paul bit? (Nods gravely.) You're right. For one thing, I don't get taken seriously. People just see my name in the credits, and a smile forms on their faces.

Q: **Which is preferable to days of old, where people saw Basil Rathbone's name and hissed, right?**

A: True, but then he got to be Sherlock Holmes. See, *I'll* never get that much of a turnaround. It'll always be Paul Lynde, funnyman.

Q: **Comedians aren't really considered actors, are they?**

A: Not versatile ones. The irony is that if you can do comedy well, you can do drama. But it doesn't follow that if you're a good dramatic actor, you can do comedy at all.

Q: **Because of timing?**

A: Yes. It's something you can't get or build, like the craft of acting. Being funny is what you *are*; we all know people in real life who are naturally funny, and they've probably been told they should go on a stage or do a stand-up act.

Q: **Whereas most actors start out going to Hollywood because they're handsome or beautiful, right?**

A: Yes. Somehow they think looks are a qualification for acting. Or that modeling to acting is a *natural* transition! My ass! But comedy is *rough*—ya don't go from *Vogue* to comedy. Thank God!

Q: **Can I ask you whether you were snide or sarcastic as a kid?**

A: Are ya trying to say, "Were you *always* like this?" (Laughs.) Basically, I was. I'm just *better* at it, now.

Q: **Who were your comedic influences?**

A: I always liked Eve Arden. I liked her in anything she did, and the way she elevated the scenes she was in. She'd appear in some gooey, icky-poo romance movie and, for a few minutes, breathe fresh air into it. And some down-to-earth sarcasm and insight.

Q: **She was acerbic but likeable.**

A: So am I—I hope!

Q: **Who else?**

A: Well, I like Pangborn. Always enjoyed him immensely, but I didn't want to pattern myself after him. I think he was too much of a stereotype. It wouldn't work today.

Q: **Why not?**

A: Because now it's all in the open. More or less. Then, you didn't ever have a homosexual. Not acknowledged as such. Now you do. Now the jokes tell all: "Do you have a fairy godmother?" "No, but I have an uncle we're not too sure about."

Q: **In show biz, are you that uncle?**

A: *Moi*?

Q: **Well, you were Uncle Arthur on *Bewitched*. . . .**

A: Yes, but. . . . Oh, I don't know. I s'ppose I am. But not *explicitly*.

Q: **Does it come easily when you play a father?**

A: Of *course*! That's why they call it acting. I could play Sherlock Holmes, or a kidnapper, or a father, or someone with a lisp or a limp, or anyone who's not remotely like me. I *act*.

Q: **Do you think being the center square in *Hollywood Squares*, you've been at all overexposed?**

A: That's the nature of TV. It's a blessing and a curse. Elizabeth Montgomery will be forever known as Samantha on *Bewitched*, and nothing else, no matter what she does.

Q: **Some do transcend their TV roles. Look at Sally Field, who was Gidget and the Flying Nun.**

A: Very, *very* few.

Q: **A few years ago, you toured with Wayland Flowers. . . .**

A: We did summer stock. I love summer stock. Ya get to go out and meet the people, and believe me, they are *fans*. From that quiz show, they think they all know me, and they come to see me be someone else or do something new.

Q: **Do they know the real Paul Lynde at all?**

A: My God, I hope not! (Waggles.)

Q: **Who is the real Paul Lynde?**

A: *That's* a question ya answer in the bedroom, kiddo.

Q: **Are you inviting?**

A: Well, I'm not rulin' it out, sweetlips!

Q: **Do you ever long for a dead-serious role, just to impress people with your range?**

A: I wouldn't mind, if I could win an Emmy for it. And if everyone saw it, and I didn't play a murderer or something *too* gruesome.

Q: **Being liked is important?**

A: Within certain parameters, I'd say . . . *absolutely*!

Q: **What about retirement? Do you ever contemplate it?**

A: Only on Sunday mornings. . . . The thing about retiring is, it pays off only if everyone knows you're doing it. Like Sarah Bernhardt used to do—her retirement tours were legendary. She'd announce she was retiring, you know, real casual-like, and everyone would beg her not to. *That's* the way to do it. If you announce it, and people just yawn, it's no good.

Q: **This may be a peculiar question, but do you think if you were still fat, you'd be funnier?**

A: It's not peculiar. Look at the comedians whose shtick is

being fat—Totie Fields, James Coco, all the way back to Fatty Arbuckle. *I* wouldn't be funnier fat, 'cause I'd be too insecure, looking that way and feeling awful. I hated being fat. Some people just don't care, but I was miserable.

Q: **Also, fat people are supposed to be jolly, whereas your nervous image goes with being thin.**

A: True. Fat does not go with my image. I have to *look* good.

Q: **How would you describe your public taste in clothes?**

A: I'm not a picky dresser. So long as it doesn't itch and it's not Hawaiian, I'll wear it. I like color, and I like prints, but nothing *too* loud. 'Course, nowadays we can wear clothes that even Franklin Pangborn wouldn't have dared; times have changed. But one thing I try and avoid is dressing too young—nothin' shows up an old queen like tight armpits or ass-hugging jeans!

Q: **You seem very comfortable with yourself.**

A: Ya like?

Q: **I like.**

A: Well, why not? I'm the only me I got, I may as *well* be comfy.

Like most people, I never saw Wayland Flowers perform live, but I caught him in the gay "comedy" film *Norman, Is That You?*, in his own video special, on *Solid Gold, Hollywood Squares*, several talk shows, and in "his" TV series *Madame's Place*. I even skimmed the autobiography of his Southern-cracked-belle puppet Madame.

One afternoon in mid-1988, I was in Beverly Center, the huge mall which despite its name is in West Hollywood. This makes it probably the gayest mall in the world. I'd finished lunch and was passing B. Dalton bookstore on my way to my car—an '80s Mercedes had replaced the '70s Ford that Paul Lynde had described as "serviceable."

Out of B. Dalton bustled Wayland Flowers, with a large shopping bag. He himself was rather large, so it amazed me when only months later I heard that he had AIDS and was near death. I contacted his personal manager Marlene Shell and learned that Wayland was spending his final days at Hughes House on Ogden Drive in Hollywood. The small, intimate hospice for patients in the final stages of the disease was later forced to close due to funding constraints; however, it reopened in late 1989 and was renamed Flowers House, in honor of the gent behind Madame.

I was informed that Wayland wasn't seeing most potential visitors, so instead I sent flowers to Hughes House. The card said, "Thanks for the wonderful talk at Beverly Center."

That day at the mall, I had followed Flowers up the escalator to the food floor. To my delight, he headed straight for the Muffin Oven and ordered one of my favorites, carrot cake. And coffee. I milled about a few minutes, and since he didn't look to be expecting anybody, I ordered a cup of coffee and headed his way.

Our eyes met, and he smiled a tight but expectant cruising smile.

"May I join you?"

"Be mah guest." He moved his bag from the table to the spare chair.

"My name's Boze. . . ." After a swig of coffee, I said, "I wrote a protest letter when they canceled *Madame's Place*, and I have some of the episodes on video, including 'Barbra Streisand Nose,' a parody of " 'Bette Davis Eyes'."

"Well, now," he drawled, "a man right after mah own heart." He sidled closer, and I offered him a cigarette. When he declined, I put the pack away. "Honey, Ah gotta be careful what Ah put in mah mouth. All the good things are taboo now," he winked.

He told me a bit about himself, his background, and Madame's genesis. He laughed uninhibitedly—heads turned— when I mentioned that for some reason Madame always reminded me of Mary Martin. Then he told me an involved Mary Martin lesbian joke.

In the way of most celebrities, he didn't ask much about me, outside of what I did for a living. I told him I'd interviewed Paul Lynde. . . .

A: Where did it appear?

Q: **The part that appeared was in a women's magazine distributed solely to beauty shops across the nation.**

A: Paul would have loved *that*!

Q: **What sort of man was he?**

A: Very, very funny. Underrated.

Q: **Not by gay people.**

A: No, just everyone else. The guys who run television. Ah swear, he had more *pilots*. . . .

Q: **Sexually?**

A: (Guffaws.) Yes, well, he *may* have, but Ah meant TV pilots.

Q: **I wish he'd done more movies.**

A: *You* wish. . . . But he was a big, big star in summer stock. In his home state of Ohio, he'd regularly break all the box office records in the cities. He used to say he could run for governor in Ohio.

Q: **Maybe he should have.**

A: Honey, no! Paul was no Harvey Milk!

Q: **You knew him closeup. Did he have to work at being funny, or was it all *there*?**

A: He worked on his expression. Like the head thing?

Q: **The waggle?**

A: Tha-at too.

Q: **Richard Deacon told me Paul Lynde's body language was just naturally funny.**

A: Sweetie, *no*body is "naturally funny." You gotta groom it.

Q: **And you gotta have a gimmick? Like you with the puppets, and Paul's nervous, kvetchy manner, right?**

A: A gimmick, I'll grant you. But you gotta stay flexible within your range. Old Richard has no range. I mean, *had*.

Q: **He was funny in whatever he appeared in.**

A: In a stiff way. I'll grant you that.

Q: **You've been called campy, and so has Paul. Do gay comedians ever mind that?**

A: Depends who says it. We *are* campy. That's why people come back for more. But if some lard-butt newspaper critic says it, he means it derogatory, like it's beneath him. Straights don't even know what "campy" means, honey. Some jerk once wrote that Lily Tomlin's one-woman show was "campy." Now, the girl may be butch, but she's no bitch—not like Joan Rivers is bitchy and campy. Joan just appropriated gay humor.

Q: **So did Bette Midler.**

A: Bette's an honorary gay man.

Q: **Do you think Paul Lynde was too campy for his career's own good?**

A: Who can say? How do you second-guess fuckin' life?

Q: **Can you offer a few words or an impression of the individual if I mention some gay comedians of the past?**

A: A verbal Rorschach test? Shoot!

Q: *Paul Lynde.*

A: . . . Brilliant, funny . . . temperamental.

Q: *Franklin Pangborn.*

A: You know what he reminds me of? Whenever you see him in some old movie, he looks like he's just discovered an unpleasant smell in the room. A fart-finder!

Q: **Hmm.** *Wally Cox?*

A: Ah dunno, ask his ex-roommate Marlon Brando. . . .

Q: **I mean Wally Cox as a comedian.**

A: . . . Small reaction. Mr. Milquetoast. He was "Mr. Peepers," wasn't he? How far can you go doing *that*?

Q: *Jack Benny.*

A: Ah *loved* his swishy walk. And his body language, his long, questioning stares. He was a hoot! And gutsy too, doin' what he did in *those* days.

Q: **James Coco.**

A: The jolly pink giant? What can Ah say? Honey, he is such a closet queen—or *was.* Did you talk to him too?

Q: **Yes.**

A: When did you meet Paul?

Q: **In '78.**

A: *One* interview, right?

Q: **Two. One at his home, one at a restaurant. Why? Was one his usual limit?**

A: In or out of bed, you usually only got one chance with Paul. He didn't think he could impress people, time after time.

Q: **Really. Well, how about *Divine*?**

A: Very, very funny. Even just the way she looks. Oh, shit! *Looked.* (Divine died in March, 1988.) She was real smart, because it's the height of camp to turn female impersonation over on its head by being a glamour queen, but a 300-pound one! She was fabulous!

Q: **Billy De Wolfe.**

A: Fussbudget! He was good. Funny. Not *that* funny, but Ah never saw him in drag, and he was famous for it.

Q: **What about those who say drag puts gay people down?**

A: The whole *world* does *that.* Doesn't mean gay people can't let their hair down and party. Straight guys have locker room humor, which is *vicious*, honey! Ah've had firsthand reports. *We* don't do vicious, we don't hurt nobody. Anyway, fuck 'em if they can't take a joke.

Q: **Bette Midler's line.**

A: No, she *borrowed* it!

Q: **What's the difference between heterosexual and homosexual humor?**

A: Ah just said! Men are vicious. Gay men aren't. Where's the harm in a Dynel wig?

Q: **As opposed to locker room talk ruining a woman's reputation. . . . How about *Arthur Treacher*?**

A: Oh, yeah. Merv Griffin's sidekick. Well, Treacher was always the butler, till he ganged up with Merv. I've done Merv—his *show*. Who was that other English guy who did butlers? In the old movies.

Q: **Eric Blore?**

A: That's the one. See, honey, Ah'm from the South. Ah don't find servants funny, I'm sorry.

Q: *Richard Deacon*, **or dare I ask?**

A: Ah loved him on Dick Van Dyke's show. What else can Ah say? Honey, can Ah ask you a personal question? Did you ever go to bed with him?

Q: **No.**

A: Just wonderin.' Ah guess nobody did. Ah'd love to know if under that old stiff upper lip there was any . . . *you* know.

Q: **You mean you can tell about a man from his upper lip?**

A: (Laughs.) Honey! You've been around!

Q: **The mulberry bush. *Edward Everett Horton*.**

A: Ah *loved* him! Best thing in those boring Fred Astaire movies! He was priceless!

Q: **The "boring" Astaire-Rogers movies?**

A: Don't make it sound like they was filmed in parchment, honey! They are *dull*. Granted, the dances are magnificent, but the plots? You could plotz from those plots. And old Fred had all the sex appeal of a gnat. Though I grant you, next to Miz Rogers, he did look good!

Q: **Wasn't it Katharine Hepburn who said he gave Rogers class, and she gave him sex?**

A: *If* she said it. Ah grant you, it's a little true. Ginger needed acting classes, and Fred needed macho lessons. Every time he danced, they had to pair him with a framed photo of some girl or with Miz Rogers.

Q: Or with a female coatrack. You know, I read where Astaire once called Horton a "pansy."

A: Look who's talking! Mr. Macho mincing-toes! Puh-lease!

Q: What did you think of Danny Kaye?

A: Danny *Gay*? Ah heard a rumor or two. . . . He was funny—not side-splittin'. When he was *young*. He got older and lost it. It's kinda like sex appeal, is laugh appeal—some people lose it once they're older. But *un*like sex appeal, you can *get* laugh appeal once you're older.

Q: Can you give an example?

A: . . . Nancy Walker. She did a few movies in her youth. But she was homely, not funny, sorta pathetic—played these desperate, men-hungry characters. Then she shows up, years upon years later, as *Rhoda's* mom, and she's great, and unless she wants to be, she'll never be out of work again.

Q: Wayland, what makes you laugh?

A: *Me!* Madame! Madame is me, and I'm Madame.

Q: Like Flaubert said about *Madame Bovary*.

A: Madame *Ovary?*

Q: The French novel.

A: Sure, Ah heard of it. But *Flaubert* sounds like a runny relative to Camembert.

Q: Moving on to women. . . .

A: Honeychile, the only women who's skirts Ah'll willingly put my hand up are my lady puppets. . . . It's true! Ah always keep women at arm's length.

Q: That's funny! You mentioned Nancy Walker, Tomlin, and Rivers. Are funny women very different from funny men?

A: Oh, honey, who *cares?* Do you know this is the cruisiest shoppin' center in La-la-land? Half the guys workin' here are *gay!* Gorgeous critters. Looky there at *that* one. . . .

Q: They could recruit for *Dynasty* in this place. But moving on to women—

A: Bite your nasty tongue, boy!

Q: **Are women funnier?**

A: Gay men are funnier.

Q: **Why?**

A: Ah'm gay. Paul was. All the men you said: their names, they were gay. Name some funny heterosexuals. Go on.

Q: **(Jokingly.) How about . . . Shecky Greene?**

A: (Seriously.) *Augh!* I've seen him in Vegas. Typical Shecky joke: "What's the difference between my wife and an ice cube with a hole in it? My wife retains water. . . ."

Q: **Oh, God. What do you think of Pee-Wee Herman?**

A: He has Venus envy.

Q: **Huh?**

A: We're talkin' *straight* comics. Anyway, you get my drift. Does anybody not heterosexual honestly find Steve Martin funny? Or gutter-mouth Eddie Murphy? Now, Ah grant you, the *women* are funny. Bea Lillie was aces. Androgynous, too. She'd have been no funnier if she was a gay man—and I heard *those* rumors, too! Lucy was funny, but she got less funny the older she got. Of the newer ones, Ah like Elayne Boosler, also Judy Tenuta, Roseanne Barr, and . . . that's it. But Ah like people who aren't vicious.

Q: **Women comics don't tend to be vicious about womankind anymore.**

A: No, but some lesbian ones go way overboard, they do a whole routine about me-chasin'-a-man. They do it to *pass*. A gay comic can't do that; if he made jokes about his wife, no one would believe it.

Q: **That sounds like you're saying gay funny men aren't masculine, and masculine gay men aren't funny.**

A: You catch *on*, honey.

Q: **You really believe that?**

A: Was Tyrone Power funny? How about Rock Hudson? Or—

Q: **I get the idea. You do have _some_thing there.**

A: Ah got a lot here, honey. . . .

Q: **Wayland, about Paul Lynde. Why do you think he's become a cult figure?**

A: 'Cause he's dead.

Q: **That's all?**

A: No, but Paul had a huge gay following. Everyone always asks me, "How come there ain't any other gays as funny as Paul Lynde was?"

Q: **What's the answer?**

A: Ah think gay comedy died with Paul. He was the end of that line of comedy great gays (sic). All those guys you named—Horton and Pangborn and the rest. Paul was one of them, and he was the last one. The last great one.

Q: **Then, in your opinion, what killed gay comedy?**

A: Cock Robin. . . . _AIDS_, honey. And demographics—you gotta appeal to the scum o' the earth if you wanna do movies, also TV—my show didn't have a chance; people loved it, but not enough people . . . and if you do TV, you gotta keep it clean or have Paul's gift for staying clean but soundin' filthy. These are seriously aggravated times, honeychile!

Q: **The Aching '80s.**

A: Don't Ah know it.

JAMES COCO

(1 9 2 9 – 1 9 8 7)

February, 1987, saw the passing of three gay celebrities: James Coco, Liberace, and Andy Warhol. Only the one who died of AIDS was noted in the media as homosexual.

Coco was the least "out" of the three, due to his protected status as an actor and because of his weight. He confessed to *After Dark*, a crypto-gay '70s magazine, "When people see me, they don't automatically ask themselves, 'Is this guy married, single, what?' My weight puts me in another category, sort of androgynous. I'm not the type most people wonder if I'm available next Saturday night. Sunday brunch, maybe. . . ."

The self-described "butterball" was an actor destined for comedy who emerged as a lead in numerous stage, TV, and film projects, not all of them comic. "I've been shockingly lucky," he felt. *Motion Picture* magazine called him "the most popular big-screen fat man since Fatty Arbuckle and Oliver Hardy" (or at any rate since Laird Cregar, a gay actor of the 1940s who tried to diet his way out of villain roles, even though they were leads). Instead, Cregar died before age 30.

Coco had a lifelong weight problem. His peak weight was 315 pounds. "I'm a self-made man," he mock-boasted. "It took a lot of pasta dishes to get where I am today." After losing 120 pounds, he authored a diet book and appeared on *Donahue* to promote it. Almost inevitably, he regained some of the weight and died partly because of his loss/gain.

The likeable, pudgy actor broke through in the '60s as Willie the Plumber in TV Drano ads. He began in children's theatre but in 1959 won an Obie award for drama in *The Moon in the Yellow River*. To support himself—he later regretted having bypassed college—he worked as a salesman at Saks, a soda jerk, a Santa Claus, and a switchboard operator. In 1964 he won a part as a sailor in the nonhit movie *Ensign Pulver* (which was a sequel to a hit). Coco worked mostly as a stage character actor until 1968, when he starred in Terrence McNally's tailor-made *Next* as an over-aged draftee.

That led to starring in Neil Simon's heterosexual stage hit *The Last of the Red-Hot Lovers*, which resulted in a string of substantial roles on screen and two 1970s tries at his own TV sitcom. His talent was well-showcased—he could play "droll or deranged, adorable or murderous," he admitted—but a lack of moviegoers reassigned him to supporting parts.

I first met Jimmy in 1973 via a mutual friend when he was living in Greenwich Village. He cooked us a memorable Italian meal and complained ingratiatingly about the high cost of living in Manhattan and having to "live all by my lonesome. I mean, I'm not asking for a hunk, just a close friend, someone loving." Years later I read an interview in which he was asked why he lived alone (i.e., why he was not married), and he explained:

"I only live alone because I need my freedom. I couldn't live with anyone else. . . . My kitchen is so messy, no one could put up with it." His kitchen in '73 had been spic and span.

I contacted James Coco for an interview after the 1981 release of *Only When I Laugh*. It yielded a Best Supporting Actor Oscar nomination, and I wanted to talk with him about his gay role for a future book. We met in New York and ate Italian food at a restaurant of his choice. "I have a cute joke for you," he said. "It's supposed to be a Liberace riddle. What's better than roses on your piano?" I gave up. "Tulips on your organ!" he roared with laughter, almost crying.

For the waiter, Jimmy recited his most famous line from the Neil Simon movie—"I always wanted to have a neck like Audrey Hepburn." Then he turned to me and whispered, "Hell, I always wanted to have a *neck*."

Q: **It's ironic that you dropped to 260 pounds to play Roscoe "Fatty" Arbuckle in *The Wild Party*, or someone based on him.**

A: Isn't it awful?! But that's all people remember about him, that nickname, other than that manufactured sex scandal that ended his career.

Q: **He was tried, more than once, acquitted, and even so, was boycotted by Hollywood and the public.**

A: Yeah, I read about him. It was (shakes head). . . . The public was real mean then. All those powerful, prudish ladies' censorship groups.

Q: **Plus the even more powerful men in politics and pulpits.**

A: I like that word, "pulpit."

Q: **Does it remind you of citrus fruit?**

A: Reminds me of . . . how could I forget his name? Cardinal Cook, the gay one. Am I allowed to say that?

Q: **If they're allowed to closet people, you're allowed to say who is or was factually gay, lesbian, or bi.**

A: Didn't Truman Capote call him Cardinal Cookie on TV?

Q: **It sounds Tru.**

A: Well, it's sort of like Michelangelo—a *paisan*. After he died, I read one of his relatives got paid for publishing his secret love poems. Only first he changed all the *he*s to *she*s.

Q: **Relatives are generally notorious for that. But back to *The Wild Party*, from Merchant Ivory.**

A: Before I knew them, I thought they were importers or something.

Q: **I've heard both James Ivory (the director) and Ismail Merchant (the producer) are gay. Did you find out?**

A: They are, but they're low-key as a couple. I know they want to do a gay love story (they filmed E.M. Forster's posthumously published gay novel *Maurice* in 1987). But so much for them. (Laughs.) Not really. But . . . it wasn't "Fatty" I played, and I showed the darker aspects of the character, a movie star in spite of his girth, shall we say. *Not* a jolly fat man, which is a tiresome stereotype. The movie flopped bad, but I got good things out of it. . . . I do get tired of the funny sidekick, but I know that leading-man roles are more rare now.

Q: **Why? Aging?**

A: Well, I am getting older. Which does not help. But I'm no longer flavor of the month. I don't fear not working, but I sort of get antsy about being repetitive or getting offered only junk. That's why when people like Merchant Ivory come your way, you'll take almost anything they have to offer.

Q: **I noticed *The Wild Party* had its alleged requisite share of homophobia, despite the producer and director. . . .**

A: . . . Oh. Yes, I know. It did. But I'm only an actor.

Q: The homophobia didn't concern your character, otherwise that couldn't be an excuse. In Otto Preminger's *Tell
Me That You Love Me, Junie Moon*, your character—
Mario, right?—is described as a "lifelong bachelor,"
which is often a half-correct euphemism for someone
gay.

A: Yeah, maybe just a bachelor towards girls. (Grins.)

Q: Yes. But Mario fires Ken Howard, who is epileptic,
when a customer complains about his "odd" behavior.
And Howard's character is called a "pervert." How did
you feel about that?

A: I had a tiny role in that. The stars were Liza (Minnelli),
Ken Howard, and Robert Moore. So I had no input at all.
But I think it's . . . maybe it's there to show that people use
words like that without knowing what they mean. The
only person the epileptic was trying to . . . molest or
seduce was Liza.

Q: How would you define "pervert"?

A: Gee. Mostly a child molester. Or one of those crazies who
can rape a little girl or an old lady. To me, that is incom-
prehensible.

Q: *Junie Moon* was not a hit.

A: I have had the dubious distinction of being associated with
several very prestigious, exceptionally pricey *bombs*. But it
was a fun movie. You know Robert Moore's gay, and he's a
director too (the director of the stage hit *The Boys in the Band*
later died of AIDS), and he was always studying Otto or trying to get him to tell stories about one of our favorite
movies, *Laura*. Like how Zanuck didn't want Clifton Webb
to play Waldo Lydecker because he thought Webb wouldn't
walk across a set, he'd *fly*. And how all his life Webb lived
with his mother—

Q: The famous "womb with a view."

A: (Laughs.) Oh, God! And how the mother was even more affected than he was. They were great stories.

Q: **Moore later directed you in the all-star movie** *Murder by Death.*

A: A bona fide hit at last! That was the best time of all, working with people like Truman Capote and Maggie Smith and Elsa Lanchester and David Niven and Peter Sellers and . . . God!

Q: **You played a takeoff on Agatha Christie's Hercule Poirot.**

A: Yes, with a marcelled toupee and a rather juicy chauffeur who slept with me. If you've ever read the books, she wrote him like he *could* be gay.

Q: **Which is surprising. Old Agatha was full of prejudices.**

A: My God, she was an ace bigot! Hated everyone. A friend on Madison Avenue told me they used to censor her books for the USA, removing the anti-Jewish and anti-Italian slurs.

Q: **I've read all her novels, and one of her recurring themes is an abhorrence of anything Latin.**

A: But again, I wasn't really playing Poirot.

Q: **You know the first actor to play him on screen? Charles Laughton.**

A: Oh, I loved him! Talented, gay, overweight—no, fat, he was *fat*—and downright . . . not handsome. Yet a star and such a talent.

Q: **So likeable when he chose to be. Have you seen** *St. Martin's Lane* **with Vivien Leigh and Rex Harrison and Tyrone Guthrie as an apparently gay character named Gentry?**

A: Wait a minute! *St. Martin's Lane*? I saw a movie with the same people. It was in London, about street entertainers, and she becomes a star but Laughton stays in the gutter.

Q: **Same movie! Let's see . . . the American title was** *Sidewalks of London.*

A: Augh! How stupid to change titles.

Q: **They did that a lot with Agatha Christie. She had one famous novel known as *Murder on the Calais Coach* in America. The original title was *Murder on the Orient Express*.**

A: Someone should explain *that*.

Q: **How was Truman Capote to work with?**

A: Mad. Mad as a March hare. Wicked sense of humor. He said one thing to me, that if he'd said it in front of our whole assemblage, I'd have died. But maybe it was my fault. I happened to say, 'cause I'd seen him in New York, "Truman, you've gained weight." Quickly remembering to add, "haven't you?"—like that would give him a chance to say no, despite the visual evidence.

So he comes right back, glaring at me, "Yes. And if I keep on gaining, someday I'll be as fat as you."

Q: **. . . Cripes.**

A: You mean crêpes. Anyway, I was mortified. And embarrassed. But then he goosed me—which totally shocked me—and burst out in this little barklike laugh. So we forgave each other. Although I did not goose him back. Or ever cross him again. I later told Bobby Moore about it. He said if he ever wrote a book, he'd put it in there.

Q: **Wasn't Robert Moore one of the directors of *Rhoda*?**

A: You're right. Boy, you retain things. Charlotte Brown was the producer. It was the '70s.

Q: **You retain things too.**

A: Mostly water. . . . I remember one *Rhoda* story about Bobby. One episode he directed, with an anti-gay . . . slur, that's the word—like a slurp. And it was in there, even though *Rhoda* was more progressive than most TV shows. So someone wrote in and complained about the slur. But Bobby never saw the letter. Till years later, somebody mentioned it to him, and he was really . . . he took it very personally, even though this had taken place years before. Bobby was quite sensitive.

Q: But not to homophobia. Even though he was in a position of power.

A: He was ambitious. If you speak against bigotry, they think you're gay.

Q: So what? (Pause.) There are two kinds of homophobia. Heterosexual homophobia, which might be partly excusable because of ignorance. And homosexuals' homophobia.

A: Which is not. I know. I know. (Sighs.)

Q: Who was the funniest cast member of *Murder by Death*?

A: God. . . . Peter Sellers kept breaking me up. He was playing a Chinese, and he kept lifting his gown and asking, "Wanchee lookee underneath sheath?" You had to be there.

Q: How was Elsa Lanchester?

A: Like me, she was a takeoff on an Agatha Christie. She played Jessica Marbles, from Miss Jane Marple? She told me a few Charles Laughton stories—'cause I mentioned her late husband, how much I admired him, and she said, "He'd have liked you too." She seemed a bit sarcastic but happy to be working. She was open about his being gay but closed up about her own life. I think some of the wilder stories about her and her Hollywood girlfriends will come out pastamously (sic).

Q: Posthumously?

A: I didn't do that on purpose! It's posthu-, not pasta—it's a weird way of saying after somebody's dead. But she looked after Estelle Winwood. Who doesn't look a day over 90. Very protective with her. Sisters under the skin, I guess. Ho-hum.

Q: You've worked with women like Elizabeth Taylor, Sophia Loren, Raquel Welch, Liza Minnelli. . . .

A: Yes, and they all loved me. Everyone loves a fat man. Well, maybe not Dyan Cannon. But we won't go into that.

Q: **She was married to Cary Grant. Part of his matrimaniac lineup. They had a child. His only one, and he was about 65. The media kept saying how incredible of him. No one tried to ask why he hadn't had one before, especially with so many wives.**

A: I heard he and Howard Hughes always made love on water.

Q: **What, a waterbed or at the beach?**

A: On Howard Hughes's yacht.

Q: **You worked with director George Cukor in the Soviet-American musical flop *The Blue Bird*. With Elizabeth Taylor, Ava Gardner, Jane Fonda. . . .**

A: The first *and* the last Soviet-American coproduction! Horror-time. That is one country where I can diet. They don't do anything well there. Not the food, making movies, anything. I became pals with Elizabeth because we both loved to eat.

Q: **And Ava and Jane didn't? We *all* love to eat. Alas.**

A: Yes, but some of you do it on empty stomachs. Anyway, Elizabeth would fly in chili from Chasen's. So *that* was bearable. But the Soviet crews were beyond inept. So I panicked. So did Ava—last time I saw her, she was guzzling vodka out of a milk bottle, yelling, "Get me the fuck outta here!" I decided to get out of Russia *and The Blue Bird*. Which I did in a rather dramatic fashion—I had my gall bladder removed!

Q: **How was Jane Fonda?**

A *Thin*. (Sighs.)

Q: **You were an excellent Sancho Panza in *Man of La Mancha*.**

A: I'm happy to agree with you. But . . . another flop. Huge hit as a (musical) play, huge flop as a movie.

Q: **Somebody said it takes as much work to make a flop as a hit.**

A: When you're filming, you don't know *what* will happen. Nobody knows. We all thought *Man of La Mancha* would be a hit, from moderate to humongous. And it was a long shoot, eight months in Rome.

Q: **Otto Preminger again—you had a large role in *Such Good Friends*.**

A: All my roles are large. . . . Get it? (Giggles, sighs.) An unhappy set. Otto and Dyan Cannon became bitter enemies. Don't ask—I wasn't that involved in that. But another colossal flop.

Q: **Does it ever surprise you how many leads you've had?**

A: Because I'm fat? Yes, yeah, sometimes. But if you act too surprised, or grateful, then they think less of you. So I take it all in my stride. Officially.

Q: **Do you believe fat is armor?**

A: Absolutely. It is. It keeps the world at bay.

Q: **Also lovers?**

A: I was never handsome. And I didn't get fat as an adult. So I've always had a low self-image. One of the things I like least about the gay community is the looksism. You get judged on looks, almost entirely.

Q: **Looks and the swimsuit competition.**

A: (Laughs.) Don't even say "swimsuit" to a fat person.

Q: **Of course, heterosexual men judge women on looks too.**

A: Wrong! Heterosexual men will screw anything that moves, preferably female, of course. In New York I see all these handsome or okay-looking guys, and they're accompanied by some gross, fat-assed girlfriend or wife. No, heterosexual guys *don't* use taste in choosing their sex partners. At least gay men do.

Q: **Some heterosexual men don't, some do. But look at how many attractive women seem to choose unattractive men.**

A: Ah. That's monetary. He can be old, fat, ugly, but if he's rich, he's the one. And frankly, that's prostitution, no matter how you label it.

Q: **For the most part, fat is a choice. Do you agree?**

A: Too true. I know. Nobody forces you to eat. It *is* a choice, but in me the craze to eat is so strong, it might as well not be a choice.

Q: **And the key is how much you eat, not just what you eat, right?**

A: Yes, and I eat like a pig.

Q: **Is it any comfort that Americans are getting heavier?**

A: Not when I have to look at them! But even in front of the fat ones I'd like to look good, though I know I'll never be thin—I'm not *that* dumb. Or hopeful.

Q: **Nowadays, due to AIDS, I know several gay men use that as an excuse to get overweight or fat. They figure, at least no one will think I have AIDS.**

A: That is beyond dumb.

Q: **I saw Wayland Flowers not too long before his death from AIDS, and he was still quite overweight.**

A: That's another . . . misapprehension. That they're all skeletal. Anyway, I'll never have to worry.

Q: **About AIDS, or being skeletal?**

A: Listen, I wouldn't mind being kind of skeletal! I meant AIDS. People who look like me, my dear, do not get AIDS.

Q: **You mean it's men who are younger and quite attractive?**

A: The ones everyone's dying to have. Like, to have a hunk, you practically have to be one. But I am going to lose sizeable weight, it will happen. Someday.

Q: **Did you ever hear the bad joke about Mama Cass and Karen Carpenter? (The former died choking on a sandwich, the latter from anorexia.) They say that both women, both singers, might be alive today if Mama Cass had just given Karen Carpenter her ham sandwich.**

A: (Shrieks.) How gruesome! But how true! It's horrible. Still, you can't eat, or diet, for anyone else. It's literally the most personal thing on earth.

Q: **Do you think some young gay people gain weight to shield them from their own sexuality?**

A: Absolutely. Do you mean me when I was young? When you're young and you know you're different, sexually, and everyone will hate you for it, you do eat out of insecurity or lack of self-confidence, and you keep eating till you become asexual.

Q: **Asexual to other people, perhaps. You still have sexual feelings.**

A: Yes, and fat is like armor, but it changes nothing. It just keeps the world farther away. And then you can use it, the jolly fat tub of lard thing, to be funny and hide your pain.

Q: **Paul Lynde told me that after losing quite a bit of weight, he felt much happier and sexier.**

A: Yeah, Paul was fat, once upon a not so jolly time. He also used to be handsome. (Sighs.) I'm totally oral. I eat everything, and I mean everything (leers). . . .

Q: **A varied diet. Hmm. I once saw a man on TV. They asked him what he thought of oral sex, and he said, "I suppose it's okay to talk about it sometimes."**

A: Augh! He thought oral sex is talking. Well, *now* oral sex can mean just phone sex. As far as I'm concerned, that's not sex. It's like eating a candy bar through a condom.

Q: **Good grief. Have you ever thought of writing?**

A: To who?

Q: **Never mind. Was getting Oscar-nominated the high point of your career?**

A: Oh, definitely one of them. (Later he noted, "Losing was such a bummer. I almost felt as if they might give it to me out of sympathy. You know, a fat actor. . . .")

Q: **In Britain it's titled *It Hurts Only When I Laugh*.**

A: Really? Don't tell Neil. He might spit.

Q: **Your *Only* costar Joan Hackett was nominated too.**

A: Her and Marsha Mason, everyone except Kristy McNichol.

Q: **You've heard the lesbian rumors?**

A: About Kristy? *Oh.* Joan. Yes. I asked her. But she told me not to reveal what she said. If I tell you, you mustn't repeat it.

Q: **That's okay, you don't need to tell me.**

A No, it's all right. I can tell you. (He does.)

Q: **Your gay character in *Only When I Laugh* has no sex life.**

A: You saw him. Were you surprised?

Q: **Never mind. Point is, most supporting gay characters, unlike hetero ones, have no gay friends or partners.**

A: . . . Mmm. Neil Simon means well.

Q: **Did you see his *Plaza Suite*?**

A: The movie? Weeks ago on TV! I know what you're gonna say. The homophobia. Walter Matthau says his wife left him for another woman, so he says, "I married a faggot."

Q: **Charming of Simon and Matthau.**

A: Neil *usually* means well. In *Only When I Laugh*, I say, "There's nothing as great as dishing with the girls." That's not homophobic, is it?

Q: **Of course not. Many, not all, gay men might say that. Homophobia is name-calling and put-downs. Of the sort that no longer get said on screen about other minorities.**

A: When people stand up for themselves . . . it's true about minorities that the wheel that squeaks loudest gets the grease.

Q: **Squeak your wheels.**

A: You know what Cary Grant's nickname was? El Squeako.

Q: **Why? I can't imagine him speaking out for anyone but himself.**

A: Not for that. It's because he's so cheap. A friend of Dyan's told me that. He's known as El Squeako to his friends.

Q: **Wonder what his enemies call him?** *Oh*—**probably homophobic names. Or sobriquets; that's a nice word for names.**

A: I heard Howard Hughes hated English movies and actors.

Q: **Other than Cary Grant.**

A: The exception. Maybe he just hated Englishmen he couldn't get into bed.

Q: **I've heard kinky stories. I'm not sure Howard ever did it in bed.**

A: I heard he was right in there, in the witch hunts.

Q: **Many from the radical right were anti-England. William Randolph Hearst actually said—on top of being isolationist and pro-fascist—that England "deserved" to lose World War II.**

A: Thank heaven they didn't. I love England. Except the food.

Q: **Their food's better than people think. Tea and scones, toad in the hole, sherry trifle . . . many others.**

A: Toad in the hole? Tell me more. . . .

Q: **I thought you were oral.**

A: I'll bet Paul Lynde would have a good comeback for that!

Q: **Do you think he's more widely perceived as gay than you, and why?**

A: Yes. Of course, yes! Why? For so many reasons, and I'm not putting him down. On the negative side, for me, I'm fat, so I'm not sexual-seeming, period. On my plus side, I've done a lot of theatre, regular parts, but I think Paul did nothing but funny parts. And I don't think he ever carried a project. And he was on *Hollywood Squares*, which only encouraged him to camp it up.

Q: **Did you ever consider contractual marriage?**

A: Consider it what?

Q: Always the joker. Do you recall Lionel Barrymore's famous quote? "Half the people in Hollywood want to be discovered. The other half are afraid they will be." I paraphrase, but is that as true today as back during the, uh, "golden age"?

A: Just as true. But do you know about Lionel?

Q: Bi or gay, you mean?

A: One or the other. He loved young men. Often.

Q: How many people told you that?

A: Enough that I finally believed it.

Q: Like that Chinese saying: The first time you hear a rumor, you don't believe it. The second time you hear it, you don't believe it. The third time, you believe it.

A: Where there's smoke, there's fire.

Q: There usually is. Let's move to TV. You had a couple of series, but they didn't last long.

A: Understatement! On the stage and even in motion pictures, I had great luck and success. And movies have far more class and status, so I'm not really kvetching. You know this word?

Q: Do I know this word! Proceed—as Clifton Webb might say.

A: TV is something no one can figure out.

Q: Didn't Noel Coward say TV isn't something to watch, it's something to be on?

A: If he didn't, he should have. Anyway, I was in *The Dumplings*—don't you love that title? I loved it, and I hated it. And way back, I did *Calucci's Department*. TV wanted to present me as a fat Italian-American. Where *I* feel I can play *any* nationality of fat.

Q: Jackie Gleason was very big on TV.

A: And in real life. That's one good thing about TV, you can be fat and still a star. Movies is more . . . looksist.

Q: *Laṣt of the Red-Hot Lovers'* movie version starred Alan Arkin.

A: That was awful. For me. But that's the rule—if you're in the Broadway show, you're not in the movie. They go for "Hollywood stars" (sarcastically). Except Arkin wasn't one. (Pause.) Did you see the movie? (I nod.) And?

Q: I hate to tell you, it's hilarious. Arkin, Renee Taylor, Paula Prentiss. It's one of the few I can watch every time it's on TV.

A: How *nice* for you (in a Bette Davis voice).

Q: Have you a favorite actress?

A: Have I? Yes, but not Bette or Garbo, or anyone you'd guess. It's Priscilla Lane. I even have Priscilla Lane scrapbooks.

Q: Well, somebody has to.

A: How mean! (Laughs.)

Q: I'm kidding. Didn't she do musicals at Warners?

A: And comedy.

Q: What makes you laugh?

A: *Not* fat people!

Q: Ever have a crush on an actor?

A: *An* actor? What, I'm only allowed one? Tab Hunter. He looked good enough to eat. I mean head to toe. Back then, you had to look like that to bust into the movies.

Q: There was Sydney Greenstreet. . . .

A: Well, thank goodness. . . . Speaking of funny, I like food humor. But not fat people humor. Anyway, what's the difference between a last will and testament, and a man who's eaten all he can?

Q: Tell me.

A: One's been signed and dated. The other's been dined and sated.

Q: Good one. Did I read correctly that a gay playwright

wrote a play for you?

A: You did. My friend Terrence McNally wrote me a play called *Next*, about a fat man who gets drafted. He's a fine writer.

Q: **And a fine man, I've heard. So you're from the Bronx?**

A: If I'd stayed, I'd have had two choices—join the mafia or open a grocery store. No contest. I love food and hate blood.

Q: **Reminds me of the guy who wanted to become a tree surgeon, but he couldn't stand the sight of sap.**

A: I like that. . . . Do you know what led me to acting? *Snow White and the Seven Dwarfs*. I was the wicked witch. In drag. I loved it. *Acting*. I said, "This is for me."

Q: **So you headed for Broadway?**

A: I detoured into commercials. But they liked that I was fat. Acting is one area where if you're fat, it can help. Fat people have always been entertainers. Probably the first court jester was fat.

Q: **Or a dwarf.**

A: Or a fat dwarf. Double the laughs!

Q: **What woman do you think is really funny?**

A: Dody Goodman. That weird, fabulous voice. She's a riot.

Q: **Any funny men?**

A: In New York City—are you kiddin'? (Laughs.) Oh, you mean the competition. Like Paul Lynde. Good question, but I've gotta go. I have a cooking class to prepare for. But we are gonna talk again. (Gathering his things, keeps talking.) That could even be a fabulous theme for a book, about gay comedians and gay humor and all that.

Q: **You could be one of the interviewees.**

A: Me in a book?! I wouldn't mind. But as an expert, not one of the subjects. I do want to keep working, you know.

In 1982 Jimmy sent me a thinking-of-you card enclosing a handwritten tortellini recipe. Over the next few years we talked on the phone a handful of times. The third time he called he said, "I appreciate that you let me call. Most people, if I gave them my number, they'd call too often or want something every time they called." He inquired regularly after my book project, originally intended to comprise actors discussing gay or lesbian roles and how they related to their careers and lives. In 1984 I switched to a broader picture—gay- and lesbian-themed movies, their stars, makers, characters, and critics. *The Lavender Screen* was published in 1993, preceded by Parker Tyler's *Screening the Sexes* in 1972 and Vito Russo's *The Celluloid Closet* in 1981.

Q: **I interrupted you in a movie?**

A: One of my favorites. It's okay, I have it on video. I'll watch the rest later or tomorrow.

Q: **Which one?**

A: *To Each His Own* (1946). Olivia de Havilland. It won her her first Oscar.

Q: **I saw it once. How come you like it so much?**

A: Cheap sentiment. It's so full of it. It's about an unwed mother who doesn't get to say she's her own child's mother. It's kind of so awful, it's good. I think it was one of the first movies to deal with that whole theme and the taboo.

Q: **Bette Davis did an earlier film on the same subject, *The Old Maid* (1939).**

A: Leave it to Bette. Well, this one's so . . . emotionally gaudy. And it had this fabulous gay director (Mitchell Leisen), who used to be a fashion (no: costume) designer, so it's very campy.

Q: ***The Old Maid* had a gay director too, Edmund Goulding. Not very campy, though.**

A: I can send you a videocopy of it, if you like.

Q: **Thanks, Jimmy. But honestly I don't recall much enjoying that movie. It seemed rather forced.**

A: It has one thing going for it, besides the great ending where the big lug (John Lund) finally realizes she's his natural mother. It's the part where Olivia gives up her baby forever. Her dad convinces her, because of what people will think. So she keeps silent and becomes very rich but lives in all this emotional turmoil.

Q: **Hiding her secret because of what people will think.**

A: As if they do! Right?

Q: **I remember that now. The point is, if she and others like her didn't keep silent and give in to prejudice, the stigma attached to unwed motherhood would be far less, and the turmoil too.**

A: It's like that AIDS group (ACT UP) motto, *Silence Equals Death*.

Q: **Self-oppression.**

A: What's the last good movie you saw?

Q: **Good or fun? Let's see . . . some days ago I caught *Stalag 17*, which I think I saw as a child, but all war movies blurred together then. But I saw it all, though I didn't intend to. It grabbed me, it was very interesting, the writing, the cast, particularly William Holden as the anti-hero and Peter Graves as the surprise traitor.**

A: Didn't Holden get an Oscar for that?

Q: **Yes. And I'd have voted for you for *Only When I Laugh*.**

A: You're sweet. And noncaloric. But I do think I was gypped.

Q: **Yet it wasn't that much of a metamorphosis. . . .**

A: Augh! (Guffaws.) How nasty!

Q: **No, no. A gay actor playing a gay character?**

A: A gay overweight actor playing someone gay and overweight.

Q: **You brought *that* up.**

A: Not overweight, *fat*. I know I keep bringing it up, but . . . if I keep mentioning it, maybe I'll *do* something about it. It's just something my friends have to put up with.

Q: Aren't people lovable by the pound?

A: That's really sweet! Guess what I'm eating. An apple danish.

Q: They can be good. I bake a wonderful apple crisp.

A: Oh . . . don't even tell me. Or next time I'm on the coast I'll have to come over and eat you, I mean your dessert. *God.*

Q: Ahem. Who do you admire among actors? I mean besides Olivier and Brando.

A: They're overrated anyway. At least a teensy bit.

Q: Bet you wouldn't say that in public.

A: Some things one doesn't say. Party line: Olivier's the best English actor, Brando the best American one. Ho-hum. Who do I admire? . . . Richard Burton. You know he's like me? An addict. But to alcohol. Which isn't why I admire him. But he's handsome, talented, he has charisma and that fabulous voice, and I read he said something like, I used to be a homosexual but it didn't work out. Do you believe that? The *guts*. . . . I guess he made it with the wrong guy.

Q: Or he felt more comfortable being approved of. But I can hardly imagine any Hollywood star making a statement like that.

A: Especially a gay one wouldn't. That self-oppression hang-up.

Q: Yes. Of course, it's easier to say what he did if one is married to Elizabeth Taylor. But it's still brave.

A: Bisexuality's more common in Europe.

Q: Or reality about its existence.

A: And they eat less. I mean food. (Snickers.)

Q: Have you been to Vienna?

A: You mean the food? Or the Vienna sausages . . . ?

Q: The desserts. A city renowned for its cakes, but I think they're better here.

A: Did you try the Sacher torte?

Q: Yes, and it's good but not spectacular.

A: I could go there for two weeks and just eat.

Q: You'll eat just as well in New York. Where I wanted to go was Mayerling.

A: Where?

Q: That's the hunting lodge where the Austrian crown prince shot himself and the young woman he loved but wasn't allowed to live with.

A: Didn't they make a movie of that?

Q: One with Danielle Darrieux that I've always heard about— my father attended the Sorbonne, he's a Francophile.

A: I love franks too.

Q: I'll ignore that. You probably thought I meant Oscar Mayerling? (He giggles.) But it never shows anywhere, and the '60s color version with Omar Sharif and Catherine Deneuve is stunning. So were they. And the music is sublime.

A: Omar Sharif! He was so sexy! Then . . . poof! *Nada.*

Q: They both were, but she looks better now. Than him, I mean. It also had Ava Gardner and James Mason as his parents. You must see it when it's on TV.

A: Straight love stories, I dunno. So boring and routine.

Q: Most are routine, but not all are boring. This one's not, with that ending and the music, plus it's history.

A: But fictionalized.

Q: Most movies are, to some extent.

A: No, I mean this wasn't as romantic as you think. He killed her.

Q: It was a suicide pact.

A: Well, I don't know when they found this out, but that's just the official story. She cut his thing off, or things, with a big hunting knife. He was drunk, and then he got mad and killed her. And then himself.

Q: **Where did you read this?**

A: Somebody gave me the whole story. And it was on TV.

Q: **Are you sure?**

A: Of course. Maybe you don't read enough *modern* history. Your father taught ancient history?

Q: **Yes, but—**

A: I'm sorry, Boze. But that's the real truth that the royal family covered up. They preferred the story about star-crossed lovers.

Q: **Who couldn't live without each other. . . . I'm amazed.**

A: Most princes are schmucks. He'd already lost interest in her. What was her name?

Q: **Maria Vetsera. He was Crown Prince Rudolph. Go on.**

A: You really didn't know? I think he found another woman. Maria found out, and when he got really drunk—

Q: **At the hunting lodge?**

A: Yes. Where the hunting knife was. Sorry.

Q: **I'm amazed.**

A: Don't always believe the movies, Boze.

Q: **I'm supposed to know that.**

A: This one was no fairy tale.

Q: **More like a fatal *Who's Afraid of Virginia Woolf?* I *must* read up on this. . . .**

A: Movies are better than life in one way—the people look better.

Q **Right. Look at Cleopatra. In the few likenesses, she looked nothing like Elizabeth Taylor. Or even Claudette Colbert. More like Theda Bara, but not even.**

A: I saw a picture of her, on a coin, in a book. Just a fat Greek with a hooked nose.

Q: **I don't think she was fat, but she was plain. . . . What's the worst thing that ever happened to you?**

A: . . . When my mother died. I was just hitting puberty.

Q: **I'm sorry. I didn't mean . . . to get that answer.**

A: It's okay. After that, things could only improve for me. She could never have dreamed I'd be so successful, you know. When I won an Obie, there was this story in the local paper. But I was almost glad my mother couldn't read the headline. It said, "Local Boy an Autistic Success on Stage." (Laughs softly.) I considered suing. For about two seconds. Finally I showed the paper to my relatives who hadn't seen it, without any comment. They read the headline and congratulated me. They didn't know from artistic. They were from Sicily.

Q: **By the way, congratulations on your Emmy.**

A: Thanks! I wondered when and if. . . .

Q: **You were a popular win. Someone asked me if your escort (actress Doris Roberts) was your fiancée.**

A: He thought I'm . . . ? Oh, God! He must be straight.

Q: **That, or he's spent his life in the Louvre.**

A: Doris is my official escort, and me hers. We've worked together, laughed together, cried together, we go way back. Have you read *The House of Breath*?

Q: **No. Did she write it?**

A: Her husband did. William Goyen. He was bisexual. You should read it, it's famous, though it's real old (published in 1950).

Q: **Ah, literature. Yes, I must. Some time. Do your traditional relatives ask, "How come you're not married?"**

A: Not so often as they would if I wasn't a star. I just make it sound like I have to continue exactly as is, to remain a success.

Q: **"An artist walks alone."**

A: You know that I used to be addicted?

Q: **To what? Pasta?**

A: Worse. You asked about the worst thing in my life, but the worst times in my life were much of the 1960s. I was hooked on amphetamines because of my weight. So I had a Jekyll-and-Hyde personality and lost most of my friends.

Q: **How awful. What brought you back?**

A: Success. Nothing succeeds like excess, right? Once I became the toast of Broadway, I was okay. Okay enough to kick amphetamines, but not okay enough to become thin again. If I ever was.

Q: **What motivation would that require?**

A: I suppose a live-in hunk. No: *reincarnation.*

Q: **What about gigolos?**

A: A few years ago, this brazen hunk at some party said to me that he'd be willing—wasn't he kind?—to move in with me on a temporary, no-strings basis. *If* I paid all his bills, gave him a general allowance and a "small car," probably an Alfa-Romeo, and so long as I didn't ask any questions about what he did on his own time.

Q: **And you didn't take him up on it? (Both laugh.)**

A: I told him if I did all that, he wouldn't *own* any of his own fucking time!

Q: **Why not rent him for a night? Or a few hours?**

A: . . . You *are* innocent. Apart from my frequent feelings of physical self-consciousness, I'd get to see the repulsion in his eyes. And the contempt afterwards, and then have to live with the dread that he'd go out and sell his story to that vile *National Enquirer.*

Q: **Or *Star* or *Globe*.**

A: Those rags are completely all anti-gay. They don't give a damn what they say, or how.

Q: **No, and neither do their gay readers. Or their readers with gay relatives.**

A: So I have my success—the money and fame—but that's the only specimen of good-looking guy that ever gives me the time of day. (Sighs.) So it's all a trade-off. *Ouch!*

Q: **What happened?**

A: I bite my fingernails. I just did it too deep. Like I said, I'm very oral. You know what drives me up a wall?

Q: **Dare I ask?**

A: Awards.

Q: **Not winning Oscar? You got Emmy.**

A: God love her. No, it's those jerks who do win and get up and say, "Thank you, God," like they were divinely picked over the nominees who didn't win. It's so stupid. *And* condescending.

Q: **There's more of that in music awards than acting ones.**

A: It drives me up a wall!

Q: **How about the winners who—hetero or not—thank their heterosexual spouses?**

A: It's like saying it without saying it: "I'm straight!" Big deal.

Q: **How about the people who say, before or after the awards, "The important thing is just being nominated"?**

A: That's like getting . . . a brownie and not getting to eat it, then saying, "The important thing was looking at it," while somebody else takes it home and eats it.

Q: **It's called having your brownie and eating it too.**

A: (Sighs.) What can you do? When your last name is food. . . .

Q: ***Coco*. That's a restaurant chain in California. It could be worse. I knew a man in Hong Kong, a slim businessman. Mr. Fat.**

A: Oh, God! "Are you Fat?" "Yes, me Fat."

Q: **He spoke the Queen's English.**

A: Was he . . . ?

Q: **Not to my knowledge. He had four daughters.**

A: You know what they say about men who can only produce daughters.

Q: **Do they ever say anything about women who have only**

sons?

A: You always have a question, don't you?

Q: **Thank you. Speaking of weight and stereotypes, it amazes me that in the West, so many people assume the Buddha was fat. What they're picturing is that fat Chinese good-luck-and-prosperity symbol.**

A: Those fat porcelain figurines?

Q: **Yes. They're mythical figures, like Santa Claus. The Buddha was not fat. Or Chinese.**

A: Yeah, probably no more than Jesus was. But anyone fat, even a religious figure, would be put down for their fatness, no matter what was inside.

Q: **Well, this is a lack of information, but many journalists and authors make the same mistake. They should know better.**

A: They don't teach much about other religions.

Q: **It's a do-it-yourself project. The media pushes one sexuality and one religion, and that's it. But back to you. You once said in an interview, "I love people and I want them to love me." Can you expand on that?**

A: Honey, I can expand just looking at a hot fudge sundae! I meant that I love it when the public treats me nice after they recognize me. They smile at me.

Q: **Don't some show biz people want to be loved so much— or rather, approved of—that they try and conform to what they think the average public wants?**

A: Sure. But that's being insecure. Which I used to be. People go through stages . . . they mature. Some of us get very rounded. . . .

Q: **Another quote of yours. "I don't think I'd see a show that had been panned. Yes, I'm definitely influenced by critics and agree with what they say—even about me!" *Jimmy!***

A: Not too smart, huh?

Q: **It's your choice whether to follow critics, but why give them that power over what you see and don't see, and how you feel about yourself? If you've given a great performance, you *know* you've given a great performance, so what matter the critics?**

A: . . . Sometimes when I get interviewed, a lot depends on who's asking, and how they're asking. I know I shouldn't, but I can get intimidated by the reporter or the place it's going to be printed.

Q: **Be yourself, that's all.**

A: But for an actor . . . *which* self?

Q: **The one you like. The one that's real.**

A: And if they're not the same?

Q: **Then something needs fixing. Or adding—self-esteem maybe.**

A: Most actors have little enough self-esteem. But fat actors, are you kidding? And fat actors who're sexually different from the great unwashed public? Not easy. . . .

Q: **No, but the more you care what others think, the less free you are.**

A: That's why I couldn't ever do stand-up (comedy). A role, it's different. The lines are already written for you. It's all there, all you do is shed yourself and pretend to be that other person. With stand-up, it's *you*, and there's no retakes. You gotta be glib and confident. . . . I could never do what Paul Lynde did. Like on *Hollywood Squares*. Not a regular gig. I know they coached them beforehand, but I'd have to be a wit. Paul was a wit, and his delivery was more aggressive than mine would be—unless I'm in character. You have to be able to think on your feet. The only thing I can do on my feet besides walk is eat.

Q: **It always comes back to food?**

A: Of course. (Sighs.) If I had a tombstone, it could say, "He ate
and he acted." Or "He acted and he ate." Except the first one
would be more accurate. Oh, well. . . . I'm hungry, aren't
you?

In 1983 Jimmy had won an Emmy Award for *St. Elsewhere*, in
which he'd guest-starred with Doris Roberts. He was also working on the diet and book that would earn him new media promi-
nence, for a time, in 1984. Later, he played a gay role opposite
Elizabeth Taylor and Robert Wagner in a TV movie of James
Kirkwood's autobiographical *There Must Be a Pony*. He said, "I
shouldn't be complaining, me who gets to work with people like
these, but I could swear that since I've shrunk, so have my roles!"

His friend James Kirkwood, who outlived Jimmy by two
years until his death from AIDS, offered, "Jimmy has a lot of
heart. He's like a great big puppy. He has lots of love to give. I
just wish he would give more of it to himself." After Coco's death,
Kirkwood stated, "It's a cliché, but Jimmy was wedded to his
career. To use another cliché, you can't take an audience home
with you. Not without, as someone said, being accused of
immorality on rather a grand scale."

The night before his death, Jimmy Coco appeared on an
episode of the TV sitcom *Who's the Boss?* A few weeks later he was
seen in a television movie. At the same time, he was appearing in
his last theatrically released motion picture, titled *The Hunk*.

AIDS

LIBERACE

(1 9 1 9 – 1 9 8 7)

In a way, the following statement encapsulated Liberace:

Explaining why he declined the role of Mr. Joyboy in the movie *The Loved One* (1965), he wrote in stereotypes, "He was an effeminate mama's boy, ten feet off the ground at all times. A great actor could get away with playing the part. . . ."

In Liberace's case, he wouldn't have had to *act*. Second, he was never offered the lead role, which was enacted by then-leading man Rod Steiger. Director Tony Richardson responded, "Liberace's off his chump if he truly believes he was up for the starring role." A *lie*. Third, Liberace did appear in *The Loved One*, in a small and surprising role—in view of his above comment and his closetedness—as a flamingly gay casket salesman! A *contradiction*.

(The camp cult movie, from Briton Evelyn

Waugh's novel about the Southern California way of death, also featured Robert Morse, John Gielgud, Roddy McDowall, and Tab Hunter. Screenwriter Christopher Isherwood noted, "I think most of us on both sides of the camera, this time around, are gay or bisexual." Richardson, aka the ex-husband of Vanessa Redgrave—whose father was bisexual Sir Michael Redgrave, so acknowledged by daughter Lynn—and father of actresses Joely and Natasha Richardson, died of AIDS in 1991.)

In his unctuous 1986 book *The Wonderful Private World of Liberace*, the man described in the book as "undoubtedly America's most beloved entertainer" wrote that he'd turned down many a nonmusical movie role because his public would "be disappointed if I did a straight acting role." Not to mention amazed.

The effusive pianist did a handful of film roles. In his first film, starring Shelley Winters and Macdonald Carey, he played, of course, a pianist. In the tropics. He recalled, "Don't remind me! It was called, I think, *South Sea Sinner* (1949), and my hair was unbelievably bad. They hired me for my ability to play, not for my looks, but jeepers! Somebody should have been looking after me. . . ." Carey later stated, "The guy has talent. But for Hollywood, that isn't crucial.

"Apart from his private life, which is up for grabs, he has a very different type of persona. I think he's smart; he's stayed in the musical arena and thrived there." The "very different" personalities—and physicalities—of music stars like k.d. lang and Michael Jackson prevent their musical popularity from translating into movie popularity. Actors *act* (well, many do), but several musical luminaries are forever their unique, a-traditionalist selves, at least outwardly (Jackson, a walking contradiction himself, *wishes* to project an ultra-traditionalist image).

Isherwood commented, "Lee's [Liberace's] hopes of any sort of movie career must have been past by the time of *The Loved One*, or else he'd never have taken that part. . . . The one thing which seems odd now is that he ever did have one vehicle tailored around him [*Sincerely Yours*, a 1955 misnomer]. In it, he had not one but two love interests, both of them actresses. Proving once again that on the silver screen, fiction is stranger than truth."

Regarding fiction, in his book—not his first, though supposedly "my most personal gift to my public"—Liberace offered his recipe for Liberace Sticky Buns (no comment necessary), confided that Mae West once requested him for a "gift," and vaguely purported how he lost his virginity at 16 to an "older woman" named Miss Bea Haven. Such was Bea's impact, that she forever spoiled Lee for women his own age!

The book's illustrations posed him beside "friends" like Michael Jackson, Debbie Reynolds, and the Reagans, and his (companion and final love) chauffeur Cary James (the 24-year-old blond was with him at his deathbed). The book also featured a closeup of Liberace's first screen kiss, from *Sincerely Yours* with Dorothy Malone. The flop film's monumental bad taste was later lampooned in books like *The Golden Turkey Awards*.

When I asked the pianist who his favorite movie actor was, he hesitated, then said, "There are *so* many wonderful movie legends. It's *so* hard to choose." Finally he named Clifton Webb (best known for *Laura*, 1944, which made him a screen star in his mid-50s). Why? Because Webb was gay? Never wed (like Liberace)? Was a witty, waspish, unique performer? "I liked him because he was very good to his mother." (When Webb's mother died in her 90s, he carried on so loud and so long that pal Noel Coward drily sympathized, "It must be tough, being orphaned at 72.")

Like Webb, Liberace well-remembered Mama, beyond her death in 1980. The Sheik-loving Frances had named her youngest son Rudy (his offspring would be disinherited by Uncle Lee) and given son Wladziu *Valentino* for a middle name. (Did she ever suspect the Italian "sheik" seldom if ever entered a lady's tent?)

Her eldest son she simply called George.

Wladziu Valentino Liberace, aka Lee, the Wizard of Ooze, King of the Stardust Ballroom, the Sultan of Glitz, and the Grand Poobah of Kitsch, worshipped his "Queen Mum," for whom he fashioned a special throne. "I'm proud of my mother, and she's very proud of me," he said more than once. Indeed, in the 1950s and '60s he elicited frequent derisive publicity for his devotion to his mother. Strange then, that he couldn't conceive—on paper anyway—of playing "an effeminate mama's boy." Perhaps he identified more as a butch or macho mama's boy. . . .

Hours before flying to Mexico City in late 1978, I got a telephone call:

"Hello?! Is this Boze Hadleigh?" the voice drawled. It sounded almost like a cartoon.

"Yes, speaking."

"This is . . . Liberace." A pause—the pause that impresses. I nearly said, "Mr. Liberace?"

He went on to say that he was regretfully declining my request to interview him for *Talk* magazine. "All those lovely ladies under the hair dryer will *have* to struggle on without me," he chuckled. Then he thanked me for the sample piece I'd enclosed on Audrey Hepburn, whom I'd interviewed about her movie comeback in the undeserving *Bloodline*.

"I *really* enjoyed that. She's *such* a lovely lady. *Tell* me," he hush-asked, "is she really as *thin* in person as in the movies? She's *so* wonderful." The first paragraph of the article had pointed out that it was a phone interview.

"She's quite thin," I stated the obvious (the camera might add pounds, it doesn't take them away).

"Isn't that wonderful? Of course, *some* of us have to *work* at being thin. I think Audrey's one of the lucky ones." Pause. "How about you? Are *you* thin?" I said yes. "Not *too* thin, I hope. Young men shouldn't be *too* thin." I'd heard he liked some meat on his men. "Well, you're *young*. Of *course* you're thin." How did he know I was young? Come to think of it, had I enclosed my phone number with the request? (One usually had the celebrity's publicist call *Talk* in New York to confirm and to arrange about illustrations, then the publicist or my editor called me to set the date.)

"How old did you say you were?"

"Twenty-four."

"*My!* So *young!* Have you had any training in journalism or anything?"

"My master's degree is in mass communications, journalism specifically."

"Ooohh! So young . . . *already*. That sounds very impressive—a *master's*. . . . Well, we'll probably meet when you're a little older. If," he chirped, "you're persistent."

"It's very nice of you to call."

"Not at all, it's *my* pleasure. Now, don't work *too* hard. Goodbye!"

The second major star to die of AIDS, Liberace passed away in February, 1987, days before my first interview book, *Conversations With My Elders*, went to press. Removed, via the publisher's attorneys, were a few references to Cary Grant, including Rock Hudson's comments on Grant's 1930s love relationship with Randolph Scott and how they'd shared at least four different houses in Los Angeles and had all but scandalized tinseltown by showing up at film premieres together; Paramount finally put a stop to their togetherness under threat of nonrenewal of the rising stars' contracts.

Sal Mineo had declared, "If I had a real and lasting personal partnership like that, I'd have told the studio to go fuck itself. . . . Why doesn't anyone ever threaten to sue and expose the studio for practicing that kind of crap?" Probably because if money talks elsewhere, in Hollywood it dictates.

Grant died weeks before *Conversations* was published, and Scott weeks after. I'd already not included in the manuscript some quotes about "Lee" from Rock, for who could have known that Liberace would die a few months before sixty-nine—*"soissante-neuf,"* as he called it in *Cue* magazine, adding, "I just love all things French. Except rude Parisians and sauces that are wickedly caloric!"

Conversations includes a passing reference—excuse the pun— to Liberace by Hudson. A nonsexual one. But when Rock had casually alluded to an affair with Lee, I thought he must be pulling my leg. "Really?" I asked. He nodded. "When?" He paused before answering. "You really want to know about this? You can't *use* it, you know." He went on:

"It was just a few weeks—a fling, fun while it lasted." But "Lee was very patronizing. A kind man, generous, and we shared an interest in classical music. His piano-playing knocked me out. But he was quite patronizing even then, and he treated every-body like his protégé."

I asked Rock if they'd remained friends. "We're on good terms, but not friends. For instance, if I went to one of his con-certs or he came to see me in a play I'm doing, people might talk. It would be noticed."

The hard-to-imagine affair, he said, happened in the "very early '50s." At that time, Hudson was a struggling Universal con-tract player, something of a handsome lump. In his first film, in 1948, he'd required dozens of retakes to deliver a simple line. A few years later, he was better known as the Baron of Beefcake— he was an enthusiastic poser—than for his screen roles. Liberace, on the other be-ringed hand, was a TV star. His piano-centered variety series was seen in more homes at the time than *I Love Lucy*. Of course, Lee was yet a pale sartorial shadow of the glit-tering icon of excess that he would become.

Then, as later, Liberace preferred "rough trade"—gay, bi, and sometimes financially wanting heterosexual men of rough aspect and typically blue collar. Hudson was a former truck driver and mail carrier; Lee would often take fiscally disadvantaged but hardy young males and employ them as chauffeurs, assistants, or masseurs. "Men are *my* kind of people!" he informed me.

After *Conversations* appeared, the omitted Hudson quotes about Liberace were picked up by the *Washington Post* and then by hundreds of newspapers around the world. Even though the brief affair had occurred some three and a half decades before, several papers tried to establish a cautionary link between the two eventual AIDS victims' mutual intimacy. The *National Enquirer* placed the story on its cover—a dubious honor—and I appeared on *Larry King, Live,* the topic being "the late, flamboyant, and controversial Liberace" and the celebrity closet.

I'd voiced my surprise at Rock and Lee's long-ago affair to a closeted Hollywood publicist who replied, "Rock was promiscuous, but he did have a type—handsome younger hunks. That is, once he himself was older. Preferably blond ones. However in earlier years, he was less picky. He was something of a groupie. He'd go to bed with big names, or try to. Especially when he first arrived in Hollywood and was chasing after his idols Jon Hall and Errol Flynn." Though more of a chunk than a hunk, Liberace was by then a Name, and whichever way they met— Rock never explained, and grew irritable when I later inquired—his sexual interest in Hudson probably flattered the younger, less-known, and horny actor.

Liberace himself became the object of affection of certain youths. Some younger gays looked up to him as a role model, a man who combined his burgeoning and undeniable flamboyance with public success, *joie de vivre* and that Liberacian pastime known as crying—or laughing—all the way to the bank.

"Rick Shaw" is a "semi-closeted" Oriental. "I'm divorced and fully *out* at work and to friends, but my kids don't know. . . ." A former singer and actor, he was lovers with Paul Lynde and Rock Hudson and a would-be groupie of Liberace. But he never got close to his favorite, remembering, "San Francisco, 1952, was real memorable for me. I belonged to the Emporium Teen Board [of the Emporium department store], and the week before Christmas, my school choir sang carols in the store's rotunda. Lee Meriwether (one of three actresses who played Catwoman on TV's *Batman*) was working there too.

"Our carols were mostly ignored by the shoppers, who went their merry way. Then our soloist, a colored boy, stepped forward to sing. Gradually everyone stopped what they were doing and listened. That voice was clearly one in a million. It belonged to Johnny Mathis. My crush on him began when I heard him sing. I had an idea he might be gay, but in those days I couldn't have predicted that he'd ever come out." (Mathis came out in *Us* magazine in 1982, a newsworthy celebrity admission not picked up by the mainstream media—likewise Brando's early '70s bisexual declaration in France.)

"The other thing about 1952 that was so memorable was my parents buying us a television set. I fell in love with the magic of TV, and I liked Liberace's show best of all. I thought he was very appealing in a low-key way, and when he sang his theme song, 'I'll Be Seeing You,' and winked, I would pretend he was singing it only to me, winking at *me*.

"When I came to L.A., I tried to find and meet Liberace, but I guess I was never at the right place at the right time. Then I heard that he preferred blonds anyway—like that Scott Thorson [the chauffeur cum companion who instigated the famous palimony suit]. That was disappointing, but I was still beholden to the man, because in my teens I'd had to take piano lessons, which was considered 'sissy stuff' then.

"But playing the piano was what Liberace did, for plenty of bucks and stardom. Thousands of guys taking piano in the '50s were nicknamed *Liberace*. It was meant as a crack, but many of us were proud of it. He was a star, to most people the only pianist they knew about. . . . Later, when he denied being gay, that was a disappointment too, but let's face it, those were the not-so-good-old days." Or, nostalgia isn't what it used to be.

Gay TV producer Carl David reminisced, "In the '60s, you could often see Liberace cruising the Akron store on Sunset Boulevard with his little doggie in hand, dressed all in white—Lee, I mean—trying to pick up Mexicans in the store's parking lot. He wasn't discreet, he was daring and rather outrageous about it. He'd stand in the lot and try and pick up young men parking their cars. Most didn't recognize him!"

After I told an associate that Liberace had phoned in 1978 to decline an interview request, he huffed, "Of *course* he called you and was very polite." The man had been an assistant to Lee in Las Vegas, when Barbra Streisand was the superstar pianist's opening act. "Lee runs scared of the press and what they might say about him. He sued *Confidential* magazine and that English paper, but he can't go around suing everybody. Besides, times have changed. . . . He's extremely publicity-conscious. He courts the press. The way Joan Crawford did, only he telephones, he doesn't send little thank-you notes with a big *JC* on them."

And he did it again. In late 1981 I re-requested an interview, on behalf of a Japanese women's magazine. I heard nothing for weeks, until, 20 minutes before a dentist's appointment, I got a phone call. I only answered because I thought it was a relative visiting San Francisco, who I would be seeing that evening in San Mateo.

It was Liberace, politely declining the request. (So I was late for the dentist—sometimes that happens. After I got there, I waited five or six minutes, then the dentist came in, half-apologizing for being "a little bit behind today"—often that happens.) He began by chummily referring to our "chat" of three years before, and inquiring into the Japanese market. . . .

A: Would this be published in Japanese?

Q: **Yes, it would.**

A: How marvelous! (Pause.) But I'd never be able to *read* it.

Q: **Neither would your American fans. . . .**

A: Except in Chinatown. I mean Little Tokyo!

Q: **The interview could be syndicated internationally, to make it worth your time.**

A: Oh, *no.* I'd prefer if it appeared only in Japan. (A conspiratorial pause.) You know, various American stars do commercials in Japan for *big* money that they'd never dream of doing for *American* TV.

Q: **Have you done ads in Japan?**

A: (Laughs.) Aren't you the curious one! I've been *approached* several times. . . .

Q: **Remember the Audrey Hepburn article? She's done wig commercials for Japanese TV.**

A: I *know.* For a tremendous sum, I hear. I'd *love* to see them. She looks marvelous, I hear.

Q: **One thing about Japan, they don't tend to ask such personal questions. On the other hand, one can be franker in an interview for Japan, without it, um, coming back to haunt one. If you're concerned.**

A: I'd have to think about it. But I don't know. . . . I'm so busy lately. You know, Boze, I have too many candles burning at both ends, but it's the *only* way I know how to live! I have so many interests and concerns, but I *relish* all the pressure.

Q: **You should write a book about it.**

A: Oh, I *will*. They always want a new book from me, and they're always asking me to *please* be as candid as I like. But Boze, *some* autobiographies are candid—and *others* are just . . . *candied!* (Laughs.)

Q: **That's amusing.**

A: (Sighs.) I don't know. Nowadays, everyone just lets *everything* hang out. I always feel there should be a little mystery. Don't you?

Q: **Sometimes a little goes a long way.**

A: Boze, you're teasing me!

Q: **You don't give many interviews, do—**

A: Call me *Lee*.

Q: **. . . .**

A: No, I don't. My personal appearances are the very best sort of publicity.

Q: **But not in-depth.**

A: People have short attention spans. I found that out long ago. They get bored quickly, if you're not doing something exciting.

Q: **Or humorous, like Victor Borge.**

A: . . . Yes.

Q: **You don't do much TV, either.**

A: No, and I'll tell you why, Boze. People don't want to pay to go see what they can get on TV, at home, for free.

Q: **Whereas your live appearances are special events.**

A: *Very* special! I really work and slave to make them special. But it's worth it, because people appreciate it.

Q: **What about TV interviews?**

A: I have done them, and I'll continue to. My fans are always writing in, *begging* me to be on TV. "*Let* Barbara Walters interview you," they say. But if I do something at home, in one of my own wonderful houses, it has to be on *my* terms. And *my* questions. I wouldn't want to be sat down and asked a lot of silly questions by a silly woman.

Q: **You don't like Barbara Walters?**

A: *Boze!* You must *not* put words in my mouth like that. I think she's darling. But I'm not about to let down my fans and do a quickie TV segment. When I appear, it has to be a special event.

Q: **So TV's not really your medium? Even though you had such a popular series in the 1950s?**

A: You *know* about that? How *wonderful!* My younger fans often know more about those years than I do—they *study* it.

Q: **I've *heard* of your show, of course.**

A: Thank you! But there *is* one nice thing about a television interview. Unlike in the newspapers and the magazines, they can't misquote you or take it out of context. They *can* with editing, but if you go on *The Tonight Show* or something and are there for one or two segments answering silly questions, then at least the public gets your own answers, and the intonations and gestures and everything. In the *press*, my *lord*, they can make you sound like somebody *completely* else. A *stranger*.

Q: **("Stranger than who?" I almost ask.) Since I'm lucky enough to have you on the phone, I wanted to ask about your loyal older fans who—**

A: *Boze,* my fans are *all* ages. That's the wonderful thing. It's *all* ages, and all *people.*

Q: **Oh. What do you do when you're not working?**

A: Now, Boze, are you trying to do an interview with me on the sly? (Chuckles.)

Q: **Everyone's interested in the real Liberace. . . .**

A: Thank you. That's very sweet.

Q: **If you want to reconsider, I can have sample copies of the magazine sent to you. You have many fans in Japan, as you may know.**

A: Oh, I *know*. But I don't know. . . .

Q: **Or we could wait a few months, if you like.**

A: You understand, I'm trying to be *very* selective about what I do. I'm at a place in my life where I have to really, *you* know, get a *kick* out of what I do.

Q: **Well, I appreciate your calling.**

A: *My* pleasure. A rejection letter's just *so* impersonal! And since you're a nice young man who's nice enough to still be interested and pursue it, I thought I'd call up Boze and explain to him how pleased I am, and sorry I can't do it—at this time. (Pause.) It is nicer than a rejection letter, isn't it?

Q: **Far nicer. Thank you.**

A: Don't mention it. It's just a little something.

Q: **Well. . . .**

A: I guess I'd better let us *both* off the hook. But *do* keep in touch, won't you, Boze?

Q: **I will.**

A: The third time might be the charm! (Laughs.) Well, be a good boy. . . .

Q: **I'll try, Lee.**

A: (Snickers.) Just don't try too *hard*. . . . Good-bye!

Liberace was a gay autofact. He styled, re-fashioned, and molded himself into a one-of-a-kind celebrity. He was the biggest star to ride a gay stereotype to the top. Yet he slavishly sought to please the masses and periodically deny his innate nature. Despite his *outré* dress and percolating-molasses voice, Liberace defied the media to tag him. Even accurately.

In his first decade of stardom, London's *Daily Mirror* had labeled him "the pinnacle of masculine, feminine, and neuter—everything that he, she, or it could ever want." Though this was name-calling of the most subtle type, Liberace sued.

Said Quentin Crisp—who penned a foreword to *Conversations*

With My Elders— "Personally, I would regard these words [in the paper] as a compliment." Liberace informed the court that in America, if anyone was described as "it," he was thought to be homosexual. Incredibly, he won his suit and over $22,000. He won not by providing a shred of evidence refuting the admittedly homophobic paper's implication, but via the court's indignation that anyone should be publicly branded non-heterosexual. (After he died, the *DM* asked Liberace's estate for its money back.)

Crisp called Liberace's "an empty victory. He couldn't have needed the money, and his image had in no way been tarnished, because his appeal never depended on his being heterosexual or even sexual. His audience treated him as though he were an expensive Persian cat wearing a *diamanté* collar—and purring."

Of course, the Liberace jokes continued, and so did his occasional swipes at the media. In the late 1970s, during an Emmy awards telecast, cohost Robert *(Baretta)* Blake made a poor-taste remark about Liberace. Immediately following the commercials, he contritely announced that Liberace's attorneys had called the show's producers, and he, Blake, was humbly apologizing to "Lee, I love ya" for any unintended malice.

Understandably, Liberace wanted his dignity. But he didn't seem to realize that his role was court jester, not pillar or role model, and that majority "morality" wasn't central to his success. Crisp opined, "Just as crowds went to the Café de Paris to stare at Miss Dietrich rather than to hear her sing, so they flocked to Radio City to *see* Mr. Liberace, rather than to appreciate his expertise. He was a stylist; that is, he graduated from the profession of doing—playing the piano—to the profession of being— Liberace.

"I did not follow his progress closely. In fact, I have learned more about him since his death than I ever knew while he was alive. He radiated a childlike glee at being popular. I think it is very unlikely that his gaudiness was just any old way of increasing his income. I think it was much more probable that, as his capacity for dealing with—or rather, winning—his audience increased, his self-assurance grew, and he became more like the bejeweled icon that he always longed to be. As he grew more artificial, he became more genuine.

"In later years, Mr. Liberace very wisely began to parody himself without the least hint of bitterness. Everything he couldn't wear, he carried onto the stage and invited the audience to admire. He died at just the right moment: he was old enough to know that there was nothing more that he could achieve and young enough to avoid having been long forgotten."

Asked his opinion of Liberace's "absolutely fabulous showmanship" by Andy Warhol, movie actor and future AIDS victim Anthony Perkins stated, "He's damn lucky he didn't make it in film. I think Liberace did a movie or two, but he could never have gotten out of film the same gut-level, immediate response and approbation that he gets out of live performances. Actors can only envy what he does. I mean I'm not inordinately fond of the idea of getting up in front of swarms of Midwestern grannies and their descendants, but he obviously gets off on it."

Though he made but five movie appearances, all virtually forgotten (save *The Loved One*), Liberace never entirely deserted tinseltown. At one time he had a mansion above Sunset Boulevard, which he turned into a museum of himself. The neighbors complained, and he transferred it to Las Vegas and Midasized it until it became one of Nevada's top three tourist attractions. And at the end, he still had a home in Malibu.

His lover/companions notwithstanding, the cruising never stopped completely, and Liberace occasionally "stepped out" on his steady with an escort or call boy or even a runaway. (A shocking percentage of America's runaway teens are gay kids kicked out of their homes by homophobic parents, usually fathers; prostitution becomes a necessary evil for many such young, homeless, and often drug-addicted runaways; AIDS is not an uncommon end to the survivalist lifestyle forced on these youngsters by their unloving and unthinking parents who believe their sexuality is a "sin" and/or changeable.)

As already noted, Liberace was often indiscreet. "He felt he could counter that," said his ex-assistant, "by a balancing act of avoiding the press and periodic statements that his life was extremely private. He could come on strong sometimes, be aggressive when he felt threatened. He greeted most reporters with a notional rolling pin. He just didn't 'get' that after the Swinging Sixties and the Stonewall riots, he could finally relax a little.

"Liberace only ever thought he could be 'wild' in his wardrobe. His excuse for his clothes was 'showmanship', but some of it wasn't that far from drag." Lee advised the *Ladies' Home Journal* that "What people do in the privacy of their own bedrooms is nobody else's business." True, but reporter Ruth Batchelor countered, "Nobody wants to know what you're doing in there, Lee, just the gender of who you're doing it with. . . . If we know that, say, Robert Redford's bedroom partner or partners are female, are we somehow invading his privacy?" Liberace refused to continue *that* interview.

When pressed by foolish or phobic reporters about the women in his life—other than, of course, the beaming, bespectacled Frances—he would recite a litany of his three alleged "fiancées," a showgirl, a fruit heiress, and the late skating star Sonja Henie.

The first nonfictional glimpse into Liberace's wonderful private world came in 1982, when ex-lover Thorson sued him for $113 million in palimony for their seven years together (later he cowrote a book titled *Behind the Candelabra: My Life With Liberace*, which substituted a burly football player from the Green Bay

Packers for the incomparable older "Miss Bea Haven").

The tabloids had a field day—or year. It was the first major gay "scandal" since the widely circulated rumors of Rock Hudson and Jim Nabors's marriage. That story allegedly cost Nabors his TV variety series but apparently didn't hurt the more butch and famous Hudson. Liberace eventually settled out of court with Thorson, meanwhile and afterward acting astounded by Thorson's allegations and even his existence. He should have been heartened (or genuinely astounded) that the lawsuit and the blond's revelations didn't hurt his popularity. The "crass classic," as he was sometimes dubbed, continued to play to capacity crowds.

He garnered $4 to $5 million annually, his hold on the Polident generation seemingly unbreakable. In 1985 he broke Radio City Music Hall's 50-year record. *The Advocate* described a typical RCMH performance: "He danced with Diane from New Jersey, and when they were done, he gave her gifts—a Liberace neck scarf, etc.—and went down into the audience to meet her husband Eugene. 'Does Eugene like to dance?' he asked Diane, who stood beside her husband sitting in a spotlight. 'Oh, he *does*? Some other time, Eugene,' he laughed, and everyone laughed with him.

"Then he wagged a finger. 'I *heard* that, Eugene—why didn't you get a ring or something? You gotta do more than *dance* for *that*, Eugene!'"

Despite such innuendos on stage, Lee remained as tightly closeted as ever. Unlike Rock Hudson, he was able to delay confirmation that he had AIDS until after his death. Early reports had him suffering from watermelon-induced anemia and weight loss. When the *Las Vegas Sun* broke the story that Liberace was dying of AIDS in his Palm Springs home, his physician, a Dr. Ghanem, asseverated, "The rumor of Liberace having AIDS is as ridiculous as Elvis having a drug problem!"(!).

Rock Hudson did not voluntarily come out, but his illness was used to help launch an AIDS foundation and awareness of the disease and indirectly helped boost funding to fight AIDS. But both men, "of a certain age" and a social and political disposition inimical to gay rights and any sense of community—each of whom left an estate worth many millions—left not one copper penny to benefit AIDS research or People With AIDS.

Of course, the mainstream media didn't care about or report this. The immodest Liberace had already been taking credit for paving the way for such unusual music stars as Elvis, Michael Jackson, and Boy George. But ABC-TV's *Nightline* went so idiotically far as to suggest that Liberace had "inspired gay liberation."

By contrast, fashion publisher James Brady asked, "What would candor have cost Liberace? Do you think the blue-haired ladies would have smashed their records and torn up their tickets to the Music Hall if, a few years ago, he'd talked openly? I doubt it. He wasn't selling macho up there, you know.

"The man never committed reticence once in his life, yet as he lay dying, the people around him threatened lawsuits if anyone suggested he was gay or had AIDS. Sadder still that Liberace didn't grab the opportunity for one final standing ovation, a last curtain speech, in which he told Middle America just what it was that was killing him and how they, and all of us, ought to be doing something about it."

Or as the *New York Native* put it, "Yes, the beloved Liberace died a liar."

By the mid-1980s, after I saw Liberace perform in Las Vegas, I frankly had less interest in interviewing him. For one thing, what could he possibly say that was new or sincere? And by then, few periodicals were interested in an unrevealing interview with what many considered a clichéd or overexposed—or embarrassing—celebrity (ageism also played its part in the disinterest).

Then I was contacted by Tom Clark, publicist and Rock Hudson's close friend. He hoped I could help "Rock's people" publicize his latest—and increasingly rare—feature film. He knew I knew Rock socially and had published a standard "fan interview" that omitted Hudson's private life save for citing the statistic of his one "marriage." Tom joked about Rock's current schedule being "busier than Liberace's wardrobe." So I brought up Rock's admission of his ages-ago affair with "Lee."

"Rock doesn't usually talk about his star-fucking days. . . . Have you interviewed Lee?" I explained the two telephone "chats" we'd had and which I'd enjoyed. "You'd probably enjoy him less in the flapping flesh," said Tom harshly. "His face is so taut from facelifting, unlike his old neck, and I think it's affected his brain." He didn't explain this and wasn't really one to talk, as years later he cowrote a "tribute" book to his late friend that unscrupulously avoided Rock's and his own homosexuality (except for the unavoidable affair with Mark Christian—who sued Hudson's estate and won—whom Clark characterized so negatively that he sued).

When *The Advocate* queried Clark why he'd been so closet-y on paper, he replied that he was afraid of what his elderly mother and "the other ladies" at the beauty shop might think!

"I can fix it for you to interview Lee, if you think anyone would publish it." I said I doubted it, at least in the USA. "If you help publicize Rock's movie, I'll get in touch with Lee's publicist. Is a phone interview okay?" I said that by now, anything else might seem strange. "Smart. If you met him, the moment the publicist left the room, Lee'd be spluttering all over you." Before the interview, I ascertained noncommitted interest from *Cleo*, an Australian women's magazine.

In mid-1985 I got the call (I wasn't given *his* number, he was given mine, a more typical practice; I never did ask "Lee" which home he was calling from). . . .

A: Is this Boze Hadleigh?

Q: **Speaking. This must be Liberace.**

A: *"Lee!"*

Q: **How are you?** *Again.*

A: I am *so* disappointed, Boze.

Q: **Why?**

A: Third-time lucky, and we're *still* speaking on the telephone. I wanted to *meet* you.

Q: **I did too, but . . . maybe someday.**

A: (Sighs.) Oh, well, Now, this is for Australia? Only Australia?

Q: *Cleo* **magazine.**

A: A ladies' magazine? How nice. I think Australians are my kind of people. They're very loyal fans.

Q: **They're big on the Village People—the only place left that is.**

A: *Oh.* Well, they're fun, aren't they?

Q: **The Village People?**

A: Yes. Fun to look at. But it's not a *real* group. Only *one* guy sings, and he's not so special. But they are fun to look at.

Q: **What do you think of Boy George?**

A: He seems sweet. I like his music or *their* music. I do think he could tone down his makeup a bit! (Chuckles.)

Q: **Elvis was said to be a fan of yours.**

A: He *was.* *Such* a tragedy, his dying so young.

Q: **What did you think of him?**

A: He was darling. Really. A very sweet, unspoiled boy. When he did what he did, he didn't *know* he was being sexual.

Q: **He didn't?**

A: He was, what's that French word? A *naïf.*

Q: **Gerry Mulligan (the saxophonist and composer-arranger) once said about you, if you don't mind a quote . . .?**

A: About *me*? Go right ahead. Quote him.

Q: He said you're a very good pianist but that you'd rather play "Three Little Fishies" than Mozart or Chopin.

A: *Well!* I play Chopin all the time. He's *Polish*. Who does he think he is? No one ever heard of . . . whatshisname until he lived with Judy Holliday (both were bisexual or gay). . . . I'm not upset, it's just a very uninformed quote. He's clearly never seen me perform. I play what I like, which is mostly classical music, and what audiences seem to like. If I played only the classics, I suppose I'd be accused of being a snob. I'm *not* a snob. But perhaps that man only likes jazz and doesn't *know* about anything else. At least jazz *is* a great American art form.

Q: Biographies of Judy Holliday have come out which reveal that she had a policewoman for a live-in lover.

A: *Really?* Oh, I love to dish the dirt!

Q: Well, this isn't "dirt."

A: No, no, of *course* not. I'm very open-minded. Judy Holliday . . . she was a great comedienne. Didn't she win the Oscar?

Q: Yes. In her first major film.

A: Boze (whispering), the tale I heard was that—and this is *not* for *Cleo* or any other ladies' ears; turn off the recorder, please.

Q: Okay. It's off, for now.

A: (Regular tone.) I heard she left the Isle of Man for the Isle of Lesbos. Do you catch my drift?

Q: I caught it. She traded a boyfriend for a girlfriend?

A: No, the other way around! She swapped *her* for *him.*

Q: You had your islands reversed, but I know what you mean. Do you think, though, that was motivated by her becoming a public figure?

A: I have *no* idea what goes on in ladies' heads or regions below. We all know what *men* do. . . .

Q: Men in the public eye?

A: Yes. Now let's end this rather dangerous topic, then you can switch on your machine.

Q: **You know, very little is said about public figures' responsibilities, only their rights—the right to privacy.**

A: Oh, most of them willingly give *that* up! (Snickers.) If you want total privacy, stay anonymous.

Q: **True enough. But public figures are role models, for better or worse. Usually for worse, when it's a lie on screen and off. . . .**

A: (Tone hardens.) Do you mean actresses like Judy Holliday?

Q: **And actors like Judy Holliday.**

A: Well, switch on your recorder and let's have some more pertinent questions. I *don't* have a lot of time. Is it on now?

Q: **It's on.**

A: (Tone softens to near syrup.) Now what was the next question, Boze?

Q: **What do you think of Stephen Sondheim?**

A: Well, he's *very* musical. He's done some wonderful tunes. I *love* "Send in the Clowns."

Q: **And Jerry Herman?**

A: I think he's easier to hum. *Wonderful* music. They're both very talented men.

Q: **If someone ever did a movie of your life, who would you want to play you?**

A: Oh, I *wouldn't!* How horrible. No one could play me, and I would *never* want my life filmed. (There was a posthumous, homophobic TV movie—twice: two networks, same approach.)

Q: **Little Richard said if they filmed his life, he'd want Michael Jackson to play him.**

A: Really. The same casting couldn't apply in my situation.

Q: **Why do you think Jackson is trying to feminize his appearance?**

A: I don't know. I think he wants to look better.

Q: **But he was a good-looking black boy. Now he looks more and more like a white girl. A strange one.**

A: That has nothing to do with me. What's the *next* question?

Q: **What's your favorite room of the house or houses?**

A: You know, I love and enjoy *every* room. And I have the best cooks in the world, but sometimes *I* take over. I rule the roast! (Laughs.) Not too often! If one eats like Miss Piggy, one won't look like Twiggy.

Q: **That's cute. Do you have a weight problem?**

A: Boze! That's almost *rude*.

Q: **It's a question *Cleo* often asks.**

A: Well, I'm sure most *ladies* wouldn't answer. But being a gentleman, I'll just say that . . . dieting *is* my *weigh* of life. "Weigh"—as in *weighing* yourself on the scales each morning.

Q: **How clever. What do you think of plastic surgery?**

A: I don't condemn anyone who tries it. Why *not* look your best?

Q: **Have you tried it?**

A: Boze! I don't *need* to. But if someday I do, I'll definitely give it serious consideration. There's nothing *wrong* with it.

Q: **If you hadn't become a pianist, what would you have been?**

A: Oh, that *is* difficult. I love great art. I've always admired the great masters—the painters, especially in the Renaissance.

Q: **Most of them were gay.**

A: Really?

Q: **The Renaissance was in large part a gay arts and philosophy movement which turned away from the church's restrictions on art and thinking, to draw inspiration from Greco-Roman culture, which was far more tolerant and accepting of homosexuality and bisexuality.**

A: Oh, by *far*. (Pause.) I mean that's very *interesting*. They were very intelligent men.

Q: **So you might have been a painter?**

A: Not exactly, Boze, though there *are* a lot of house painters in the Midwest. (Chuckles.) I'd have been an amateur painter, I'm afraid. I always knew where my real talents lay.

Q: **You could have painted for fun. Many actors do.**

A: Not for fun, for soul-release. You know, Boze, the word "amateur" has been degraded and misunderstood in our society.

Q: **That can be said about a lot of words.**

A: Yes. But "amateur" means, it's from the Latin, . . . *lover*. Somebody who *loves* what they do. *That's* an amateur. Someone who does it for love, not money. So you see, an amateur painter is more pure in his motives than a painter who does it for money.

Q: **Though presumably less talented. For the Renaissance artists, painting was a career and their way of life.**

A: I just *love* their painting. What else did you want to ask *me*?

Q: **Were you very surprised when *Sincerely Yours* wasn't a success?**

A: . . . The people, my fans, who saw it *loved* it. I think the timing wasn't right. Timing is *so* important. For anything. But by the time they asked me to do another movie, I was too busy. As I say, I know where my real talents lie.

Q: **People prefer to see you in person than on a giant screen?**

A: Well, I love the concept of a closeup, but I'm not exactly an Adonis! (Giggles.)

Q: **Like Tyrone Power?**

A: Wasn't he nice-looking?

Q: **And then some. What do you think of biographies that disclose the facts of his life?**

A: . . . I'm of a very mixed mind about that, Boze, since you ask. Very mixed. I don't think we want to go into that here. Okay, then. *Yes*. You are right. Men and women *much* prefer to see me live.

Q: **People prefer to see you live. Do you think that's partly** because when you're yourself on a stage you can dress and act in a manner that has to be far more subdued for the screen?

A: Let me think. . . . I suppose so. I always want to give my fans the best of myself. I love to shop, and I love to *share* that with my fans. They get a vicarious thrill out of seeing my belongings. I couldn't deny them that.

Q: No, one shouldn't deny. . . .

A: I beg your pardon?

Q: You have all kinds of fans.

A: *Yes* (purrs).

Q: Including gay ones—this isn't for *Cleo*, by the way. You were a pioneer in some ways. Do you find you get less-bigoted reactions from critics now than before?

A: Critics are *paid* to be critical. If they were *amateurs*, we might all be better off. They want to make it a life's work. . . . But they're not all bad, and *I* have no problem with them. I think most of them like me. I don't know. I never get to read reviews. I do know somebody once said that I'm "critic-proof." The critics have nothing to do with my shows. If they like my shows, I'm delighted. But it's the audiences who buy the tickets, and they can never get enough of me. The proof is in the box office (chuckles).

Q: I thought it was in the pudding.

A: You know what, Boze? I rule the roast, but I'm also king of the box office! So they always *tell* me. (Sighs happily.)

Q: Well, you do live like royalty. What about when someone says your shows play to people's love for kitsch?

A: I'm Polish-Italian, I don't speak German. *Next* question?

Q: What do you think of Johnny Mathis, who came out of the closet a few years ago?

A: . . . His voice? I don't think diabetics can listen to him for long. You said he . . . ?

Q: Yes: "came out of the closet." Which takes guts, doesn't it?

A: Isn't it a little *redundant*, in his case? Please do *not* print these questions and answers about Johnny Mathis. I don't want an interview where I talk about others and give my opinions. . . .

Q: **I can strike it. *Cleo* need never know. Do you prefer it when others—noncritics—give their opinions about you?**

A: No! Not at *all*. I don't want to talk about them, or them about me. I want to talk about *me*. *That's* what people want.

Q: **You seem to be an expert on what people want.**

A: I should be. I've been at it quite a while! (Chuckles.)

Q: **Not all people want the same thing. (No reply.) Did you know Rock Hudson was a big fan of yours?**

A: Really? He's a darling man. (Aside.) Let's *not* talk about his health (in 1985 Hudson was revealed to have AIDS).

Q: **You once knew him socially, didn't you?**

A: Did he say I did?

Q: **Oh, yes.**

A: Well, . . . one of the *wonderful* things about show business is the people one gets to meet. Ordinary people *and* movie stars, everybody you have *time* to meet or would want to. It's a *real* joy.

Q: **Is there a special someone in your life now, Lee?**

A: I *never* give up hope—I'm always looking. *When* I have time. (Coolly.) Did Tom Clark tell you to ask about Rock and Mathis and all this?

Q: **No. Why?**

A: I wouldn't put it past him. And he's *not* Rock's lover—anymore.

Q: **Would you be willing to be interviewed for a gay magazine?**

A: . . . What? *Why?*

Q: **Coming out didn't hurt Mathis' career, and he dresses less . . . flamboyantly (than Liberace).**

A: (Acidly.) Is he a closet Reagan supporter? I think he's been around even longer than I have.

Q: **Ronald Reagan?**

A: *Mathis!* (Exhales audibly.) What's the *point* of this? "Coming out" is for younger people who want to stay in the headlines all the time! I don't need or like headlines, and I don't *need* to. . . . You really have upset me.

Q: **Of course it's a personal choice, but—**

A: *Oh!* I hear the doorbell. And the butler's not around. I have to *go*. (Shifting tones.) It *really* has been a pleasure, Boze— mostly. (Shifting back.) Just make *sure* it's legally safe, do you understand me?

Q: **I understand, and it *is* legally safe. A lot safer than it *could* be. You better answer your door. . . . It is ringing, isn't it?**

A: *Thank* you.

Q: **Thank *you*.**

BRAD DAVIS

(1949 – 1991)

Brad Davis was best known for starring in *Midnight Express* (1978), which he half-jokingly felt had "done more harm to Turkey's image and tourist industry than all the movies before put together." He was also known for starring as the lusty *Querelle* (1982), director Rainer Werner Fassbinder's final film; the openly gay German had declared that Davis's white sailor pants were so tight, they revealed what religion he wasn't. On TV, Davis portrayed one of his heroes in *Robert Kennedy and His Times*.

He received more publicity than ever after dying of AIDS in 1991 at age 41. In the movie capital, his passing garnered more newsprint coverage than any AIDS death since Rock Hudson and Liberace. The main angle was fear. Davis had known he was HIV-positive since 1985, the year he'd appeared in Larry Kramer's AIDS-

169

themed play *The Normal Heart* in New York. He'd kept the information secret, and although a dues-paying member of three actors' unions, he had paid his own bills and insurance out of fear that his medical status would otherwise be discovered and his career ended.

The revelation that Davis had to live secretly with AIDS for some six years helped lead to the foundation of Hollywood Supports, an industry organization supportive of People With AIDS and working to end anti-gay discrimination. (For example, by 1996 every Hollywood studio but one was offering spousal benefits, including health and dental coverage, to domestic partners of its gay and lesbian employees. The holdout is Rupert Murdoch's 20th Century Fox, known in some quarters as 19th Century Fox.)

News coverage empathized with Davis's plight and his understandable anxiety over not getting more work if he were found out. However, he kept his secret even after work seemed impractical, and novelist Armistead Maupin opined, "I'm tired of people being congratulated posthumously on their brave battle. It wasn't that brave if we didn't know about it while it was going on."

The publicity also stressed Davis's widow and their eight-year-old daughter, without stating his bisexuality. Davis had met Susan Bluestein, his agent, in 1971. They were "friends" for five years, he said, and then married for 15 more. With Lily Tomlin and others, Davis appeared in gay activist Vito Russo's *Our Time*: "It was a modest educational entertainment," explained the actor, "mostly for gay viewers, and even though it was gay-themed, I wanted to be part of it. I wanted to contribute something without being front-and-center out there."

Russo offered, "I know Brad from way back to unknown. I remember he was in this off-off-Broadway play, *Sissies' Scrapbook*. He was devastatingly sexy to me, a hustler type, and then the play was retitled *Four Friends* and moved to a bigger theatre. But it didn't do well and closed.

"Brad was nonchalant about his gayness before he headed out west. He was always horny, and the first to say so. . . . I had no idea he had a bisexual side. He either hid it well or going Hollywood just coaxed it out of him—if *out* is the right word, and in this context it ain't."

The ambitious Davis never achieved superstardom but hit temporary stardom with *Midnight Express*. Ironically, he played a real-life individual who was openly bisexual in the memoir upon which the film was based. The movie—surprise—made Billy Hayes entirely heterosexual. Even in prison. Even in a Turkish prison.

But Davis's big screen success "made me more restless," and his bigger income went partly to drugs and alcohol. In 1981 he joined Alcoholics Anonymous, and after Fassbinder's death in 1983 from a drug overdose, Davis confessed that he, too, had tried "every known drug under the sun, singly and in combinations.

"I have this excess of energy, and when I'm not working, one thing I try and do with it is to write. I'm not a professional writer, but I write about me and the things I go through."

After he died, Ms. Bluestein revealed that a book would be forthcoming based on Brad's journals covering the years of hiding and dealing with his illness and that it would be a strong indictment of how Hollywood treats its own. Thus far the project hasn't been published, despite its potentially riveting subject. The grapevine alleges that "the industry" applied pressure to keep its close-up picture of movieland homophobia and indifference to suffering from seeing the light of print. Others say the publishing world decided the book had a "limited" audience. Both reasons for nonpublication are possible, the former one more so.

Ron Vawter, an openly gay stage and film actor (*Philadelphia, The Silence of the Lambs*) who acknowledged having AIDS, believed, "Hollywood was shamed by Brad's death into reacting, to a limited degree. Behind the camera, of course. With the usual tsk-tsk-ing about why didn't the poor actor feel he could come to us with the truth? Brad was able to experience more commercial success than I was, but his trying to re-create himself as a mainstream, married hunk pushed him deeper into the closet. It made the lies more pressing.

"Toward the end, I saw him a few times, and he looked like a scared, unhappy man. When you're living out your final few years, by then you hope to be able to experience some measure of inner peace and freedom from worry or pretense. Brad was once so joyous, even reckless, but the last few times I saw him, he just looked haunted and guilty."

Vito Russo noted, "Hopefully Brad has his family's acceptance, if not his own. But the mere fact of his heterosexual lifestyle and his presenting himself now as a mainstream actor work against his ability to be honest on any level. . . . I know lately the talk is that Brad has been distancing himself from gay and bi characters. He's rejected some good roles because they don't fit what he's now trying to project.

"I wouldn't call him homophobic, I think it's more his galloping ambition. For some reason he's turning his back on a past of artistic risk-taking, so something must be up. . . ." This was in the late 1980s, when Davis and Russo each knew he had AIDS.

Several in Hollywood knew that Davis visited the occasional gay bar or adult theatre and a geographical assortment of bathhouses. A few admitted to having slept with him. One was Timothy Patrick Murphy, who played Mickey, Charlene Tilton's lover on *Dallas*. Before he died of AIDS at 29 in 1988, he informed *Gold* magazine:

"I caught Brad in (Joe Orton's) play *Entertaining Mr. Sloane* in the early '80s, and a few years later he was living in Studio City near L.A. I had a friend there, on Camellia Drive, who I used to

trick with. I knew Brad informally, and at some point I mentioned Studio City and my friend, who was tall and not very dark
but awfully handsome. [My friend was] *not* an actor, which was an
inducement, because actors prefer having sex outside the industry, when possible. . . . Brad had one physical insecurity—he was
on the short side. So he had a thing for tall dudes with long legs.

"To cut a long story short, we used to drive over to Camellia,
separately, and have three-ways. But when my friend moved out
of town, Brad had nothing more to do with me. I'm not exactly
chopped liver, or short-changed in any way. I think he fled
because he didn't want it to possibly get around that he and
another actor were making it together. Like *I* was gonna tell!
This is *Hollywood*, where the money's big-time and the closet's as
wide and as friendly as Texas." Put another way: Hollywood,
where the truth lies. . . still.

Just before *Midnight Express* came out, I was assigned two
interviews by *Showbill*, a Canadian magazine. One with newcomer Mary Steenburgen, discovered for film by Jack Nicholson—
Goin' South, directed by him, would be a flop. As for *Midnight
Express*, which would prove a hit, I was asked whether I preferred to interview Billy Hayes, whose story it was, or Brad
Davis, the actor playing him. I chose the nonfiction version and
enjoyed the interview with Hayes, whose book I'd just read. I'd
not yet seen the movie, which of course compared unfavorably
with the less self-conscious and xenophobic, more honest book.

I did think of trying to interview Davis after *Querelle*, for my
eventual book *The Lavender Screen*, but didn't get around to it.
Then in 1987 I got a letter in which Brad Davis introduced himself as "the screen incarnation of Genêt's Querelle de Brest, by
way of my great friend and colleague—and your excellent interview [sic]—Rainer Werner Fassbinder." He enclosed a clipping,
an interview in which he allowed that he cried for two weeks

after Fassbinder's death. And another note reiterating that he'd "loved and was mesmerized by your dramatic encounter and interview with Rainer, which makes me very hopeful that you will answer at your soonest convenience and we can arrange to meet soon."

(The Fassbinder chapter was one of six interviews with gay men of cinema—three directors, two actors, one designer—in *Conversations With My Elders*, so titled by my editor because I was between 18 and 28 when I met the celluloid sextet.)

The letter had been sent via my publisher, but Brad didn't enclose his phone number—on purpose?—so I sent a reply with my number, and within days he called. I'd recently moved to Beverly Hills, so when he asked at which restaurant we should "do lunch," I left it up to him. He chose the French Quarter in West Hollywood. "It's great. It's a gay hangout, and all the waiters I know are gay, but it's straight-owned and it doesn't matter if you're spotted there." By "you're" he, of course, meant his acting self.

Bear in mind that when I interviewed him—we lingered for hours but never met again—I had no idea he was HIV-positive or would die in four years. Stereotypes, again: although I'd heard through the grapevine time and again that Brad Davis was gay or bisexual, the fact that he was married and a father put any notion of AIDS that much further from my mind. Vito Russo wrote, "More often, it [AIDS] strikes the closeted male who engages in frequent and preferredly anonymous sex than it does the gay male involved in a longtime relationship with another man and who seldom, if at all, cheats on him and typically not as secretively as the closet case who sneaks out to cheat on his wife, whether or not she's aware of his dominant sexuality."

Brad Davis had enacted a small part in *Chariots of Fire* (1980), starring Ian Charleson as the fanatical or devout runner. The sexy and talented Scotsman later costarred in *Car Trouble*, in my opinion one of the funniest British film comedies, with the even-more talented Julie Walters. Charleson, the same age as Davis, would die of AIDS a year before Brad.

A: Did Rainer say things about me that weren't in the book?

Q: **Yes. There's not always room for everything.**

A: What did he say?

Q: **. . . You're very attractive.**

A: He did?

Q: **Didn't he tell you in person?**

A: He was shy. What do *you* think?

Q: **About what?**

A: Attractive?

Q: **Oh, yes. He also said you're sexy and that it's not always the same thing.**

A: (Laughs.) For sure. What else did he say?

Q: **Um, that you had guts to accept such a homoerotic role, that few Americans would have, and no Hollywood star would have.**

A: Oh. . . . Well, it's a great book.

Q: **Thank you.**

A: But his chapter's my favorite. I'd love to play Rainer in some classy, honest little art film. I could even direct or cowrite it. As a homage, but also it could make a great human-interest story.

Q: **And a cautionary tale about drugs and excess?**

A: That's the human interest. His career was gangbusters, non-stop. He *was* German film. But off the set, a wreck, emotionally. He had no self-esteem.

Q: **Several who knew him said he put on all the weight because of that lack of self-esteem.**

A: I'm with that. Rainer just felt he was worthless, so he might as well look worthless.

Q: But that's so sad, a self-fulfilling prophecy.

A: He didn't even always enjoy food. He punished himself with it.

Q: He did the opposite of what some young women lacking self-esteem do via anorexia.

A: People ought to love themselves more.

Q: That's like a line—applicable to Fassbinder—from *The Boys in the Band*, at the end: "If we could just learn not to hate ourselves so much."

A: Yeah. . . . Like I said, I'd be the best actor, of anyone, to option that chapter from your book. (Makes a tsk-ing sound.) But I know I'd face this opposition from my crowd. . . . For sure I'd need European financing. It'd have to be done in Europe, a coproduction, German-French or something like that.

Q: It would be worthwhile and would have a market—over there. But time will tell.

A: Yeah. And I couldn't afford to pay much for the option, at this point. . . .

Q: You were born Robert Davis. Is it true there was one on the Screen Actors Guild rolls?

A: (Laughs.) Brad's a better name for me. *Robert's* blah. Brad's more butch, isn't it? (Laughs.) When your name's real ordinary and you want to be an actor, sometimes it forces you to be creative and rig up a new moniker.

Q: Like the British James Stewart. There already was an American one, so he became Stewart Granger.

A: No kidding! That's lots better anyway.

Q: *He's* bisexual. . . . (My tone/emphasis meant to convey: He was bisexual *too*.)

A: No kidding. But jeez, your chapter about Rainer . . . I haven't read all the rest of the book—I skimmed the ones with Rock Hudson and Sal Mineo. But I bet it's the wildest chapter, huh?

Q: **At the time, it was frustrating and frightening. Now I'm glad I had to go through it because it reads interesting.**

A: I could play him. I can do a German accent, you know.

Q: **Oh? (No sample given.) I . . . you don't look like him.**

A: No, but I could pad up. And a beard, the accent . . . I got to know all his mannerisms and expressions, we worked so close.

Q: **You would, of course, depict him as he was? (No reply.) It wouldn't be a fictional Hollywood version?**

A: (Grins.) No way. If you mean gay, I know he was gay. He made no bones about it. To tell you the truth, he wanted to spank me.

Q: **Oh. Well, there's spanking and there's spanking. Two of his lovers committed suicide. That may indicate something. . . .**

A: He was very unhappy, some of the time.

Q: **A biography—book or film—should include the highs and lows, don't you think?**

A: Yeah, and a movie about Rainer would have plenty of lows. Highs too, but lows are more dramatic. It's always more visual when someone's sad. Or angry.

Q: **You know that, briefly, he had an actress wife? Some said for show. . . .**

A: I knew that.

Q: **A movie could include that but shouldn't dwell on that.**

A: I know what you mean. That was the exception, not the rule.

Q: **And it didn't define who he was, it was more reflective of the society he lived in—its expectations.**

A: Yeah. There's this German director, one of her movie titles says: "It Is Not the Homosexual Who Is Perverse, But the

Society That Persecutes Him." Something like that.

Q: **Very similar. But Rosa Von Praunheim is a man.**

A: She is? He is? *Rosa?*

Q: **Well, there's Sir Carol Reed, the British director.**

A: I guess you can't always judge by . . . you know.

Q: **One can rarely judge. Covers are usually convincing.**

A: To tell you the truth, Rainer was very jealous, professional-ly. I don't know about in his personal life. 'Cause I hap-pened to mention this other German director who admitted he was gay, and he did gay movie stuff, Wolfgang Petersen, and Rainer got very jealous, became real cold. He said, "When you go back to Hollywood, you can work for him!" He got real heated, but only for a few seconds.

I didn't even know if he ever worked in Hollywood. But I liked *Das Boot* (helmed and written by Petersen), and it was about Nazis in a submarine! So I said, "I thought he was here in Germany," and Rainer shouted, "He'll wind up in Hollywood, and then your dearest dream can come true!" (Petersen later moved, and directed Clint Eastwood in *In the Line of Fire* and Dustin Hoffman in *Outbreak*.)

Q: **Fassbinder was a very dramatic man. One of his quotes was, "I don't throw bombs. I make films."**

A: That's cool. Scary too.

Q: **And as a workaholic, he averaged one motion picture every three months, over 13 years.**

A: Yeah, and directing and writing's more time-consuming than acting, even the star parts.

Q: **There's also pre-production and postproduction. . . . I have one of your quotes (reading from notebook).**

A: (Beams.) Let's see if it is.

Q: **After accepting to play *Querelle*—"I realized that if I let the fear of being persecuted by the industry stop me from doing something I felt was right, then my whole life was a lie."**

A: For sure. I still feel that way, and I'm proud of *Querelle*. It didn't do so hot, but that's okay.

Q: **It was a very sexual film. Was it comfortable kissing male to male for the screen?**

A: It would have been *uncomfortable* in L.A. Rainer made it very everyday. I asked myself, later, how people I knew at home would react.

Q: **Despite doing gay roles on screen and stage, you were allowed to play Robert Kennedy. That's progress, isn't it?**

A: There was some resistance, but hardly anyone saw *Querelle*. And what you do on stage hardly counts.

Q: **Why?**

A: . . . Stage and Hollywood are two different things. Like, you can do anything on stage. And if it's in New York, it's almost like doing it in Europe.

Q: **After I saw *Midnight Express*, a friend asked if I liked the book better than the movie.**

A: Dumb question, isn't it?

Q: **A better question would be, "How different are the book and the movie?" I did say the book. . . .**

A: Of course.

Q: **Of course. And she said the book might be good, but it couldn't have Brad Davis's butt.**

A: (Laughs.) My butt! I got a great one too! People do say I have a great body (shyly).

Q: **And some probably say, "If I tell you you have a great body, would you hold it against me?"**

A: (Laughs.) I would! I do think, physically, my body's better than my face. It's okay, and my teeth are good, although—

Q: **You look fine. All right, more than fine.**

A: But when you're not taller than average in Hollywood . . . (Shakes head.)

Q: See that guy? He's one of the managers. You're tall next to him.

A: So's everybody.

Q: So it's relative.

A: But not in Hollywood.

Q: That's true. Hollywood is a business of absolutes—it's either/or.

A: . . . Didn't you like the movie? (*Midnight Express.*)

Q: It was very emotionally involving. Repulsive at times— like the combination of anti-Turk, anti-gay emotion in the scene where it looks like the guard's going to demand oral sex, then the sudden, applauded violence. Killings, biting a person's tongue off or whatever—I had to close my eyes during that—and of course, keeping the drug-smuggling hero straight and narrow. . . .

A: It made a lot of money.

Q: Then it succeeded. In Hollywood terms.

A: Have you ever been to Turkey?

Q: The first time when I was 12. Istanbul is a beautiful and exotic city. Outside its prisons, obviously.

A: Personally, I'd have let Billy, my character, be bisexual in the movie. But I don't know if it would've made as much money.

Q: Do you think one brief, nonexplicit scene of male-male pleasuring in a prison, of all places, would cause audiences to stampede out of the cinema? Especially with such a riveting plot?

A: You should've interviewed Billy Hayes.

Q: I did.

A: You did? (Slightly disappointed.)

Q: He sent me the book, but my deadline meant I couldn't see the film first. Anyway, the piece focused on the real-life drama and how a movie had actually been made of it!

A: So daring of Hollywood! (Both laugh.)

Q: **Exactly. Did you do much research into prison life for** *Midnight Express?*

A: (Pause.) It was so long ago. I don't think I did a whole lot. Why?

Q: **One thing I wondered is whether someone in prison would cry a lot—daily?—or become inured to tears, or try and hide them, conditions and most other prisoners being so hard.**

A: That would be something someone could find out.

Q: **Preferably secondhand! Oscar Wilde, who was jailed for homosexuality, wrote that a day in prison when a man didn't weep wasn't a day of happiness, but a day in which his heart was hardened.**

A: They should make a movie about him. A good new one.

Q: **Would you want to play him?**

A: I don't think so. His height, looks, accent . . . too different from me.

Q: **He had a wife and two sons. Why do you think he married?**

A: To get ahead. Then, especially!

Q: **What about today?**

A: Would he marry if he was alive today? Gee, I don't know. It would depend on what he was aiming at. How come?

Q: **Or how he felt about himself?**

A: I guess. . . . I read someplace that he was so wild—sorry, I didn't mean to make a pun—he was so, like, flamboyant, that he needed a wife for a cover.

Q: **I can think of two comic actors whose non-macho was surprisingly camouflaged by their having long-term wives. One of them deceased. . . .**

A: . . . Jack Benny?

Q: **So several have said.**

A: Who's the other one?

Q: This one, I know two older gentlemen who had affairs with him when he was younger too. He not only hides being gay, but Jewish. Changed his name, of course, and he's never looked back. (I mention his name.)

A: He's Jewish?! I knew he was gay, I didn't know he was Jewish.

Q: Then, he's half-succeeded, by his and Hollywood's standards.

A: I think he's one of those guys who always needs to have a wife he can mention on a TV talk show. (The actor has since remarried, to a female decades and decades his junior.) But about Oscar Wilde, what bummed me out was reading how the reason he got sent to jail, and having to do hard labor, was that he led such a reckless life.

Q: Who wrote that?

A: I don't remember. But it bummed me out because it wasn't about his being reckless or . . . flamboyant. It was the law. If you were homosexual and got caught, the law sent you to jail.

Q: Or bisexual. Non-heterosexuality was criminalized. As it still is in most of the world and not just abroad.

A: (Shakes head.) Bummer.

Q: In one of his later poems (*The Ballad of Reading Gaol*), Wilde wrote, "For he who lives more lives than one/More deaths than one must die."

A: A real bummer. He was deep. When I was in Europe, I found out where Oscar's buried, in a cemetery in Paris. The same place where Jim Morrison's buried.

Q: And Gertrude Stein and Alice B. Toklas, together.

A: Yeah? So I wanted to know where he died, 'cause that would be more personal—where you're buried isn't really part of your life. A friend of Rainer's told me Oscar died in this hotel in Paris, the Hôtel d'Alsace, I think. It's still there. I wanted to go and see the wallpaper, 'cause he hated the wallpaper. I mean, what about having to die in a room where you couldn't even stand the wallpaper!

Q: **I wonder if it's the same wallpaper now?**

A: I don't know. I was surprised the building would be there that long.

Q: **In Paris that's not so long. You were in *Chariots of Fire*.**

A: (Beams.) Yeah. Nobody knew it was gonna take off like that.

Q: **Did you get to know Ian Charleson?**

A: In a way. (Warily.) He's okay. How come?

Q: **Do you consider yourself bisexual, Brad?**

A: (Eyebrows jump.) Well—had—didn't someone once say everyone's bisexual, deep down?

Q: **Not everyone acts on it.**

A: James Dean said he didn't want to go through life with one arm tied behind his back. Why do you ask?

Q: **Did you know, making the movie, that Ian Charleson is gay? He's admitted it—actors actually do that in England, sometimes. He said a British movie producer tried to get him to pretend he wasn't, which he went along with until he saw he wasn't going to get much work in Hollywood.**

A: Wow. I knew. He sort of . . . came on to me.

Q: **Did you react? Or come on to him?**

A: (Laughs shyly.) He's cute.

Q: **Do you ever get involved romantically or furthermore with costars?**

A: I don't think business and pleasure should mix. A little masturbation can save all kinds of complications. (Grins.)

Q: **Since you bring that up—pun not intended—**

A: *I* like it. . . .

Q: **Wilde said, "To love oneself is the beginning of a lifelong romance." Anyhow, I heard you began an interview by telling the writer that before she showed up you were** feeling kind of low, so you . . . took matters in hand. Is that true?

A: That I told him—it was a guy—or that I jerked off?

Q: Either. It's a provocative way to begin an interview.

A: That's the idea. You got to make yourself known as a stand-out interview, 'cause you're competing with every other actor who's a potential interview, and if you're not in a new hit movie. . . . I've done it a few times, mostly in Europe. I start the show by saying I was feeling yucky, then I masturbated, and now I'm ready to begin the old question-answer.

Q: How do journalists respond to your statement?

A: If they're guys, they smile—they're either embarrassed or turned on. If it's a gal, one was . . . like indulgent, the other pursed her lips—she thought I was lying or scum.

Q: Is it just an attention-getting device or a statement of fact?

A: Once it was both. Another time, I did it after the interview was over. On account of the interviewer. (Grins.)

Q: Appealing?

A: (Nods.) Yah-man.

Q: Jamaican?

A: No, he was . . . *oh*. I mean I don't remember. I'm kidding anyway. I didn't do that. Jamaica, huh? There was this old, old joke: Man says, "My wife and I went to the Caribbean." His friend says, "Jamaica?" Man says, "No, she chose to go." (Laughs.) Yeah, Rainer told me about some of his lovers. One of them was Turkish, and he liked *Midnight Express*. He has blue eyes.

Q: Many Turks do. In French, that's what *turquoise* meant, "Turk's eye."

A: Lots of Jewish people have blue eyes.

Q: Especially Jewish actors, from Newman and Bacall to

Streisand, etc. Yet Jewish characters seldom do, or have light hair. Hollywood stereotypes.

A: It sure does. People always say I have a real American face. What does that mean?

Q: Yet you played *Querelle*. For Fassbinder. . . . I saw you on TV in that short movie, *The Greatest Man in the World*. You were playing an aviator based on Lindbergh, weren't you?

A: Yeah, but it wasn't really a movie. He was a creep. Lindbergh and my character. It showed the public side, where he was a hero for what he accomplished, and the private side, where he was a creep around most people.

Q: Lindbergh was quite a bigot.

A: People didn't know that, then.

Q: Far more of them shared his prejudices, then.

A: Yeah. That's interesting to me, about fame. How it covers up so many things, not just bad ones. Say, what do you call it when it's a lady flier?

Q: An aviator. The old term is aviatrix, like Amelia Earhart.

A: That's who I meant! Amelia Earhart. She was a lesbian, but this guy promoted the hell out of her, like a circus act or a novelty. He called her the lady Lindbergh.

Q: And got her to marry him. For her image and his publicity.

A: And maybe so he could control her more.

Q: That almost goes without saying.

A: Wasn't it Gore Vidal said something like, "Wife, therefore a slave"?

Q: Could be. He's said so much.

A: Do you know him?

Q: We correspond. Don't say "To what?" (Both laugh.)

A: Yeah. 'Cause I was reading something he said about Amelia Earhart—that's a funny name. Like he knew her or something. Could be he did. Maybe he's older than he looks.

Q: **Or younger than he writes.**

A: You know, I always wanted to play someone aristocratic. A Gatsby character, like.

Q: **What's your background? Born in Tallahassee?**

A: (Laughs.) That's a funny name too. Once, this casting director asked if I had a girlfriend—it's like asking if you're gay. I just said, "Yeah, I got a lassie in Tallahassee." He liked that.

Q: **I'm sure. Did you want to be an actor when you grew up?**

A: (Shrugs.) Well, in high school I got into plays, and then I got into Atlanta, then New York. Then getting into, or onto, the New York stage, that part wasn't so easy.

Q: **Did your looks or sex appeal help?**

A: Thanks! (Smiles.) Like the casting couch?

Q: **You tell me. If you wish.**

A: Yeah. I had guys after my . . . me. And not only guys. But I got some sexy roles. Showy roles, 'cause in the theatre you get to show more of yourself.

Q: **Physically, too.**

A: That's what I meant. But I'd rather talk about today.

Q: **Who do you admire today?**

A: I admired Rainer (closes eyes).

Q: **Who do you not admire?**

A: Reagan. He's bigoted and ignorant and no leader at all. Maybe in foreign policy, they all gotta do that. But in domestic issues, like for instance AIDS, he's so arrogant he wouldn't say the word in public.

Q: **Even after his supposed friend Rock Hudson died.**

A: Maybe he said it by then, finally. But only because the guy was a Hollywood star.

Q: **And a Reaganite.**

A: You're kidding.

Q: **Never underestimate self-hatred. I once asked Rock,**

who often used to visit San Francisco, what he thought of hippies during the 1960s—

A: He looked down on them?

Q: Yes. Disapproved strongly. He said, "They deviate from the norm."

A: What a dumb reason!

Q: Blue eyes deviate from the norm. So do left-handed people, gay people. . . .

A: You know, I'm not into leather. I don't know if you've heard that. Some people spread it around that I am, I dunno why. You can't even wear a leather jacket once in a while. . . .

Q: A town of spies?

A: Like a nest of spies. The second you leave your house, it's potential publicity.

Q: What do you think of the Hollywood closet?

A: Well, it exists.

Q: So does the pope.

A: Someone else I don't admire. Maybe I shouldn't . . . (frowns).

Q: Don't worry. The so-called Legion of Decency is dead.

A: What's that? A censorship thing?

Q: It was a Catholic censorship body that helped keep gay and lesbian characters off the screen from 1934 to 1959, and its influence lingered after that. . . .

A: You know how they call him the "holy father," and he's neither.

Q: Tell me about the Hollywood closet, which is real.

A: What can I say about it? (Glares.)

Q: . . . Not much.

A: I'd rather talk about censorship.

Q: It *is* censorship. . . .

A: No, I mean the movie ratings board of Jack Valenti. It's this small bunch of parents from the [San Fernando] Valley, and they can keep a guy's . . . male nudity off the screen by saying it gets an X-rating, and no one, the moviemakers or the studios—

Q: **The distributors. . . .**

A: Yeah, them, no one wants an X anymore. But the actresses get to show everything, or have to.

Q: **That board also gives a gay or lesbian love scene an *R* or an *X*—which usually means it gets cut—where they'd give an equivalent heterosexual scene a *PG*.**

A: They're out of touch and out of date.

Q: **Censors usually are. Especially about anything gay or lesbian. They preach about "protecting" their children but always leave out their gay and lesbian ones.**

A: Well, that's *it*. Somebody said once, maybe in some play, that contrary to what most people think, gays don't come from pods.

Q: **Parents also underrate the strength of the heterosexual impulse in those who are hetero or primarily hetero. Nobody can be forced to be homosexual. *Or* heterosexual.**

A: Yeah, most parents don't want to think about it. But gays are America's kids too.

Q: **Precisely. But they should at least let their parents and families know. Acceptance begins at home.**

A: Yeah. It's not like telling your boss, who can fire you. Your parents can never fire you.

Q: **No, but some parents actually throw their gay kids out. And then the kids become runaways. . . .**

A: Parents like that should be sued, at least. Or shot. It's real sad, but most older gays don't even want to get involved.

Q: **One reason they don't is that it's so easily misconstrued. If they show interest in the young runaway's plight, society and the law think the interest is just sexual.**

A: That's what bums me out about how they talk on the news. They talk about "gay lifestyles" or gays wanting more acceptance for their "lifestyle."

Q: **A "life" is serious, a "lifestyle" is not.**

A: But it's not a choice.

Q: **No more than heterosexuality.**

A: They never talk about a heterosexual lifestyle. Like I have, for instance.

Q: **Like you've chosen. The media give the impression, deliberately or ignorantly, that everybody's heterosexual but some insist on adopting a gay lifestyle.**

A: Which gay lifestyle? There's a lot of 'em.

Q: **And even with AIDS, there's no encouragement of committed gay relationships. Even Dr. Ruth, who avoids gay topics in her quest for popularity, has said there should be encouragement.**

A: She's good. She knows where it's at.

Q: **And then there's bisexuality. . . .**

A: She's from Europe, she knows about that.

Q: **Have you ever had sex with a man?**

A: Well, who hasn't?

Q: **I can think of a few women, for starters.**

A: Everyone's experimented.

Q: **But Brad, much of Hollywood says you're actively bisexual.**

A: (Gestures helplessly with hands.) Most men in the whole world. . . . If you've been to Turkey, which is just one Middle Eastern country, you know how all the men have . . . they do homosexuality, it's real common. But they all have wives and kids.

Q: **And consider themselves entirely heterosexual. I know the mindset you're describing. It's widespread throughout what one calls the Third World.**

A: Yeah, and the big . . . distinction they make is who does what to whom. Right? They don't go by gay or straight, they say masculine or feminine. If you screw, you're masculine, if you get screwed, you're feminine.

Q: **Where does oral sex fit in?**

A: I don't know. Or "69," huh? (Winks.)

Q: **Yes, where both perform the same role, simultaneously.**

A: Yeah, and oral sex is a lot safer than anal sex.

Q: **Such societies are very either/or; it's all black-and-white, even the languages give a gender to every noun, every item. Differences are always stressed and exaggerated.**

A: They're not very compassionate cultures. They treat women almost as bad as they treat animals.

Q: **They're extreme patriarchies. Subtle but strong dictatorships.**

A: But the women put up with it. . . . (Shrugs.) The good thing is, when you travel, like Turkey or Latin America, a guy can have sex with almost any local guy, if conditions are right.

Q: **That's stretching it, but . . . it also depends what he's willing to do. Money also often enters into it in such countries.**

A: 'Cause they're poor.

Q: **Also because the guy playing the butcher role often doesn't want the foreigner to think he did it for pleasure. He wants money or a "gift."**

A: It's interesting about Turkey, that whole culture, their Moslem culture. A friend lent me this book about Christianity and Moslems and how they treat gay people. I didn't get to read it, but it looked like the guy did his homework.

Q: **John Boswell? (Author of the 1980 book *Christianity, Social Tolerance and Homosexuality*.)**

A: I think so. It told about the rotten things our society's done to homosexuals for centuries and how Moslems are supposed to be better.

Q: **It's very relative. I wouldn't say better. . . .**

A: Wait, here's what happened. I gave the book to a friend who had the time to read it, and after he did, I said I ought to maybe read part of it, and then he showed me this article that was all about, like, rejecting the things the writer said about Moslems.

Q: **Islam.**

A: This article showed how a lot of things in the book were wrong or . . . out of context.

Q: **Or mistranslations?**

A: I think so, and how Islam hasn't done a whole lot better than Christianity. And far worse towards women, for sure. Still, what's cool is that if a guy's interested, the Middle East lets him get his rocks off.

Q: **Again, depending on what one's willing to do. And certainly tenderness is not involved, let alone relationships. Those are all heterosexual or familial.**

A: I wouldn't ever want to live there, but I'd like to travel more, on my own.

Q: **What's your current or next project, Brad?**

A: A movie where I play a cop. (Grins sheepishly.) Oh, well. It has Sharon Stone and Adam Ant, the English singer. (Whispers behind his hand.) Somebody said he's heterosexual. I was surprised—if it's true.

Q: **There are what are stereotypically called "gay-acting straights."**

A: And straight-acting gays.

Q: **Correct. Mostly you act for the camera now. Do you miss doing steady theatre?**

A: . . . Not really. And when you live in L.A. . . . I think theatre's more for younger actors.

Q: **Or English actors?**

A: Yeah. They never get enough theatre (laughs).

Q: **What can't you get enough of?**

A: (Covers mouth, then laughs.) Acclaim. I love being in demand.

Q: **Do you think most actors are too fond of attention and other people's opinions?**

A: Probably. Someone said that with actors, none of us got enough love in our childhood.

Q: **Why do you think a bigger percentage of gay or bisexual men become actors than, say, become accountants?**

A: Not that there's no gay accountants! I know one or two (laughs). Because when you're different, you have to start acting right away. You pretend, to get by.

Q: **To pass.**

A: Yeah, so you're already doing a role as a kid or a teen. We *all* act, but if you're not straight, you act even more. And acting's exciting. I think most gay kids look at their parents' lives, and they want more.

Q: **You played a sailor in *Querelle*. Did the uniform aspect of the project or role appeal to you?**

A: Is that what you've heard? Did Rainer say that?

Q: **Many people fancy a man in uniform.**

A: Or, better, out of it! (Grins.)

Q: **Were you eager to play a sailor?**

A: To tell you the truth, every sailor I've ever known wasn't heterosexual or homosexual. I think most of them are bi. In Rainer's movie, it went mostly homo, so that wasn't so accurate either. But it kind of made up for all the Hollywood movies where every guy who ever wore a uniform was heterosexual.

Q: **Despite many of the actors and stars playing them. (Davis notes the bisexual Gene Kelly in *On the Town* and other musicals.)**

A: Hollywood never shows homosexuals in the army.

Q: **Not quite true. Remember *Reflections in a Golden Eye* with Brando and *The Sergeant* with Rod Steiger, to name two of the '60s ones? And a few more since, including British and Continental. Interestingly, almost nothing on lesbians in the military.**

A: That's funny, 'cause I'd bet the average dyke's more interested

Cesar Romero

The Silver Fox

"The Gay Caballero" and Tyrone Power's lover

The New Valentino

Paul Lynde

"I'm no Hollywood square, sonny!"

In drag, opposite Robert Vaughn in *The Glass Bottom Boat* (1966)

Opposite: Funny man of the big and little screen

Oscar nominees: Coco, Joan Hackett, Marsha Mason in *Only When I Laugh* (1981)

James Coco

"I'm a self-made man. It took a lot of pasta. . . ."

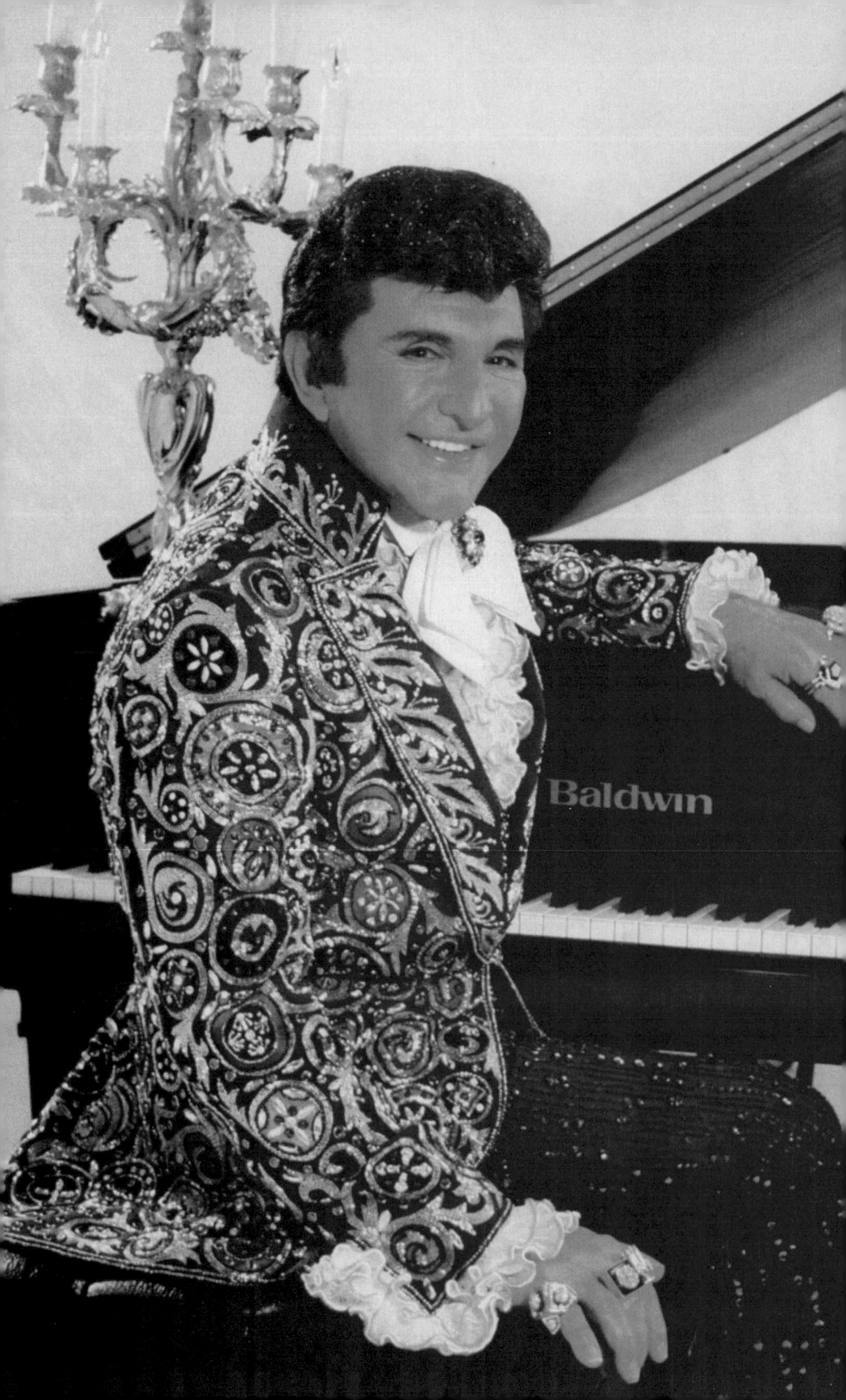
Baldwin

Liberace "The Wizard of Ooze"

Oppisite: Aka the Kitsch Kid . . .   . . . and the Queen of Denial

Brad Davis

Q: Have you ever had sex with a man?

A: Well, who hasn't?

As the gay sailor Querelle in Fassbinder's *Querelle* (1983)

The hunger: Davis and Franco Nero in *Querelle*

Anthony Perkins

Young and gay: Paramount pretty

Truman Capote:
"Tony became
more and
more like
Norman Bates."

Older and closeted: *Psycho-analyzed*

Cary Grant

Chevy Chase called him "an old homo"...

Tall, dark, and handsome:
Grant in 1933

Opposite: Telegram: "How old Cary Grant?"
Answer: "Old Cary Grant fine. How you?"

Randolph Scott

Cary Grant's other—
and richer—half. . . .

Grant and Scott on beach

Opposite: Tall, blond, and handsome: Scott in 1935

David in 1929, the year he and
Jimmy met

David Lewis

Joan Crawford
called him "the
prince of
Whale's". . . .

Director James Whale in 1929

William Haines

Joan Crawford said he and Jimmy Shields were "the happiest marriage I've seen in Hollywood."

Haines's last movie was aptly titled *The Marines Are Coming* (1934). He's the big guy in the middle.

Back: Caught on a cot: Haines's career was ended because he had another man in his bed at the "Y."

in enlisting than any average gay guy.

Q: **Well, who wants to wake up that early?**

A: Are you doing a book about it? Gay movies or something?

Q: **You guessed. It will include *Querelle*. And many other movies, mostly nonmilitary.**

A: Right on. Send me a copy, will you?

Q: **Yes, but don't hold your breath. Most editors love the manuscript, which I update every few years, but they feel Vito Russo's book captured the whole market. They're wrong.**

A: Someday I want to write a book.

Q: **About what?**

A: The actor's life. This actor's life.

Q: **Nonfiction?**

A: (Grins.) Yeah, mostly. I've encountered a lot of very interesting people.

Q: **And vice versa.**

A: Thanks.

Q: **Were you intimidated, preparing to play Bobby Kennedy?**

A: I don't think so. Not in any way that showed.

Q: **What do you mean?**

A: I just . . . it was a good script. I loved starring in it. But I knew he was taller than I was. Which you can get around that . . . like, I always heard Alan Ladd was bi, and he was real aggressive, like trying to make up for both things. Being shorter too. But what I meant was, Bobby Kennedy was supposed to be hung like a mule—down to his knee. . . .

Q: **I never heard that.**

A: I doubt to his knee, but. . . .

Q: **The size of caught fishes—or fish—and men's appendages, even if already impressive, is so often exaggerated.**

A: Nothing physical is ever big enough. Most people would say.

Q: **You know which one is really stupid? "You can never be too rich or too thin."**

A: Oh, no, I'd like to be too rich.

Q: **Too rich is debatable, but too thin—that's a thoughtless statement.**

A: . . . You know, nobody ever asks actors about aging. Actresses get asked all the time. What I really dislike about movie acting is it's *all* physical, and by the time you learn how to make a juvenile character, a young lead, interesting, by then you have one too many lines on your face, and those big roles get yanked away from you. Older roles are better. Better written. But younger roles get the most build-up and the most money.

Rainer was always saying Hollywood's too youth-oriented and too establishment-oriented, and he was right. He usually was right about things, and he used to give good advice to his friends. If you worked with him on either side of the camera, you were his friend. That was his world. He really didn't move through the outer world, it was all just moviemaking for him.

Q: **He was unique. It's too bad he didn't take much of his own good advice.**

A: He didn't think he was worth it.

Q: **He was an actor too.**

A: He did everything. Theatre too. And TV, I think.

Q: **With all he accomplished, it's hard to believe he had such low self-esteem.**

A: It *is* hard to believe.

Q: **He wasn't physically handsome, as you are. In what way are you more secure than Fassbinder, and how are you insecure?**

A: Uh-oh, we're going deep! Well, I'm more secure than Rainer was about my being—you could tell he was willing to throw it all away. The work was important to him, but not his own self. And he had to have work. *Had* to. I could do without

work, emotionally, but not financially. But I don't have anywhere like his smarts or his confidence about what he could
do. I think Rainer was a true genius. (Eyes have misted.)
Does that answer it?

Q: **In what way are you insecure?**

A: Well, the future. Every actor's insecure about that. Even
stars. And if you're different in any way, that doesn't contribute to being very confident, like if you don't measure up
in some way.

Q: **You mean physically?**

A: Like height? Well, yeah, but . . . everyone's insecure in different ways.

Q: **But hopefully not just about differences or nonconfor-
mity, especially when conforming wouldn't be natural.**

A: No, it's just that . . . sometimes one does get pretty down and
blue. It doesn't matter what job you have or how you look.
I think most human beings with any amount of sensitivity
get a lot more depressed than we ever let on.

Q: **Laugh and the world laughs with you?**

A: Yeah, and everyone's got his own little cluster of specialized
troubles.

Q: **That most people are happy in the same way, but sad-
ness is a specialized, individual thing . . . ?**

A: That's it. You keep your blues to yourself, and you smile at
the world.

Q: **When you feel like it.**

A: Or when you think you should.

Q: **What makes you laugh?**

A: The past.

Q: **What about the past?**

A: Things other people wouldn't find funny. Things I can
laugh at now, alone.

Q: **What makes you cry?**

A: I like this kind of catharsis. You should get a couch.

Q: **But I couldn't charge you.**

A: You could take it out in trade.

Q: **So what makes you cry?**

A: Injustice. Like in *Midnight Express*.

Q: **What makes you happy?**

A: Well, one thing is good food—served by cute waiters. Or waitresses.

Q: **What makes you scared?**

A: Casting directors and the IRS.

Q: **Interesting.**

A: You didn't ask what makes me horny?

Q: **Good food, and you're thinking about sex? Okay, what makes you horny?**

A: Do you want to go to the restroom together?

Q: **. . . Is that the answer to the question?**

A: No, but it could be the start of something big. Don't you think we've talked enough?

Q: **We haven't finished our dessert.**

A: We can eat later. . . .

Q: **But—**

A: No buts.

Q: **Literally.**

A: (Laughs.)

Q: **Listen, I have to put away the machine and my notes. Why don't you go ahead and start without me?**

A: You won't be too long?

Q: **Can anyone be too long?**

A: (Leers with cocked eyebrow.) See ya. (Rises.)

Q: **Uh, likewise . . . I think. . . .**

ANTHONY PERKINS

(1 9 3 2 – 1 9 9 2)

"**I** put Anthony Perkins into his first film," said director George Cukor about *The Actress* (1953). "He had a fresh, boyish, somewhat nervous quality. I was impressed by his attractiveness *and* his difference. . . . People seem oblivious to all the pictures he did before *Psycho* (1960). It was altogether another Tony Perkins, and he was like that until about the late '60s. Then Norman Bates began catching up with him. Not merely professionally, which had already happened, but facially, particularly the eyes. . . .

"The actor playing all these lunatics and scary kooks in all these exploitation pictures is not the actor I chose. As for all the anecdotes about him making the rounds for so many years, they indicate he's not the same boy, either."

Interesting that Cukor still referred to him as a "boy," for until his death at 60 from AIDS, Tony

Perkins retained a boyish quality, albeit no longer the boy-next-door but rather an aging, haunted Peter Pan. "He went from what one Hollywood columnist described as 'Peter Pansy' to a somewhat ghoulish image," felt Brian O'Dowd, Perkins's close friend and dresser in such films as *Psycho II* (1983), *Psycho III* (1986), and *The Lucky Stiff* (1988). "If he looks like a serial murderer at times, it's just his occasional demeanor. At times he may seem chilling, but he's just a conflicted, occasionally tormented man who sometimes has a great sense of humor and can be great fun to be with."

From the start, the actor exhibited a sensitivity on screen which got him cast in more peripheral roles. His quirkily ingratiating smile and tentative mannerisms and shrugs lacked the gravity and self-confidence of typical leading men. He often played sons, employees, or kids by comparison to the male lead. Gary Cooper, his costar in *Friendly Persuasion* (1956), Perkins's first movie since *The Actress*, advised, "I think he'd do well to spend a summer on a ranch." Costar Yves Montand (*Goodbye Again*, aka *Aimez-Vous Brahms?*, 1961) observed, "He seems to drink from the fountain of youth. He looks so young and innocent. He is playing the little boyfriend of Ingrid Bergman, my mistress." (Decades later, Perkins claimed that Bergman, Jane Fonda, and Brigitte Bardot each tried to seduce him—all denied it, as did Victoria Principal, his alleged partner in what Perkins told several people was his first heterosexual experience.)

O'Dowd explained, "Tony's father was a character actor, Osgood Perkins. He died in his mid-40s when Tony was five. It seems Osgood had health and chemical problems, and he was too hard on Tony. On the distaff side, Tony would be the first to say he wished he'd had someone else for a mother. . . . He did want to act and follow in his father's footsteps. But not as a character actor. He told me he wanted to outshine his father."

Though appealing, tall, and lanky, Perkins didn't set

Broadway or Hollywood on their stereotype-prone ears. His big-time stage bow was as the suspected homosexual student in *Tea and Sympathy*. The movie version in 1956, however, starred John Kerr. George Cukor, who like many gay directors evaded gay-tinged projects, bypassed *Tea* and stated, "For that character, who is thought so 'different,' Hollywood, as ever, wanted an actor who was not, let's just say, sexually unusual.

"Despite its sensationalism at that time, *Tea and Sympathy's* moral was you shouldn't treat someone you think is different badly because they might just be normal and *shy*."

While Hollywood, specifically Paramount, was cautious about giving Perkins leading roles, critics could be downright prickly. More than one announced that Perkins as a baseball player in *Fear Strikes Out* (1957) was "not believable" or "is wanting in athletic or emotional credibility." In years to come, as a bizarre assortment of mama's boys, neurotics, "confirmed bachelors," and blatantly homophobic gay villains, no one called Perkins unbelievable. Director John Huston, a liberal politically but not vis-à-vis feminism or the gay community, helmed the Paul Newman vehicle *The Life and Times of Judge Roy Bean* (1972):

"He isn't easy to cast," said Huston of the by-then supporting (or character) actor. "Putting him in a Western is casting against type. . . . I understand he's a friend of Paul's. . . ." A critic reviewing *The Tin Star* (1957) had remarked "how encumbered [Perkins] seemed by six-guns" in that movie.

For years after *Psycho*, Perkins declined any role involving drag and/or nonheterosexuality (before his most famous movie, he'd reportedly nixed *Some Like It Hot*, 1959, because it required sustained cross-dressing of its two male leads). "All his bisexual, asexual, and gay roles were taken on reluctantly," said O'Dowd. However, Tony had already displayed drag in *The Matchmaker* (1958), where (as in *Hot*) it served as an escape route and a necessity—the case in most Hollywood movies where a hetero character "must" assume womenswear. On the tall, broad-shouldered actor, the period drag looked positively eerie, including a veiled hat and a long gown that foreshadowed Mother Bates two years later.

After *Psycho* and until the mid-1960s, Tony moved to Europe. He informed *Paris Match*, "Hollywood thrives on repetition, which may be okay for films but is death for actors. . . . Europe gives me permission to act more mature." Perhaps another motive for moving to Paris was to be far from tinseltown's prying eyes. A bachelor in his late 20s and early 30s, the *Psycho* star was the object of more speculation than ever, not just in L.A. but the American media. Fan magazines ran jejune stories with titles like "My Fantasy Girl Is Still a Dream, By Tony Perkins," "Wanted: A Wife/Apply: Desperate Tony Perkins!" and even "Tony Perkins' Secret Mystery Girl—Why You Never See Her . . .!!"

A former talent agent recalled how in spite of Paris's freewheeling attitude toward stars and sexuality, Tony insisted on deep-closet maneuvers to hide the fact of his boyfriends and male lovers. "For instance, after lunch I'd have to leave separately from Tony and his beau from the restaurant, taking the guy with me to Tony's apartment, while Tony got there on his own. I'd enter the apartment building with the guy as if it was business, then I'd leave on my own, giving Tony and his beau time to have some fun, and then I'd go back to Tony's apartment and escort the guy out and drive him home.

"Later, at night, they might meet someplace for dinner, and so that they wouldn't seem too much like a couple, I'd 'happen' to drop by and join them for coffee after their meal. Then maybe we'd repeat the whole charade if Tony and his beau wanted to get intimate after dinner. But I don't believe Tony ever let any of his boyfriends stay overnight." Did the actor imagine that spies or paparazzi were stationed outside his building and favorite eateries day and night?

Perkins's former agent, himself gay, approved the extreme caution. "You couldn't be too careful in those days." (Most in Hollywood would say the same about *these* days.)

By 1970, Perkins was starring for the small screen in *How Awful About Allan*, from a novel by the author of *What Ever Happened to Baby Jane?* The same year, he did a minor role in Paul Newman's politically correct nonhit *WUSA*, and two years later was in Newman's own *The Life and Times of Judge Roy Bean*, also featuring Tab Hunter and Roddy McDowall. In '72 he played another memorable neurotic in the cult film *Play It As It Lays*.

"I used to say that I wondered if the movies were for me," he apprised *Coronet* magazine. "I'd gone and decided that if *Psycho* wasn't a hit, I'd consider giving up acting, or at least movies. Now I just take a role and don't worry about it. I used to worry about everything. . . . I used to care about the body of work, but I think I'm resigned to being a puppet, which is what actors really are. We interpret *other* people's work. . . . At some point I'd like to direct." Via the *Psycho*-revisited phenomenon, he got his wish, but the quality of his few directed horror films left much to be desired.

Brian O'Dowd felt that "Tony grew estranged from Hollywood. He maybe stayed in movies because of *Psycho*, but that's what cut him off from the Hollywood A-list and made him come to resent film and not feel any great responsibility toward it. . . . All through the '80s he'd complained bitterly about the 'monster shit' and the 'stereotypical shit' given to him. I once suggested that he let it all go, leave the movies for a few years. But he got close to tears and said, 'It's all I know how to do now. What else can I be, a drug dealer?' I was sorry I'd spoken up, but then he hugged me, smacked my bum [bottom], and all was well."

In 1972 I was asked by Australia's *Screen* magazine to try and get an interview with Tony Perkins, to be titled "What Ever Happened to Anthony Perkins?" It was to focus on his recent roles, on *Psycho*, of course—on the upcoming *The Last of Sheila* (which he cowrote with his friend the gay composer Stephen Sondheim but didn't appear in), and—get this—his private life.

The interview wound up a cover story. Perkins had readily agreed to do it, and only after its completion wondered if he might get the cover—compared to today's publicity maze, where a cover is often expected as a condition of the interview. During our session, Perkins avoided Norman Bates and most specifics about *Psycho*, speaking instead about its prestigious director. He said little about his screenplay and less about buddy Sondheim, actually labeling him a "confirmed bachelor." And Anthony's own private life? A single paragraph:

"Everyone keeps droning on about long affairs and relationships. Why does everyone always measure everything by quantity? I know of marriages inside and out of the entertainment sphere that're long but miserable, and I know there've been relationships, affairs, what have you, that weren't long but were intensely pleasing to me at the time."

Q: **Are there any roles in *The Last of Sheila* you could have played?**

A: I can think of a few.

Q: **Why didn't you?**

A: I wanted to go around and see the other side. I helped create these fictional beings, but I don't have to inhabit them. It's a satisfying change. It's a new kind of high. Some writers say that writing's like a drug, and others do it while they're actually high.

Q: **Have you experimented with drugs?**

A: No comment. Why?

Q: **There's a perception that Hollywood is quite drug-happy. If that's the way to put it.**

A: I've experimented. Here and there.

Q: **What about feuding actors in Hollywood?**

A: It takes two to feud.

Q: **Joan Hackett was quoted as saying (after *How Awful About Allan*) that she thinks you're "nuts."**

A: That might be. I'm in psychoanalysis. She has a few kinks up her sleeve too. You know she smokes pipes?

Q: **Don't they do that in Scandinavia?**

A: I don't think so.

Q: **I do. At our Cairo hotel, every night there was a group of Danish women who'd sit on the verandah and smoke pipes.**

A: She used to be jealous of me. End of discussion. I want to say something, and I'd like this to be quoted. Most of the time, people worry about others trying to harm them—in Hollywood, and everywhere, as a matter of fact. But to me, it's funny, and I've given this some thought, how people spend almost no time worrying about the harm they can do to themselves. Think about it.

Q: **It's a good point. But how, specifically, do people harm themselves?**

A: In a myriad of ways.

Q: **Such as? (No reply.) Drugs?**

A: Yes, and others.

Q: **Like what?**

A: . . . One thing some of us do is let other people make our decisions for us. Or our value judgments.

Q: **You said you're in psychoanalysis?**

A: Yeah.

Q: **Do you think it's more necessary for actors?**

A: Actors, yeah, and it depends on your childhood. Losing a parent young is a compelling reason to visit a professional.

Q: **But are they really experts? Aren't they apt to follow** their prejudices?

A: Yes.

Q: **So shouldn't one beware taking their opinions as truth?**

A: You have to find a good shrink.

Q: **One who agrees with you?**

A: You both have to have the same goal. But the magazine doesn't want to hear about this. Your readers are probably more concerned with . . . kangaroos! (Laughs nervously.)

Q: **Who are your heroes?**

A: . . . That's not a good question.

Q: **Or, as an actor, which actors do you admire?**

A: The rich ones. Kidding! My father was a famous actor, for New York. When New York counted for much more than today. They'd say, "Let's go see the new Osgood Perkins play."

Q: **Did you become an actor because of him?**

A: . . . For me, that's not a good question. Too complex.

Q: **What other actors do you admire?**

A: I like Monty Clift and Cary Grant. Lon Chaney, Jr., in *Of Mice and Men.* . . . Then I found out Cary Grant beat up on his wives. Or not beat up, but he used to hit them.

Q: **Where did you hear this?**

A: Maybe not all his wives, but he did hit two for certain. I know people who know them or knew them. I didn't ask, but it all gets broadcast.

Q: **I imagine there's far more of that than ever gets reported.**

A: It takes two.

Q: **What does?**

A: I'm against wife-beating, of course. (Pause.)

Q: **We should talk about you.**

A: I don't like to talk about me.

Q: **You must tire of questions about *Psycho*?**

A: (Yawning sound.)

Q: Is there someone special in your life now?

A: Bad question.

Q: Do you think a friend is more important than a lover?

A: (In a hostile tone.) What do you mean, a lover?

Q: Someone you have sex with, and perhaps love. You know, an affair?

A: Having a best friend is the best, for anyone.

Q: Do you often get asked—and this can be off the record for *Screen*—why you haven't married?

A: Why don't they ask people why they *do* marry?

Q: What reasons do you think they'd give?

A: Recurring ones. Like getting away from your parents, giving in to your parents, loneliness . . . marrying for money, and some people would marry the first person that asks them—

Q: That's insecurity or very good luck.

A: But don't ask about marriage. Bad topic.

Q: Do you ever get lonely?

A: That's not relevant.

Q: Maybe the question isn't. Not being married doesn't mean being alone—or single.

A: I couldn't tell you.

Q: Being a movie star, one imagines there are thousands who'd want you, on various levels.

A: Yeah! Want a piece of you. *Any* star. They want a piece of the star's fortune, they want a piece of ass, some of the fame, a few memories, something to brag about . . . or they even want your soul. But that's usually an agent.

Q: Janet Leigh was Oscar-nominated for *Psycho*, but you weren't, and your role was more demanding as well as extensive.

A: Right.

Q: You must have been disappointed.

A: I was glad for her.

Q: **But hurt?**

A: Do you think I was?

Q: **Would there be a reason the Academy might shun you? Or shy away from nominating you as Norman?**

A: That sort of answers itself, doesn't it?

Q: **Do you ever regret having played Norman?**

A: Bad question.

Q: **This year you turn 40. What does that feel like?**

A: Wait and see.

Q: **You're still boyish, but as an actor, is aging an anxiety or a relief?**

A: I feel indifferent to it. I don't think it'll affect what they want me to play.

Q: **Will you be writing any more movies, perhaps on your own?**

A: Of course. Lots and lots and lots of them! (He didn't.)

Q: **Australians still vividly remember Anthony Perkins, as they usually call you. Partly because you went there to film *On the Beach* (1959) with Gregory Peck, Ava Gardner, and Fred Astaire.**

A: They remember me vividly? (Sarcastically, suspiciously.) What did I do to warrant that?

Q: **It's an expression. The people at the magazine seem to really like you.**

A: They haven't met me.

Q: **("Maybe that's why," I'm thinking.) I'm supposed to ask if you have "fond memories" of Australia?**

A: I just *love* Down Under.

Q: **Do you?**

A: Do you want to find out?

Q: **You filmed in Melbourne, correct?**

A: Melbourne. . . . I'd like to spend some time in Sydney. . . .

Q: Hmm. That new opera house alone would be worth the trip.

A: I've been on many a trip.

Q: Drugs?

A: No comment.

Q: Audrey Hepburn is a favorite of mine.

A: Me too. But *I* worked with her.

Q: I know. That's what I'm about to say. One of her least known but most unusual and enchanting films is *Green Mansions* (1959), where she plays Rima the Bird Girl. Made in Venezuela, I believe? (He grunts assent.) She was wonderful, and the jungle, the animals—although it was a sad story—and you . . . were extremely appealing.

A: I was?

Q: Yes. Was it wonderful to make?

A: She was wonderful to work with, like a real person, almost a sister.

Q: And then it failed, commercially.

A: Because it was good but unusual.

Q: I can see why you were a bobby-soxers' pin-up. Didn't you record an album for them?

A: Bad topic. Boring topic!

Q: Will you forgive the observation that in your pre-*Psycho* movies you smiled a lot, but since then, not a lot?

A: . . . I might. What're you offering?

Q: . . . Tea and sympathy?

A: Bad topic!

Q: It's interesting how the character of Norman Bates is so braided with that of his mother. . . .

A: I don't know.

Q: You would say he has a mother fixation? (No reply.) Some actors do, don't they?

A: Mother fixations are a boring topic.

Q: What about father fixations?

A: Boring.

Q: Have you got any interesting fixations?

A: Sexual fixations are fascinating.

Q: Tell me about them?

A: Not for this interview.

Q: You were in a (1963) French film with Brigitte Bardot whose English title was *a Ravishing Idiot*. I don't think it was released in the USA. What was it about?

A: *She* played the title role.

Q: How did you get along?

A: We didn't. This is boring, forget her. What a brainless topic! I don't think any Australian magazine would ask you to ask me about Bardot-dodo.

Q: Most of these are my questions. Do you read, Mr. Perkins?

A: Yes, I learned how in elementary school.

Q: Read any good books lately?

A: No, but I've been trying to read one by a French writer, (Jean-Jacques) Rousseau. I hate it, it's boring and dry.

Q: What's it about? (No reply.) What have you learned from it?

A: That he didn't know his ass from a hole in the ground.

Q: Is it a geological treatise?

A: (Laughs, finally.) Yes. No. He doesn't know. This Frenchie wrote pages and pages on how masculine and feminine roles are supposed to be completely natural and heaven-sent, except he's continually instructing people who read his book on how to get their boys and girls into these roles, how to make them stay in these roles. It's only the humor that's kept me reading, but I'm gonna quit.

Q: . . . Then and now, molders of society offer a vision of what they want and what suits them, and present it as if it were "natural" and desired by all.

A: Or even good for everybody.

Q: And the word "natural," and its alleged opposite. . . . Sounds like propaganda. What led you to read it?

A: I can't even remember the title. I thought Rousseau was a great thinker. But he's boring!

Q: Sounds misguided but not boring. It's an interesting topic.

A: Not to me. When I was in France, people younger than me were reading him. I thought he was some revolutionary French thinker.

Q: He may have been progressive for his time. In some things. Few people are progressive across the board. There are usually individual biases and contradictions.

A: Most of what I read, if people recommend it, is dull.

Q: Now some assigned questions. Can you name your favorite actress and actor that you've worked with?

A: Think I should? . . . I liked Shirley Booth. And Audrey Hepburn. Melina Mercouri was fun. Janet Leigh. I liked most of the actors. Not so much Gary Cooper or Fred Astaire, they were standoffish.

Q: Your favorite actor you've worked with?

A: I can't say.

Q: You can't?

A: If I did, you'd say, "Why him?" 'Cause he's not so famous, so you'd wonder why I chose him.

Q: For personal reasons?

A: So let's skip it. Some of the people I liked most, I didn't work with. Then, being at different studios was like being at different schools, and if you had a thing with someone at another studio, watch out!

Q: Was Tab Hunter at your studio? (Hunter was at Warner, not Paramount.)

A: . . . No.

Q: **One keeps hearing you were close friends.**

A: Yeah.

Q: **Both very handsome.**

A: I don't know. But he was like a Greek god, except he was blond.

Q: **So was Alexander the Great. . . .**

A: That's interesting. We oughta meet and talk stuff over. . . . But now, for the interview, you have enough now? It's not gonna be that long, is it?

Q: **Alas, no. But I would like to interview you again someday.**

A: Or meet . . . to talk, and whatever.

In 1972 Anthony Perkins was interviewed for Andy Warhol's *Interview* magazine. The photographer assigned to shoot him was Berry Berenson, younger sister of some-time actress Marisa. Brian O'Dowd explained, "Tony was in analysis since before, not after, *Psycho*. Later, he became a client of Dr. Mildred Newman, who's a . . . the way I say it is, she's an evangelist for heterosexuality—a Jewish evangelist. She egged Tony on to have sex with a woman, as well as to try writing a screenplay, and when he met Berry, they became fast friends, and Tony found he could be bisexual, though I believe it was his second heterosexual affair. She got pregnant, and in 1973 they married.

"Emotionally, they're very close, and they have two sons. Tony wanted, like his father, to be an actor and to be a father and carry on that name, like an acting dynasty." Older son Osgood is an actor. "Overall, it's worked out, though for Tony's part, it hasn't been all smooth. But I won't go into that."

The screenplay with Sondheim was the homophobic *The Last of Sheila* (1973). Playwright and novelist James Kirkwood stated,

"After I saw it [the movie], I asked Tony—we have the same shrink—why it was that . . . I mean, not as vicious as some, but backward. He smirked and said, 'You write for the stage, I write for movies.'"

Sheila costar Joan Hackett noted, "That film was a nightmare for all concerned. Most of the cast and crew hated each other's guts, and some of the vitriol from the script's malevolent atmosphere—the murder and betrayal and blood and gore—just spilled over onto the location filming."

As for Perkins the actor, he carried on with a procession of sad roles that stereotyped him irretrievably. Said O'Dowd, "He was either a hysterical gay character like in *Murder on the Orient Express* or so many others, or he was, yet again, Norman Bates. Tony thought that branching out into directing, with *Psycho III*, could change his career, but it didn't. He was wrong to go back to *Psycho* at all. It was just for money."

(He also directed the straight-to-video *Lucky Stiff*, with Donna Dixon seducing a fat man in order to eat—cannibalize—him.)

Despite the actor's self-servingly anti-gay and misleading proclamations in a postnuptial issue of *People*, Perkins was now bisexual, not heterosexual or "straight." Andy Warhol's diary recorded, "I love seeing the new *People* magazine with Tony Perkins on the cover, and it talked about him being gay, as if it were all in the past. Isn't that funny? . . . Left out Tab Hunter and Chris Makos, but it didn't say that he used to hire hustlers to come in through the window and pretend to be robbers." Or, according to three lovers, that he enjoyed sexual foreplay in which he and a male partner enacted boxers, replete with boxing gloves and fake blood smeared on Tony's "opponent."

Warhol wrote in June, 1983, "Chris [Makos] said that he visited Tony Perkins and Berry. . . . He said that when Berry went into the other room Tony started pointing to Chris's crotch and saying, 'I'd like to see you,' and all Chris could say was, 'All right,

Norman.' I never really liked Tony because he treated me badly once when he was with Tab Hunter."

Fashion designer Halston was godfather to Tony and Berry's first child. He told the press, "Tony has changed his lifestyle, not his life. He's trying something new, and I feel the relationship will last, but Tony is Tony. . . ." James Kirkwood, who shuttled between affirming himself as gay or bisexual, recalled, "Dr. Newman was always after me to 'settle down.' By that she meant a woman and matrimony. As if that would solve all my problems, rather than giving me an entirely new set.

"My particular problems for which I sought help related to my childhood and my reactions to my dysfunctional parents, not to my love life. . . . Unfortunately, Mildred's credo was something along the lines of, it's okay to like yourself—unless you are gay. Somehow it took me a while to realize that."

O'Dowd admitted, "Tony's personal demons weren't exorcized by marriage. But through it he did establish a lasting relationship that he couldn't be blackmailed or condemned for. For all his aloofness, Tony's often hunting for other people's pat on his back. . . . Above all, he wanted to be a father and live the childhood he himself never had.

"But he still hasn't been able to kick drugs." In his 1984 book *Hollywood Babylon II*, Kenneth Anger described "ever-gaunt, closeted, and neurotic Tony Perkins (the shrink blamed it all on Papa Osgood)" being arrested at the airport after Concording to London "with a supply of sensimilla and three microdots of LSD in his purse." The *Los Angeles Herald Examiner* printed:

"Tony Perkins' loping ultra-slimness isn't owed to any celebrity workout nor visits to the neighborhood gym. Were he to visit a gym, the reason, say insiders, would be other than exercise. 'Tony likes to maintain his home life,' says an openly gay poet who has known intimate relationships with a movie studio head and a record producer. 'Tony, like lots of men on either side of the fence, has no trouble separating love and sex.' Or sexercise, since Perkins's hopped-up expression and emaciated frame make Mick Jagger look very nearly the picture of health and fitness."

George Cukor offered, "We have some mutual friends . . . one of them recently came back from New York and said Tony is renowned in local show biz circles for making available and partaking of drugs at his and other people's parties. At least he supposedly does it behind closed doors. . . . Strangely, for someone so public about his marriage, most of Tony's men friends and guests are gay men, usually in show business."

Arthur Lonergan, art director of *The Actress*, explained, "Perkins and I lost touch after a brief but pleasant yet platonic friendship. But one doesn't really lose contact, it's such a small (show biz) world. I've heard that, apart from anything else, he hoped his marriage would change his image and career, but it hasn't had an impact on his career. . . . Larry Kramer, the screenwriter [*Women in Love*, directed by Ken Russell] who became a gay activist (and safe-sex advocate), used to be a patient of Mildred Newman, but apparently he left because he could accept himself but she wouldn't. Whereas everyone says Dr. Newman became a surrogate mother to Tony Perkins, one he's always eager to please.

"It must be tough, the ambiguity in such a life. Perkins's desires aren't ambiguous at all, but he does one thing, and lives another way. The conflicts and pressure must be tremendous." Even if self-imposed.

Whatever Tony felt about his conflicted private life, his career was spiraling downward. He went from playing, say, a homosexual terrorist in a B-movie starring Roger Moore to barely released junk like *Twice a Woman* (1985) in which he taunts a female, "They say you've become a lesbian. . . . Is it because you couldn't have children?" and wherein he does play a heterosexual and murders a young woman, his lover. He flew to Europe to work in some Eastern European productions, which he declined to discuss, telling a friend, "You don't even want to know."

By now, villain roles in big-budget films were beyond his reach. When *The Silence of the Lambs* proved a homophobic hit, Perkins told friends he could envisage himself as "Hannibal the Cannibal" Lecter. A writer for *Premiere* magazine opined that Perkins was the only actor besides Anthony Hopkins he could see in the role; but Perkins's version "would be a non-heterosexual Lecter." (Hopkins won an Oscar for his *Silence* role, as did Jodie Foster, playing the sexually unspecified Clarice.)

Lambs costar Ron Vawter noted, "The filmmakers did go out of their way to make Hannibal heterosexual—he's the 'good' villain. The bad villain, the serial murderer of women, is depicted as a transvestite or a gay transvestite—even though most people who kill women, by far, are straight men in pants.

"I pictured Perkins as Hannibal, but the powers that be wanted to insure that Hannibal be perceived as straight, so they cast a straight actor. Perkins never had a chance."

Eventually Tony moved with his family to the Hollywood Hills, to be closer to work. He socialized with gay luminaries, including members of the so-called "velvet mafia" who would later attend his memorial service. But proximity to the studios didn't result in much work or offers from non-independents, and his final effort was the barely seen *A Demon in My View* (1992).

By that time, Tony Perkins had become far more interesting as an entity and a case history than any of his post-Norman roles. He could have written a riveting personal bestseller—as I pointed out to him—had he been willing to be honest. He countered by wondering, "What was that Oscar Wilde said about being honest, or about the truth?" I assumed he meant "The truth is rarely pure and never simple," from the play *The Importance of Being Earnest* (1895, the same year Wilde was sentenced to prison—and hard labor—for not being heterosexual).

I interviewed Tony Perkins twice after 1972, in New York and L.A. He'd improved as an interviewee, as hopefully I'd improved as an interviewer, and the two sessions (one for British *Photoplay*, the other for *In Style* magazine) were pleasant enough and could have extended into private encounters but for Perkins's rather frightening mien and reputation. Besides which, as I reminded him at the end of our New York session at Oscar's in the Waldorf Hotel, "We each have a partner, you know, and it's the '80s, time to play it safe." He smiled sarcastically, then snapped, "Okay, you can pay the entire bill, it won't be Dutch treat!" and called for the waiter to bring *one* check.

The next and final session was to have been a phone interview, but he sweetly requested that we meet in person, never alluding to the abrupt ending of our prior meeting, and even adding, "I really enjoyed our last several interviews (we'd done two), and I'd really like to see you again." Despite it all, Tony Perkins could be disarmingly likeable, and never entirely lost his stellar charisma.

Q: **You've used the word "hate" three times in the last few sentences—twice about food.**

A: (Winces, then smiles.) Maybe I'm a hater-o-sexual.

Q: **I've heard rumors. Seriously, though.**

A: Everything's serious. Too serious.

Q: **What foods do you hate?**

A: That's far too personal. (Grins.)

Q: **In that case, what person or persons do you hate?**

A: . . . I don't hate him, but what a joke—Truman Capote. (I ask why.) He said things about me at parties.

Q: **About your marriage? Or your . . . what?**

A: About anything that came into his head.

Q: **Why do you say he was a joke? (No reply.) His seeming a stereotype?**

A: Not only that, though he was undeniably repellent. But he did stop being a writer. Bragging all those years about a novel (*Answered Prayers*) that never existed!

Q: **Other than the excerpted chapters. Did he question whether you were gay or bi?**

A: No. Whether I was gay or straight.

Q: **Why didn't bi occur to him?**

A: (Shrugs.) Actors think about it, bisexuality. It's part of acting, unless you do Westerns. Most roles have those facets to them. But writers like Mr. Capote (this time pronounced to rhyme with *compote*) are one or the other, so they only think that way.

Q: **What about bisexual writers?**

A: Name one.

Q: **. . . Gore Vidal?**

A: Ask anyone who knows him. "Bisexual" may be politically correct, but he has no interest in women. Not that way. And he's not Paul Newman's only friend. *We're* friends too, and I've heard Joanne (Woodward) saying that Gore's never lusted after her, only after Paul.

Q: **It's certainly not known to the general public that Gore has lived with Howard Austen since before I was born.**

A: Which was . . . 1957?

Q: **Thanks, 1954. I've heard that Gore himself points out that it isn't, today, a sexual relationship.**

A: (Harrumphs.) Some marriage!

Q: **It does seem needless to point it out.**

A: And *he's* (mincingly) *bi*-sexual?

Q: **Behave yourself, Norman! (He stares, his mouth open.) I couldn't help myself. It was kind of fun.**

A: (Both laugh.) One more of those, and there'll be some harsh discipline. . . . Back to our . . . what? Talk?

Q: **Conversation. Or *psycho*-analysis?**

A: You're asking for it.

Q: Gore Vidal. Okay. You're an actor who reads. What do you—

A: Not him. Not anymore. Mr. Vidal ("Veedle") is not very much for plot. Elegant, bisexual prose, but plots? You don't read a novel to be bored. *I* don't.

Q: As an essayist, he's excellent.

A: Was. Paranoia's set in. Why do you think he's so great? To me, he's a climber. He cares desperately what other people think, but always pretends he's insensitive to it. He's *so* above it all. At least Capote wasn't as pompous or paranoid. You could count on Truman for his ratty little genuine opinion. With Vidal, it's all so calculated.

Q: But he's said some—

A: Let me finish. He won't even say *he's* allegedly, supposedly bisexual. He only says that sex acts are this or they're that, but he's . . . *above* it all. He won't commit. So he's not so brave.

Q: He's far from the only one not to commit to a category.

A: Why should anyone?

Q: Because we all fall into certain categories. Sometimes several. And others will categorize us anyway, often inaccurately or prejudicially.

A: I'm married and a parent. Doesn't that say something?

Q: That since about age 40 you've been that and that, but one category doesn't necessarily exclude another.

A: You mean (mock-shocked) life is not that simple?

Q: Life isn't either/or. It's and/but.

A: Contradictions, contradictions.

Q: Also pretenses, changes, experiments, *diversity*.

A: Is it true Mr. Capote opened his heart and his mouth to you?

Q: What?

A: He gave you a blow job?

Q: How on earth could you know about that?

A: That was Truman—have mouth, will travel. He didn't only

give good prose, he was . . . *he* said he wasn't promiscuous. And he wasn't, from behind. He just reckoned that if you used your mouth, it didn't count. (Leer.)

Q: **Did you know him, or he you?**

A: Not that way. Andy Warhol had a crush on him. During the Stone Age.

Q: **Hmm. I've seen most of your movies—a varied lot. Do I recall some Westerns?**

A: (A half-smile.) It *was* varied. I do recall a few. One with Paul.

Q: **I'll bet casting directors didn't think of you as the Western type.**

A: I'll bet they didn't. Westerns are so simplistic.

Q: **Sometimes there's quite a bit under the surface.**

A: I doubt it. Comedies are elementary school, drama's high school, and Westerns are Sunday school. To simplify it for you.

Q: **What's college?**

A: Your turn.

Q: **Costume movies, I guess, historical movies. Do you like Westerns?**

A: . . . It's a genre obsessed with masculinity, and troubled by it. I find that boring. It's so juvenile.

Q: **Is it paranoia or insecurity?**

A: It's boring. Just take things as they are. Westerns aren't happy or . . . accepting. They're so predictable.

Q: **Formulaic.**

A: Archaic. Your turn.

Q: **Comedies. I imagine producers don't think of you for comedy. . . .**

A: Producers with impaired imaginations do not.

Q: **I'm told you have a wicked sense of humor.**

A: Both. And I'm very negative at times. It helps me balance the positive. So that I can appreciate it. To me, pessimism is the face of realism, and optimism is hope. Hope's not always justified, but you need it, in doses.

Q: **Can one overdose on hope? Or optimism?**

A: A public figure can. (Long sigh.) Do you often ask celebrities about people they can't stand?

Q: **A dislike-list?**

A: A hate-list!

Q: **Not usually. Sometimes it comes up—an unliked co-star, and then I ask about another co-star or a particular director. . . . But about Capote. What can you say positive about him? (No reply.) Think hard, Tony.**

A: Yes, Mother. Well, he went out in daylight. (Snickers.) If I looked and sounded like him, I'd only come out at night.

Q: **I can see you in his *In Cold Blood*.**

A: No, you can't. They wanted unknowns.

Q: **Is it true you were offered *Lawrence of Arabia*, but you didn't want to don "drag" again, after *Psycho*?**

A: I may have been a contender. It was not offered to me.

Q: **You've heard the *Florence of Arabia* joke?**

A: I have (grimly).

Q: **Can you say something nice about Truman?**

A: Good president. . . . He had a long relationship with that dancer he met so long ago.

Q: **Jack Dunphy. I think he switched from dancing to novels before 1950. It's odd that one almost never hears about Capote's longtime companion, but quite a bit about his friendships and feuds with women. Or is it odd, knowing the media?**

A: The media. . . . Phooey!

Q: **Don't you think the media intentionally cover up longtime gay relationships?**

A: I'd say they do. But so do the majority of people in those gay marriages.

Q: **This is true.**

A: It's not easy knowing the particular value or intensity to the people involved in it of any relationship or marriage or whatever. I know a guy, married a long while to a woman, and when I used to glimpse him, I didn't know. I just knew he had a kid and a long marriage. Then we had a talk, and I *knew* he was gay or bi, whatever. You know *how* I got it? He used the word "heterosexual." Straights don't use it—they don't think of themselves as having a sexual preference.

Q: **As if only gay people have a sexual orientation.**

A: I don't like either, "orientation" or "preference."

Q: **I know. "Orientation" is better because it sounds less arbitrary, but even that doesn't indicate something innate. It sounds like something one's trained for.**

A: You go to an orientation meeting, then you leave with your own sexual orientation!

Q: **Besides, sexual-this or sexual-that leaves out affection, crushes, and love.**

A: A dancer I once knew said you could tell your real sexual orientation not by who you have sex with, but who you get crushes on.

Q: **That's astute, because many closeted or repressed gay or bisexual men have never had sex with a man.**

A: So far.

Q: **You know what amazed me? I read that Tennessee Williams never had sex—**

A: No, no: *made love*. That's the Hollywood term.

Q: **Well, Hollywood *excludes*. . . . Anyway, he never had sex with another man until he was 29.**

A: I don't believe it.

Q: **It's hard to believe, till you think back to past decades. And self-repression. The closet does the homophobes' work for them. . . .**

A: Yeah, but even if he grew up on a farm . . . lots of kids on farms experiment. Most straight boys had some gay sex when they were teens.

Q: **Actually, Tom—Tennessee—grew up mostly in St. Louis.**

A: Not many farms in St. Louis. Still, . . . *29?*

Q: **It was clever of you to note that most people don't use the word "heterosexual." But did you later find out for a fact that the contractually married man was non-het?**

A: I did, absolutely. I came on to him and he said he would. I didn't intend to, I was just testing, and he passed the test.

Q: **You led him on, then when he said yes, you said no?**

A: Not in a mean way (grins). Besides, later he got divorced, and now he's been with his boyfriend for years. Which doesn't mean he isn't a good father.

Q: **No one said he isn't.**

A: He sees his kid regularly, and really enjoys fatherhood.

Q: **Yes, I can think of at least one heterosexual father who doesn't enjoy children.**

A: I think most men become fathers out of duty. They don't *want* kids, the way women do. They just feel they ought to. I'm different—I wanted kids. Eventually.

Q: **I knew one gay boy in high school who always wanted "a baby." Didn't want a wife, but longed for a baby. Of course, to get one, he had to get the other. Deeply closeted, as we speak.**

A: Yeah, and he couldn't very well have a kid, then divorce the wife and keep it.

Q: **You said Capote was phony because he apparently never completed that novel. Who do you consider a phony, period?**

A: Several people I know or knew, not all famous. . . . Joan Crawford.

Q: **Why Joan? The loving-mother image?**

A: . . . She gave herself over completely to the star-trip. The phoniness of Hollywood. That looks-is-everything philosophy.

Q: **Appearances, appearances.**

A: She even had a special outfit just for answering her fan mail.

Q: **Only one? Why do you think they say "clothes*horse*"?**

A: Because clothescow isn't as polite.

Q: **Who else is phony?**

A: Miss Michael Jackson. Best example of all.

Q: **I believe he's the only person in show biz history to have called a press conference to announce he wasn't gay.**

A: To claim he wasn't gay. . . .

Q: **Let's move on. Any other phonies?**

A: That's a book unto itself. Don't you think some people would put me in that niche? Strike that. Let's not pursue that. . . . I know another phony. Do you know Jerry Zipkin?

Q: **Who's he? He invented zippered napkins? The name rings a bell.**

A: Ding dong. He's Nancy Reagan's best homosexual friend.

Q: **That sounds like an oxymoron.**

A: His I.Q. or hers? (Grins.) He's this utterly closeted, utterly conservative, ass-kissing friend of the woman in red.

Q: **Is he the one Truman Capote said had a face shaped like a bidet?**

A: That's the one. I heard that at a party. Phony, phony, phony. (Zipkin died in 1995 and was, with Reagan, a thinly veiled character in a play by Larry Kramer.)

Q: **There's a self-destructive, or destructive, army of phonies of that type, the world over.**

A: Roy Cohn. . . .

Q: **Terry Dolan, . . . names that will live in infamy. Onward. You have an excellent singing voice!**

A: You're referring to *Greenwillow*? (His 1960 Broadway musical.)

Q: **No. You did some songs on various albums for Ben Bagley, starting in the '60s, I believe. One tuneful song** stands out, "All My Friends Have Gone to California," where you offer to service a man for the fare to L.A. (He frowns.) The lyric also says something about "where John Travolta lives". . . .

A: I like the song anyway. Ben's a fine record producer. 'Course, he wasn't *out* then, now he is, so some of what he wrote (in the liner notes) seems silly now. That closeting stuff about different celebrities who agreed to sing songs for him.

Q: One of his notes said that Noel Coward was engaged to Mary Baker Eddy Nelson. (Both laugh.) I remember another said your closest friend is your bike.

A: Was. He exaggerated. Did you read the one that said the only thing I ever went down on was the escalator at the Uris Theatre?

Q: The only thing?

A: That's for me to know. . . .

Q: Do you agree with the sentiment that sex is not a "sin" if you feel guilty afterwards?

A: Is that from the Jewish *Kama Sutra*?

Q: No, the Judeo-Christian one.

A: Seriously, guilt's a pain in the neck, but if you've got it, you have to work through it. That's where psychoanalysis comes in. Which I'm not here to rehash. . . . By the way, it wasn't *Florence of Arabia*, it was *Psycho of Arabia*.

Q: I sit corrected. Who, if anyone, was Florence of Arabia?

A: Florence Nightingale? Didn't she work, or whatever she did, in Turkey?

Q: Yes . . . some famous hospital across from Istanbul in westernmost Asia.

A: Wasn't she a dyke? Probably not very active, but she was. . . . Did you hear that?

Q: I've seen her name on lists of famous gays and lesbians. I'd like to read an unbiased book about her.

A: The establishment won't give her up easily (grins).

Q: **Why is that nebulous yet powerful group supposedly allhetero?**

A: It can't be.

Q: **No. But officially and dogmatically, it is.**

A: Because the Zipkins count themselves as honorary heterosexuals. It's ridiculous but funny when you look in these movie reference books in a bookstore or at the library, and it includes the relationships that are opposite-sex, but for gays or lesbians it doesn't say anything about their private lives.

Q: **That is, for gays and lesbians who didn't take wives or husbands. Appearances and covers. . . .**

A: What they sometimes say is, "He never married."

Q: **A woman.**

A: But if you know many of the celebrities they're writing about, it's to laugh. (Giggles.)

Q: **Most of that supposed hilarity is self-produced. Of course even nowadays sometimes a celebrity comes out, but the media try to keep him or her *in*.**

A: A conspiracy of silence?

Q: **For the most part.**

A: What tickles me is that famous saying, "the love that dare not speak its name." Like there's some unwritten law that anyone who's different, that way, has to forever be silent? Come on!

Q: **It's really "the people that dare not speak their love's name." I agree with you. When Oscar Wilde needed voices and support, where were all those men, at least in England, who were gay, and writers or artists or politicians or clergy or rich or royal, or just plain humane? *Silent*.**

A: As the tomb.

Q: Good way to put it. Gays don't know their own power.

A: Neither do women.

Q: And women have the best numbers. The majority, in fact.

A: Best numbers. Not necessarily the best figures.

Q: That's an individual thing. Do you prefer boyish women, physically?

A: (Shaking head firmly.) I'm not going to grapple with that one.

Q: Many people were dismayed when in *People* you said that you'd had gay sex but it was "unsatisfying" to you. Of course this was said after you'd gotten legally married.

A: Oh, it's all a *game*, what celebrities say.

Q: A game taken seriously.

A: . . . I meant the relationships, anyway. Sex is great. Unless all you do is watch.

Q: Were you misquoted?

A: No. But . . . it doesn't always come out the way you mean it.

Q: I've heard you like kinky sex—rough stuff. Was sex with another man competitive for you?

A: No.

Q: And do you like it rough?

A: Sometimes.

Q: Do you like the sight of blood?

A: Not real blood. Never. Another thing, I'm *not* a sadist—or the other one.

Q: A masochist. Do you find there are more and more comparisons with Norman Bates?

A: When there are, it's always blown out of proportion in print, and it's not my doing. I like Norman. He's close to me. But he's not what people think, a two-dimensional monster.

Q: You've said that you had a difficult relationship with

your mother.

A: Mildly put.

Q: You've also said, in an interview, that she somehow made you afraid of women? How did that happen?

A: Is it so astounding?

Q: For one thing, there's more to be afraid of in men than women.

A: But we grow up in a society where motherhood is . . . it's redolent with good vibrations. Nothing negative can be said about one's mother. Why is criticism so shocking? A kid doesn't arrange his mother's behavior. And my situation is anything but unique. Gore Vidal didn't love his mother, to name one. Or . . . any number of people. It's the father that usually gets the bad rap.

Q: I hear what you're saying. Fathers may be good, bad, or indifferent, but a mother is hopefully wonderful. I should hope so, since she's the first foundation.

A: Let's move on from mothers. I don't want to talk about any-one's mother, least of all my own.

Q: I'm sorry.

A: I'm over it.

Q: I understand you're a minister? (No reply.) Of course you played a minister—who wasn't unlike Norman Bates (drag and all)—in *Crimes of Passion*. For the record, although what's one going to say, are you at all into transvestism?

A: No, I am not. I've played a few TVs, and that sticks. I played a minister, I became a minister. So? . . . You know, in England they used to call boys "master."

Q: Right. There was a Bette Davis movie, *The Nanny*. She kept calling the boy "master Joey."

A: That English actor, Alan Bates . . . a friend of his said he used to be called Master Bates (guffaws).

Q: . . . Hmm. You *are* a minister?

A: In America, anyone can get a license to preach.

Q: Like going into politics?

A: Like write to an organization, send in your $10 fee, then you can give your blessing to things.

Q: What things?

A: Marriages and such.

Q: Certain kinds of marriages. I heard you "blessed" the last marriage of your *Crimes of Passion* director Ken Russell.

A: That's what I did. No "I do's" or such; we had poetry, prose. . . it was lovely.

Q: No "I do's"?

A: Only "I'll try's."

Q: That's realistic. Do you know, you did do drag before *Psycho*? Shirley Booth was fantastic in all her few movies, and you were both in *The Matchmaker*.

A: (Actually smiles.) Mm-hmm. It was *Hello, Dolly* without the music (by Jerry Herman).

Q: A piece of Americana, like *Our Town*, by Thornton Wilder, who was gay. I was in *Our Town* in San Mateo, but I didn't know Wilder was gay till Christopher Isherwood and others said it.

A: Everyone knew in New York.

Q: That's a New York specialty, knowing things.

A: What part did you play?

Q: What else?—the journalist. Not a very imaginative director. He was also the casting director.

A: You didn't act for him again.

Q: Once more. A play he wrote about Charles I.

A: What did you play?

Q: The bishop who, as it were, blesses his execution by the anti-royalists. I'd auditioned for Charles I, but a professor got the role—this was in college—because he was the

right age. But the wrong accent: American.

A: They always cast me as Americans.

Q: **I wonder why. . . . I found amusing one of your lines in** *Mahogany,* **where again you were a tortured and villainous bisexual of sorts.**

A: That movie *haд* a memorable line?

Q: **Yes. You said, "You're only young once, but you can be immature forever."**

A: I thought Freud said that.

Q: **Or Diana Ross.**

A: (A sudden thought.) About ministers . . . as a newly ordained minister, I was able to bless or solemnize Ken's ceremony, but I wasn't able to marry them. In the movies, kids who watch them must grow up thinking ministers and priests can actually perform marriages, which they can't. They don't have that legal authority.

Q: **Religious ceremonies are more visual than a marriage at city hall, so I can understand that cinematically. But what you're pointing out is the propaganda. Marriage isn't only supposed to be about religious sanctions and prejudices. As you say, movies—and TV—always tie in marriage with the church. They make it more biblical than it is, and link it, at least subconsciously, with procreation, which makes it easier to leave gay people out in the cold, despite being citizens and taxpayers with human and constitutional rights.**

A: I couldn't have put it better myself. It's very archaic. But marriage isn't primarily about procreation.

Q: **Legally, procreation should have nothing to do with marriage. That's a choice between a woman and a man. But it's used as a homophobic excuse against legal, social, and economic recognition of same-gender marriages.**

A: Gays can adopt.

Q: Usually not, legally, but the point is, most don't want to. Marriage is two people in love joining together for life. Children shouldn't be a condition of marriageability.

A: Not all straight couples have kids. Some by choice.

Q: Exactly! The radicals on the religious right—*that's* redundant—cite "family," meaning offspring—only—to them, as the aim of contractual marriage. If that were so, the marriages of childless or child-free heterosexual couples would have to be dissolved. And that would be ridiculous too.

A: I see. You're not talking about adopting or having kids.

Q: Not at all. Before two people legally marry, they're not asked, "But are you gonna have kids?" Even if the man and woman were unable to procreate, they wouldn't be denied their marriage license. But that's precisely what happens to gay or lesbian couples.

A: I see that. It's funny that so many lesbians want to be mommies. A lot more than gay men do, but that's a gender thing. . . . Then there's all the people who're against homosexuals adopting because they think they'll influence their kids to become homosexual.

Q: That's like saying that having heterosexual parents influences their kids to become heterosexual. It doesn't work that way. Individuals are who they are.

A: And there's too much reproduction as it is. Especially with the people who can least afford it.

Q: One would have thought such tragically overpopulated nations as China and India would become less homophobic out of common sense and practicality, but. . . .

A: Common sense isn't that common.

Q: *Touché.*

A: Particularly when religion enters the picture.

Q: You said it, minister, not me.

A: (Grins.) Did you say "child-free"?

Q: I've lately seen interviews and articles where a woman who's chosen not to have a child is called "childless," and she corrects them with "child-free."

A: If she doesn't want a kid, she's child-free. If she wants one but can't have one, she's childless.

Q: That's a good definition. It applies to males too.

A: I think the word "unnatural" applies to these constant efforts to make infertile people fertile. All these pills and hormones and things—with so many kids already in the world—so that a woman can end up having five kids at a time. *Shit!*

Q: Or where a woman of around 60 can now reproduce again. Some progress, eh?

A: Quantity, not quality. And at this rate, we'll have to go colonize the moon, to begin with.

Q: And then ruin the other planets too?

A: I don't think humans will last that long, to be able to replicate on other planets. I think . . . don't you think it'll all end with chemicals or viruses or something deficient in the genes? They say human sperm counts are way down.

Q: One would never know it from the population explosion. . . . The year before *Psycho*, Hitchcock did *North by Northwest*. Cary Grant was paid a reported $450,000 for his role. You were paid $40,000 for *Psycho*. Any comment?

A: I also got a percentage of the gross once it passed a certain amount. All I can say is, Grant was overpaid.

Q: Or you were underpaid.

A: And our movie's an ensemble thing, and it wouldn't have worked in color. No one dominated *Psycho*. Grant dominated that other film, and it was drabsville.

Q: In a way, it was Hitchcock who dominated *Psycho*. And

you. He said it wasn't supposed to have any superstars
in it.

A: The *story* was the star (in a strained tone). And it did a lot
better than *North by Northwest*. People liked it more. Now,
let's get off this *Psycho* kick. I did do other movies.

Q: *Matchmaker.* Robert Morse. You played coworkers and
buddies.

A: Bosom buddies.

Q: Did you know he came out as bisexual?

A: Uh-hunh.

Q: And he's a father.

A: Yeah.

Q: It hasn't hurt his career. . . .

A: I like Bobby. But he was never a movie star.

Q: In one *Matchmaker* scene, you dance together.

A: He danced divinely. Go on.

Q: Stephen Sondheim isn't an actor. All of Broadway knows
that he's gay, and he doesn't attempt to hide it. So why
doesn't he come out?

A: Ask him.

Q: He's not easy to get to.

A: He's lucky. He doesn't have to do publicity.

Q: He also seems like he doesn't want to.

A: It's not the same as an actor's ego. Being interviewed is a
nice way of getting stroked. Though not the nicest. . . .
(Leers.)

Q: Control yourself. It wouldn't hurt Sondheim's career to
come out, do you think?

A: I don't know. Would it?

Q: It hasn't hurt Jerry Herman *(La Cage Aux Folles; Mame;
Hello, Dolly)*. But why so often the homophobia in
Sondheim's work? Not just *The Last of Sheila* (he
frowns), but in lyrics—using the anti-gay *f*-word, etc.

Why that hate, and self-hate?

A: You'd have to ask him.

Q: You don't have an opinion on that?

A: (Shrugs.) Ask me what I've been reading. (I don't.) Well, nothing lately, but I was talking with a friend who says he should do a movie set in Rome. When they had emperors. He said he saw me as a Roman poet. I said I'd rather play an emperor.

Q: Which one?

A: I checked out a history about the decline and fall of the Roman empire—there were so many!

Q: If that's the famous work by Edward Gibbon, he was as biased and of his era as they come.

A: Anti-gay?

Q: Anti-truth. Not willing to accept that bisexuality was a tolerated fact of life then. With him, the "bad" emperors were gay or bi, the "good" ones were all heterosexual.

A: It's never that simple.

Q: It is for too many historians.

A: Everyone thinks historians know it all.

Q: Those teaching or writing history are often reinforcing their own biases, not necessarily presenting what truly happened or who people were.

A: It's all because of men being the historians, isn't it?

Q: Well, they say history repeats itself, and historians repeat each other.

A: History's more interesting in the movies.

Q: Than in books? I beg to differ. History books may be flawed, but compared to movie presentations, they're filled with integrity. Which doesn't mean costume movies aren't fun.

A: Just funny about the truth. (Chuckles.) You know, I got such a hoot out of your George Cukor interview (in

Conversations With My Elders). He was so funny. Such a closeted old queen.

Q: *He's* closeted . . . ?

A: *Was*—he's dead. (Grins widely.)

Q: A great director. I'm glad you enjoyed my book, or chapter.

A: I never knew Nancy Reagan's godmother was a lesbian till Cukor said it in your interview.

Q: Yes, a Russian lesbian, at one time MGM's top-paid actress, Alla Nazimova.

A: I heard something about her. But I thought she was German.

Q: You can't judge a celebrity by their surname.

A: You can in my case.

Q: You're pretty rare.

A: (Grins.) That's how I like my meat.

Q: . . . Don't let your meat loaf.

A: Safe-sex again? (Rolls eyes.) You and Larry Kramer. . . .

Q: I haven't met the gent.

A: Don't bother.

Q: I've read him.

A: I haven't.

Q: He says some important things.

A: Depressing things. Now let's eat. Enough talk. *Brother!*

Anthony Perkins reportedly found out that he had AIDS via the *National Enquirer*. He hadn't tested for the virus but saw a doctor for another reason, and the doctor secretly tested his blood, knowing Perkins was gay. The incredibly informed tabloid leaked the information. Perkins considered suing, but Berry suggested he get tested, to confirm his HIV status. However, until the very end, the actor—afraid of losing work and probably of being sexually uncovered—ignored the entire issue and kept an extremely low profile, avoiding the media, which occasionally chronicled his growing gauntness.

Ron Vawter revealed, "Mr. Perkins was contacted about taking part in some AIDS fundraisers, and he still could have done so, but he wanted nothing to do with it. A lot of fear there. . . . I don't know whether he imagined his silence could posthumously buy off the truth. Of course, merely being married and a dad insured a mostly heterosexual slant in the [news] coverage of his death. For that, he was given more respect than Liberace.

"But the unavoidable fact is that Tony Perkins almost certainly contracted AIDS from homosexual sexual activity engaged in *after* his marriage in the early 1970s. The man's relationship with his family can be respected, but his utter hypocrisy cannot be." From his deathbed Perkins issued this nonspecific statement, posthumously broadcast around the world:

" . . . I have learned more about love, selflessness, and human understanding from the people I have met in this great adventure in the world of AIDS than I ever did in the cutthroat, competitive world in which I spent my life."

Couples

CARY GRANT

(1 9 0 4 – 1 9 8 6)

Cary Grant was born 50 years before I was, in 1904. We met soon after my thirtieth birthday, in 1984, late in May. He was 80, although age was not something he would have spoken about, much less admitted.

Many years before we met, an American magazine tried to find out Grant's real age (he usually subtracted four to eight years from his true age). The magazine reportedly sent Grant a telegram: HOW OLD CARY GRANT? He responded with another telegram, one which ignored the question about age: OLD CARY GRANT FINE STOP HOW YOU? It was both vague and witty—and vagueness and wittiness were trademarks of Grant's movie persona.

The man once told the press, when asked who he'd most love to be, "I'd like to be Cary Grant." Who was the real Cary Grant? If the man born

Archibald Leach knew, he wasn't telling. Not publicly, anyway. He sometimes candidly admitted that his was a confused personality. And sometimes he contradicted himself—so numerous were his lies, which began in childhood.

In his "notorious" biography of Cary Grant (who co-starred with Ingrid Bergman in *Notorious*), Charles Higham documented a man who began life with little white lies about himself and ended it by having lived a huge lie. The portrait in that biography is not a pretty one. The charm and cool suave of Cary Grant—the Grant perpetuated by the media even after his hallowing death—are missing.

And most people want to hold on to the Cary Grant they think they knew. I have a literary friend whose best female friend is the ex-wife of a 1950s matinee idol. She claims to have had a platonic affair with Cary Grant. My literary friend told me, "She and Cary would get in bed together, naked. But they never did anything. She says he never penetrated her. And there's no reason for her to lie about it—on the contrary, most women would invent a hot, torrid affair with him, if they could!

"All they would do would be to snuggle together, and they'd eat pizza and read the newspapers and just chat. Naked. Together. In bed."

Yet this woman—who knew that the *reel* Cary wasn't the real one—chose not to speak with Higham, whose book caused fury throughout the land because it admitted—with proof—that Grant was bisexual. That is, primarily homosexual, but choosing to live a multi-wedded (if not often-bedded) heterosexual lifestyle. Why didn't the woman speak to Higham?

"Because she knew Higham would unmask Grant as nonheterosexual. So, instead, she agreed to be interviewed by Grant's widow, who is doing an authorized—but largely false—book portrait of her late husband."

A self-professed former female lover of Grant's also did a

book, called *An Affair to Remember* (titled after another Grant film). In it, she admitted that Grant preferred to hire male secretaries, because his secretaries always tended to "fall in love" with him. His feeling, therefore, was it might as well be a man doing the falling. . . . Yet the book paints Grant as an ideal and virile—in his 70s—*heterosexual* lover.

I never had any idea I would meet Grant. But my partner is a banker, and he had an associate—a closeted gay man, married to a lesbian—who was Cary Grant's banker in Beverly Hills. (This second banker has since died of AIDS, leaving behind the widow and their adopted child.) This closeted banker, whom I'll call Bob, used to dine regularly with Cary. Just the two of them.

I met Bob, and he spent 20 or 30 minutes talking to me about Grant. Of the many celebrities he got to deal with at the bank, Grant clearly impressed him most. Why? He was the biggest star among his clients. "And you *really* have dinner with Cary Grant?" I deliberately asked, more than once.

(In fact, I once saw Grant picking up a pizza at a Westwood pizza parlor. Local gossip columns often sighted him at cheap restaurants or fast-food places, picking up food to go. Grant was legendary for his cheapness. In the old days, he and Clark Gable used to swap their unwanted monogrammed Christmas gifts. Both men had experienced very poor, harsh childhoods—and Grant was emotionally abused by his mother, as Gable was by his father. Both men were homophobic and conservative, Grant even joining the Republican Party and helping raise funds for it as late as the mid-1980s, by which time it had become the party of the homophobes.)

I was needling Bob because I wanted somehow to meet, to talk with, Cary Grant—and saw no other means of doing it—and because Bob was the sort who invited needling. First, he was the type of "married" gay man who will make "fag" jokes in front of his coworkers (I knew this for a fact), and second, he was a very pretentious man. He used to make anti-Semitic jokes about some of his star clients, and found it hugely amusing that he would from time to time deign to attend synagogue services with some of them.

This, although he knew that I am Jewish on my father's side. The second time we met, Bob challenged me, "Jews have to be Jewish on their mother's side—or else they're not really Jews."

"Do Christians have to be Christian on their mother's or their father's side?" I inquired. He shrugged, like I was *meshugah* or something.

Then I took to challenging Bob, saying he'd never invite me to dine with him and Cary, because the two of them probably did more than eat steaks together. Bob was offended by my insinuation, at the same time that he was flattered that I'd think Cary Grant would find him sexually interesting (on the other hand, I would imagine that an 80-year-old man would find anything or anyone under 70 interesting).

"It is strictly platonic," Bob would insist. Knowing Bob, I knew this to be the case, for even if Cary had been 30 at the time, Bob wouldn't have jeopardized his position at the bank by diddling—much less fiddling—with him. For we'd both heard of several instances in which a movie star had a one-night stand with someone, then ended the professional relationship; stars tend to be fickle and funny that way.

I asked Bob: "Have you ever seen *it*?"

I meant Cary Grant's cock. I'd heard Grant was part-Jewish. . . .

Bob was at a loss. After a few long seconds, he smiled mysteriously. And I swear he said: "Wouldn't you like to know?" Well, of course I would, you ditzy queen, that's what I asked.

"He doesn't want to be interviewed," Bob coolly informed me. "Doesn't need it." For one thing, Grant had retired from films in 1965. At 60-plus, the very vain Grant felt he was too old for the screen, just as Irene Dunne, Loretta Young, et al. had felt when they turned 40ish.

Some critics have declared that Grant's films do not merit study. That's debatable, but some of the film titles offer a few clues, e.g.:

This Is the Night, Merrily We Go to Hell, Sinners in the Sun, Hot Saturday, The Devil and the Deep, I'm No Angel, Born to Be Bad, Wings in the Dark, The Amazing Quest of Ernest Bliss, Big Brown Eyes, The Awful Truth, In Name Only, Suspicion, The Talk of the Town, Mr. Lucky, Once Upon a Time, Notorious, I Was a Male War Bride, Crisis, People Will Talk, Room For One More, Monkey Business, Indiscreet, The Grass Is Greener, Charade.

Some kind of autobiography is embedded in those titles. They weren't his best films, but perhaps his most revealing—and more so, if not arranged in chronological order!

George Cukor helmed various of Grant's better or more interesting films, including *Sylvia Scarlett, Holiday,* and *The Philadelphia Story.* During my extended sessions with Cukor at his Cordell Drive mansion in the Hollywood Hills, we discussed most of the stars this fabled "women's director" had worked with. Detesting that label, Cukor tried to focus on the men he'd directed especially the ones he'd guided to an Academy Award and the ones he'd discovered. But then, after the shop talk, would come the gossip, which Cukor loved to dish.

A: Cary and Randolph Scott were probably the handsomest couple I ever saw. Of course, Cary aged so much better. He was still handsome at past 50. Randy just turned to leather . . . out in the sun too much. Still, as a Western star—which is all he ended up being—it didn't hurt him. His films were leathery, and so was he. They could have wrapped him 'round a book and gilded or embossed his spine!

Q: **There has been so much talk over the years about their** having been a couple, living together—even during their marriages—and working together by request (as in *My Favorite Wife*). Do you know whether Grant eventually denied those stories?

A: Oh, Cary won't talk about it. At most, he'll say they did some wonderful pictures together. But Randolph will admit it—to a friend. He has a male nurse, you know (Scott was housebound in later years). He's shown the nurse his scrapbook on Grant, and when the nurse asked him if *it was true*, Randolph just smiled and nodded. . . .

Q: Do you know the nurse?

A: I have a friend who picks up books for me at A Different Light (a gay bookstore in Silverlake, a partly gay Los Angeles suburb). He's met the nurses there, and they've talked.

Q: Did the Grant-Scott relationship end because of studio pressure or talk?

A: That had something to do with it, of course. But so did Cary becoming a much bigger star, although at first it was Randy who seemed to have the brighter future.

Q: So there was love, but also competition?

A: More competition than with a husband and wife—men and women can't compete for the same roles!

Q: David Lewis the producer told me that when Mae West found out Cary Grant was lovers with Randolph Scott, she decided against casting him in her next movie.

A: James Whale (Lewis's late lover) told me the same thing.

And so she did—or rather, didn't. Mae always claimed, falsely, to have "discovered" Cary Grant. She put him in her 1933 *She Done Him Wrong*, which was her second film but first vehicle at Paramount. She subsequently stated that prior to it, Grant had had only bit parts in "minor" movies. One such bit was a male lead (the other lead was Herbert Marshall, a star of the time) in a Marlene Dietrich vehicle directed by Josef Von Sternberg, *Blonde Venus*. Rumor had it that West never bothered watching other people's movies, and so she may have been unaware that Grant had already played consort to an actress of at least her stature.

After *She Done Him Wrong* proved a monster hit, West again cast Grant in *I'm No Angel*, which was an even bigger hit—West claimed that the two films helped stave off Paramount's bankruptcy during the Great Depression. West was supposedly ready to use Grant a third time, but on the set of *Angel*, she found out about his homosexuality in this way:

Mae was playing Tira, a carnival "hootchie-coochie" dancer—one step above a stripper (remember, this was one year before a more puritanical movie code strangulated Hollywood with a new censorship that would last, unchallenged, until the mid-1950s). Tira had a big trunk, the inside top of which was plastered with photos of her beaux, most of them ugly brutes— boxers, ruffians, pimps, and hoodlums. But West needed some more hunk-photos for her lid, and Grant volunteered to loan some pictures of his roommate and lover, Randy Scott.

According to gay film producer David Lewis (who oversaw *Camille*, among other classics), "Cary made a comment that he had photos of his own 'favorite man', and Mae didn't arch an eyebrow, she just said, 'Let's see 'im.' Scott was of course a great-looker then, and she wound up using his photos on her trunk's inside—you can see Randy there, in the film and in film stills. But she suddenly became cool to Grant, and when his name was mentioned as a lead in her next Paramount extravaganza, she crossed him off the list, without any explanation."

In other words, Mae could tolerate gay boys in the chorus of her plays, or in minor parts in her movies, but not as her leading men, not as the gents supposedly paying her sexual court. She may well have known about Grant by reputation—he'd lived

with gay men in New York prior to moving to Hollywood, where
he still lived with a man, against Paramount's wishes. But she
may have soured on him when he "publicly" declared his and
Scott's romantic connection—a naiveté which he soon lost.

Back on Broadway in the Roaring '20s, Mae had become
familiar not only with the gay chorus boys she enjoyed putting
down, but with their argot, or "secret language." The word "gay"
was occasionally used to mean homosexual, but a more popular
term was "sophisticated." The term "out of the closet" was not
unknown either, and in one of the dialogue bits she created for
I'm No Angel, there was the following exchange between Tira and
a male admirer (*not* one played by Cary Grant).

Tira: "I like a sophisticated man to take me out."
Admirer: "Well, I'm not really sophisticated."
Tira: "You're not really out yet, either."

Like countless actresses before and since, West was not
averse to gay escorts. As she once declared, "It's not the men you
see me with that counts, it's the men you don't see me with. . . ."

After their two films together, Cary and Mae's public relationship was stiffly formal, though following a certain
Hollywood etiquette. Mae continued to praise Grant's attractiveness, as proof of her good taste, and continued insisting that
she'd discovered him. Cary never contradicted West on this point,
and would only carefully, slightly condescendingly allude to their
two "really wonderful pictures." After West's death, he finally
told a reporter that he and others hadn't cared to be around Mae
much, for "she lives in a dream world, and she doesn't deal with
reality, and everyone always had to be so careful about what
they said."

"I still think of her in a dream world." Interestingly, Grant
used mixed tenses when speaking about Mae West, as though she

were part of his past and yet somehow impinging upon his present. Unusually, West later chose Randolph Scott as one of her two male leads (her movies always had more than one male vying for her affections) in *Go West, Young Man*. But by then, West was no longer big box office, and couldn't easily reject name actors for her projects.

Scott no doubt knew about Mae's slighting of Cary, and when in the 1950s he was asked how it had been to work with Grant and with West, his response revealed more than a little: "Working with Cary was always a breeze. He's a pleasure to be with, and very professional, yet fun-loving. . . . Miss West was quite demanding, but possibly her age had something to do with it. She had a habit of playing characters well younger than herself."

Scott's estimation of working with Grant was not shared by all of Grant's leading women, though few dared buck his image as Mr. Wonderful. Joan Fontaine (they did *Suspicion* for Hitchcock) labeled Grant "an incredible boor." Ingrid Bergman publicly praised him, but privately told gay British comedian Kenneth Williams, "He was not only stingy, he worried about everything . . . the vainest man I ever met!" Bergman and Williams worked together in London's West End, and she told him, "I never had an affair with Cary—but, then, who among his leading ladies did?"

One who claimed to have done so was Sophia Loren. The alleged revelation helped make her autobiography a bestseller, but it was privately (only, for her claim "helped" his public image) denied by him. They did do two movies together, but there was no affair, he said.

Grant, whose lightweight image at times bordered on milquetoast, was very rarely teamed—once he became a star himself—with strong actresses. Bette Davis would have eaten him for breakfast, metaphorically speaking. Ditto Joan Crawford, who once wrote to a gay fan, "No, Mr. Grant and I never teamed together. It was suggested, but we never found the right story . . . I'm not sure our teaming would have been wise, for either of us, unless it had been a gender-reversal comedy of some sort." Like *I Was a Male War Bride*, which he did with Ann Sheridan.

George Cukor told me, "Grant was very, very selective about his roles, from the late 1930s on. He needed to play irresistible types, but men who weren't physical. He could never have played an athlete, for example. . . . Playing Cole Porter, who was gay, was a natural for him—you had one urbane closeted gay man playing another one, with beautiful music in the background and lots of penthouse suites and artifice."

In real life, Grant aspired to that posh lifestyle and blue-blooded circle, although his education was nearly nil and his background anything but urbane. Cukor felt that Grant wed billionairess Barbara Hutton because "she was not only rich, she was American royalty." The couple, nicknamed Cash 'n Cary by the press, didn't last long.

Grant's ex, Randy Scott, married a DuPont, and eventually grew wealthier even than Grant, whose estate was valued at over $20 million. Scott was a shrewd investor and had extensive oil and property holdings. He was also one of the few among actors to be allowed to join the blue-blooded Los Angeles Country Club; Scott's ancestors had settled very early on in Virginia. The club did not admit Jews, and as pointed out in Higham's book, Grant may well have been Jewish—on his mother's side. . . .

Grant's relationship to the homosexual rumors that cropped up was the expected one, though less vehemently homophobic than some. When Kenneth Anger's book *Hollywood Babylon* noted the infamous "Tijuana Bibles", which featured Cary Grant's face and asked "Who's a Fairy?" Grant never considered suing. To do so would have blown the matter up out of all proportion.

Besides, who reads books?

It was another matter when alleged comedian Chevy Chase called Grant "an old homo" on Tom Snyder's TV talk show. Grant sued, to protect his image, but of course dropped the suit before it went to court. In the '80s, when asked about the persistent rumors, he jocularly replied, "Everyone's been accused of that. And don't get me wrong, I know some wonderful homosexuals. But I'm certainly not one of them."

Did Grant join the Republican Party as a beard? Liberal actor Melvyn Douglas thought so. In his autobiography, Douglas explained that when the McCarthy witch hunts hit Hollywood, Grant refused to help fight them (unlike, for instance, Douglas, Bogart and Bacall, Gene Kelly, and Katharine Hepburn). He wanted no part of controversy and was not prepared to "help others. He buried his head in the sand and soon after joined the Republicans."

Douglas had to edit from his book the fact that "certain personal peculiarities in Grant's life led him to ally himself with those very forces who might have been the first to condemn him, had he adhered to their self-righteous moral standards." Douglas was married to Congresswoman Helen Gahagan Douglas, who in one political campaign was smeared as a "pinko" by a young Richard M. Nixon.

At the time that I met Grant, I was aware of his bisexuality and his acquired conservatism, but like most—especially pre-Higham—I was charmed by his movie image, never mind how repetitive it was, or how false. I did eventually finagle a meeting with Grant out of banker Bob; I won't go into the how of it here, except to briefly say that it had to do with business and a potential new client whom I later delivered, in exchange for the meeting.

We met, in May, 1984, in a bank conference room, after the dinner for two that Bob had had catered in. I was introduced as "one of our best customers," although not wealthy—not by Beverly Hills standards, anyway. Grant seemed charmed (or was this his standard how-dee-do?). I was gently disappointed; I had only seen photos of the elderly but dapper Grant, all white-haired with large, black glasses, and looking marvelous for 80ish.

In person, however, the facial lines—why do I hesitate to call them wrinkles, for that's what they were—were more pronounced, and of course more mobile than in a photo. But worse, Cary Grant—who was after all an old man; how not?—moved like an old man. He was slow in his motions, as if moving through water. And his voice had a certain hoarseness due to age; it lacked the staccato rhythms often heard in his film heyday.

Still, he *was* Cary Grant, and I was awed. I had to make an effort not to stare, although *he* was staring. He was no longer paying attention to Bob. Neither was I (not to be cruel, but I always wondered what Bob had done to get where he was, or whom he'd known). I wished Bob would go away, so I could talk with Cary Grant—the questions I had to ask would embarrass both of us in front of the banker-man.

No sooner wished, than done. Bob excused himself—I was beginning to finally like Bob—to go make a phone call. To Tokyo or somewhere where it was already the next afternoon, though between nine and ten PM in California. Beverly Hills, to be exact.

Grant beckoned for me to sit, and went to the sideboard and withdrew a glass for me, then poured into it and into his from a bottle at the table. A green bottle with flowers stuck on it—I knew that Bob only ordered the most expensive food and drink, which the bank was only too ready to indulge him and his clients in.

I'd planned to first ask Grant about how it came to be that he was the first man in movies to use the word "gay" to mean homosexual. I refer to the scene in *Bringing Up Baby* (1938) where he is wearing a woman's nightgown, and is queried why by some old biddy, and he shouts, "Because I've suddenly gone gay!!"

But how could I ask that, as an opener to a conversation with Cary Grant?

Besides, this old man, though world-famous seemed beyond sex—in years, if not in his now-faraway image.

So, for five minutes or more, we talked about costume designer Edith Head and about George Cukor, about whom Grant seemed to have forgotten much. Alas, during that introductory time, most of the interesting things were said by me, so I won't reproduce them here, for I'm not famous. Halfway through the session without Bob, Grant began looking toward the door, anticipating Bob's return.

"Good banker," I inanely said.

"Is he?" Grant answered, but it was a bored comment, not an interrogation. Seconds later, he thought to inquire how I came to "know Bob so very well . . . ?"

"I don't know him *that* well," I said. I smiled. "I know *you* much better."

"A true fan of mine, are you?"

"A fan." My smile leveled off, as I sensed that Grant was averse to those who liked him too much.

"Do you want to get together again—somewhere. . . without Bob?" Cary Grant actually asked me. Even though he knew I was a sometime actor. (Even Bob didn't know I was a journalist, and I never denied that I was, I just didn't bring it up. Would you, if it meant getting to meet Cary Grant?)

A week or so later, Bob asked me, "Did you ever find out about *it*? Did you *see it*?"

It took me a while to realize he meant Grant's cock. He'd misunderstood. "Good grief, I didn't want to see it or anything—I just was curious. You know how people in Hollywood love to discuss cock size."

"Yes?"

"Well, it's always interesting to know what actors are biggies and which aren't."

"Who's big?" Bob avidly asked.

"You mean nowadays? I have no idea. Most of them are so dull anyway, it wouldn't matter. But in the old days, they said that Charlie Chaplin and Humphrey Bogart and George Raft were really hung. And, among TV people, Milton Berle and Forrest Tucker. Plus, Rock Hudson certainly is."

"I heard Nick Adams was too," said Bob, mentioning a largely forgotten, shortish but attractive actor of whom it was said big things come in small packages. Adams had been the roommate of James Dean, and had reportedly hustled while looking for acting jobs in the early to mid-1950s. I would later learn that Adams was one of Bob's favorites, from some old TV Western or other.

"Do you think Cary Grant is charming?" Bob asked.

It seemed irrelevant, for Cary Grant was Cary Grant. And I didn't say that, no, I found the actor in many ways disappointingly human yet somehow fascinating—for one thing, his fame had overtaken him, had surpassed his career, and with a legend like that, facts didn't seem important.

"Are you meeting again?" he asked.

"Yes." But I didn't say where, for Bob wanted to arrange the next meeting, if there was one.

I was house-sitting for a friend, and one day I got an afternoon phone call. "Are you alone there?" It was *him*. I was alone, and so, several minutes later, a white limousine pulled up—a stretch-limo, natch—and a minute or two after that, the chauffeur opened the rear door, and out stepped Cary Grant, with a brown paper bag and two marigolds in his hand.

He walked cautiously up the entry, looked to both sides, and rang the bell. Suddenly, I felt foolish for not having opened the door before he had to ring, but that would have proven I'd been looking for him through the window.

"Come in!" I said effusively, warm about his actually stopping by. But he was not at all a man you'd reach out to and touch, much less hug. We didn't shake hands, because he didn't initiate it. He came inside, looked behind him, and handed me the marigolds.

"I was walking in my garden, and I picked these. . . ." It sounded like something he'd said in a movie, for it was the same voice, only an old man's very good imitation. But somehow, I didn't feel like Ingrid Bergman in *Indiscreet*.

I'd guessed that the brown bag contained liquor. It did—a minor brew, as it were: Cold Duck. *Pink*. (What did he do with all his money, while he lived??) "Do you travel at all, Mr. Grant?" He never told me to call him Cary—and how could I?

"Not as a rule, no." He held onto the revealed bottle. "Not if I don't get paid for it."

"I asked, because I wondered if you ever long to go somewhere where you aren't recognized." That was the wrong thing to say, as I should have known.

"Oh, I'm recognized everywhere," he stated matter-of-factly. And factually.

I'd asked because in my experience, the more intelligent celebs do travel, while the ones without much curiosity about anyone or anything else don't. Look at Elvis or Mae West or Lucille Ball—all the money in the world, and hardly went anywhere. Unlike MacLaine or Jane Fonda or John Gielgud. To me, an affluent person's degree of travel tells much.

"Sit down, please." He occupied the armchair, to my relief. I was on the couch. I'd wondered what might happen if he sat next to me, then nearer to me, then nearer yet. For, this had once happened at the home of a 1950s movie star, a faded one— professionally and literally. He'd been inebriated during our interview. Without a publicist to run interference, the man had pounced on me with all his former Brooklyn energy, and I'd had to keep guffawing to pretend it wasn't really happening.

Grant set the bottle on the coffee table. It was moist, and left a ring on the table, which I wiped quickly with a pillow the moment Grant got up, later. "I really can't stay," he said. "Say, do you have a couple of glasses here? What did you say your friends do?" The semi-mansion belonged to a husband-and-wife medical team. Then he asked me how much they each charged for house calls; I didn't know, but gave him their business cards.

I opened the bottle, and he poured. We'd transferred to the sunny, cozy kitchen. The living room was large and impersonal—like Grant's body of work. And its picture window was, for me, marred by the grillwork that served to keep would-be robbers at bay.

Later in our session together, Cary Grant asked, "You're not an interviewer, are you?" He had on a very small smile.

I too smiled minimally, aware of his suspicion. Then I couldn't help myself, and smiled wide. "I'd make a lousy interviewer," I said. "I only ask questions *I'm* interested in—the sort of things they'd never publish. . . ." I wasn't lying, for I knew this interview, done unawares, couldn't legally be published, and so it freed me to ask things I found of interest, rather than something like, Do you still believe in marriage, Mr. Grant? Or, have you ever feared aging?

"Very sound, very sound," he repeated himself. He reflected a bit over the bubbly, then said, "It's true. They [journalists] don't ask the interesting things, do they?"

"Not if they're afraid of the answers," of getting at the awful truth. "I think conversation is especially stimulating with somebody who's really lived. . . ."

"True. The young really have lost that art, haven't they?" he asked, as if I were no longer one of them.

"Well, I feel that one doesn't learn anything new by talking to oneself." It was a trite observation, but he found it most amusing, and laughed, then giggled. I said nothing more, as we had liquid seconds.

At length, he asked, "What do you do with your time?" He seemed eager to know. Why? Somehow, I felt nervous. Was I really sitting here, talking about time with Cary Grant? Then I remembered that for some reason I'd never understood, he had been one of the first celebrities to try LSD, under controlled circumstances. What did that mean?

"Oh, let's not talk about me," I said. I didn't want to have to lie and say I wasn't a journalist, if he knew something.

"All right." He cheerfully changed the subject. "Let's just drink and talk. . . . What do you want to talk about?" He was wary.

"You probably get so bored talking about your career."

No, he said, he didn't.

I didn't need any more urging than that. I refrained from anything more than sipping, and began asking some of the questions—those I could think of—that I'd long wondered about.

Q: **What was it like working with the director Josef Von Sternberg?**

A: How do you mean? (I found out that he needed very specific questions.)

Q: **He was reputed to be a tyrant on the set, but also a genius. What about that? True, false?**

A: Yes, he was a tyrant. Genius? I don't know. I don't think there's any such thing.

Q: **It's just another word for great talent?**

A: Joe had the good fortune to be directing Marlene in film after film. She was very popular, until he got her into too many weird films.

Q: **Too esoteric?**

A: He was American, liked to pretend he was Old World. You know, stuck the Von in front of his name—if that was even his real name, I dunno.

Q: **And his films were too static, too glamorous, for American audiences?**

A: (Ignoring my question.) After that censorship came in (in 1934), he had to lighten up, and that wasn't his style. Joe was very dark, moody. Introspective.

Q: **Was he an unhappy man?**

A: Well, *I* don't think introspective means unhappy (glaring at me).

Q: **Neither do I. But he seemed a tormented man.**

A: (No response.)

Q: **Did you ever read his autobiography, *Fun in a Chinese Laundry?***

A: No, can't say as I have. (I felt like asking whether he ever read, period.)

Q: **Dietrich was gorgeous, in that movie.**

A: Yes. She appealed to everyone. Men, women, alike.

Q: **That sequence where she enters in a gorilla suit, then is revealed—the birth of the blonde Venus—is one of the most stunning in pictures.**

A: Yes. . . .

Q: **Was Dietrich easy to work with?**

A: . . . Not easy, not difficult. Mostly, she did what Joe said she should do.

Q: **Did you?**

A: Had to. (For Grant was then a neophyte in film, and in 1932 he made seven films—the ones unseen by Mae West.)

Q: **How would you compare Von Sternberg's working methods with Mr. Cukor's?**

A: George *likes* actors (Grant used the present tense, though Cukor was by then recently deceased). He *likes* them. He'll always share the vision he has of a character, and he'll even play it with you. Joe never did that. He kept secrets. He'd just give you a minimal direction. Maybe *he* didn't know what he wanted, either—the actor sure didn't.

Q: **Why do you think Cukor had a higher regard for actors?**

A: Didn't you know? He started out as an actor. That always makes a difference.

Q: **Didn't I read somewhere that Von Sternberg also began as an actor?**

A: Could be. What does it matter now? Point is, all directors are frustrated actors.

Q: **Of course, Hitchcock's the one who said he treated actors like cattle. . . .**

A: Not *this* actor. (Indignantly.)

Q: **What was Hitchcock really like?**

A: Do you mean, sexually?

Q: **(Surprised.) I meant personality-wise, but yes, sexually as well. That is, he seemed sexless. Was he?**

A: Never came on to me! (Laughs.) Nor to any actress I ever saw.

Q: **Even though one's read about how he tried to flirt with or even seduce Tippi Hedren in *The Birds?***

A: Did he really? They printed that?

Q: **Something of that sort, yes.**

A: . . . Well, I never saw it. Of course you know (warningly) *I* wasn't in *The Birds*.

Q: **Of course not. You were in Daphne du Maurier's *Rebecca*. (I caught myself a moment after saying it; *Olivier* had starred in *Rebecca*, opposite Joan Fontaine; and Du Maurier had written both *Rebecca* and the short story upon which *The Birds* was based.)**

A: (Gales of laughter.) Do you *often* confuse Larry and me?! Oh, how marvelous! Really. That *is* funny. Do you think I'm anywhere as good an actor?

Q: **(What could I say?) It's appalling you were never given an Academy Award.**

A: Yes, well, let bygones be bygones.

Q: **All right.**

A: (Laughs.) Bye-bye, bygones! Now, where were we?

Q: **I guess we were comparing some of your brilliant directors?**

A: Oh, they're dull. Let's speak of something else.

Q: **We will, but first, can I ask if you were ever tempted to direct a film yourself?**

A: No, why should I be?

Q: **Beats me. . . . You know, Charles Laughton directed a film, an unforgettable one, *The Night of the Hunter,* with Robert Mitchum. Did you see it?**

A: No, was it good?

Q: **Good, I don't know. But fascinating. And rare to see Mitchum as a bad guy. You never really played bad guys. Did you avoid doing so, Mr. Grant?**

A: Yes.

Q: **Why?**

A: Because then the audience won't like you.

Q: **Do you think they dislike, say, Vincent Price?**

A: No, but he has a certain . . . manner. He's sarcastic, isn't he? In a likeable way.

Q: **I think he has great humor. Do you know him?**

A: Not well, no.

Q: **You worked with Charles Laughton in a film I've never managed to see on TV, and which isn't on videocassette. *The Devil and the Deep,* with Tallulah Bankhead and you and Laughton and Gary Cooper (Grant had the smallest**

role of the quartet). What a cast!

A: Yes. Who do you want to know about?

Q: **I've heard so much about Bankhead and Laughton. What about "that divine Gary Cooper," as Ms. Bankhead called him?**

A: Handsome fellow, wasn't he?

Q: **Frankly, yes. Extremely. Did you think so, then?**

A: (Smiles.) Yes, I did.

Q: **He's the sort of person—like Ms. Dietrich—whom I can imagine anyone developing a crush on, male or female. Did you?**

A: . . . Have you ever heard of *Confidential* magazine (which in the '50s used to scoop the private lives of stars, particularly gay ones)?

Q: **(Untruthfully) No.**

A: Oh. Yes, everyone was very fond of Coop.

Q: **May I bring up—as it were—something, um, indiscreet?**

A: Oh, do be indiscreet (sarcastically)!

Q: **Coop's girlfriend Lupe Velez said he was . . . well, extremely well-endowed. And she's not the only one who said so.**

A: Are you asking for a verification? Do you mean, did I ever urinate alongside him? Well, I suppose I must have done.

Q: **. . . *And?***

A: Yes, I heard the same rumor. The Montana mule, they used to call him. Say, do you have a size fetish?

Q: **No. Do you?**

A: No. Good heavens, no! Still, I'd hate to be Napoleon (smiling again).

Q: **Kenneth Anger and others have said that when he was working his way up the Hollywood ladder, Cooper wasn't averse to a male-to-male affair now and then, with a big star.**

A: Do you mean with Rod La Rocque?

Q: **He was a big star in silents, wasn't he?**

A: I don't know his exact measurements, but he was a prominent star in silent pictures, and he was said to be one of the lavender brigade.

Q: **"The lavender brigade." It sounds like a fire station—on Fire Island. (No reaction.) But wasn't he married to Vilma Banky? I mean, I shouldn't say "but"—it may well have been arranged.**

A: I don't know. If it was arranged, I mean. Yes, he married Vilma Banky. Hungarian.

Q: **Which leads us to Rudolph Valentino, for Banky co-starred with him in one of those Sheik movies, I believe. Now, he was gay, wasn't he?**

A: That's what I always heard. The subject interests you, doesn't it?

Q: **Doesn't it you?**

A: Well . . . somewhat. One can overdo on that sort of thing, you know. You want to be an actor, is what I've heard. Right?

Q: **I've been in plays since 18, just about every year. I love to act.**

A: (Drily.) We all do.

Q: **Do you have any advice—not necessarily for me—for struggling actors?**

A: Are you struggling?

Q: **Not really. I don't need it to make a living.**

A: That's a very smart attitude. Hollywood gives the jobs to those who don't need it. Need is a *killer*, my boy. If you're desperate, you're out.

Q: **Did you ever meet Valentino?**

A: Did I ever meet Valentino? (Repeating or remembering?)

Q: **Well, did you?**

A: . . . No. . . I knew a friend of his. A silent actor, Norman Kerry.

Q: **And?**

A: They were very close.

Q: **Sexually, too?**

A: Yes. That's what I was led to believe. But I don't see that it's anyone else's concern.

Q: **No, not really. But I mean, did Kerry say so to you— about him and Valentino?**

A: Why?

Q: **Because I want to know? Why not? Would anyone object if I asked if X, Y, or Z were heterosexual? I don't see why people want to be so skittish.**

A: Frankly, I don't care. But now that you ask, Kerry didn't tell me about their relationship; someone else did. Ramon Novarro told me about him and Valentino. Seems they were a very hot pair, for a while. Two hot Latin temperaments! Oh, I can well imagine it, can't you?

Q: **I'm trying.**

A: Do you like to watch? That sort of thing?

Q: **Voyeurism?**

A: Mmm.

Q: **I've, uh, never watched.**

A: Always the doer, eh?

Q: **I always think of sex as a participatory sport, not a spectator one. How about you?**

A: Oh, I like New York in June. How about you? Go ahead— now you (alluding to a famous song, "How About You?").

Q: **Moonlight, yes, motor trips and potato chips, I can take or leave (both laugh). Where were we?**

A: Bob's queer, isn't he?

Q: **That's a sudden one. You mean gay?**

A: Well, I bloody well don't mean jolly.

Q: **I don't know. Has Bob discussed his personal life with you?**

A: No, we both try to keep our personal lives out of it.

Q: **So it's a purely business relationship?**

A: Of course not. We socialize. We have dinner, we gossip—like you and I are doing—he gives me advice, as a banker.

Q: **And personal lives don't come up?**

A: *Nothing* comes up. . . .

Q: **I'm sure it doesn't.**

A: Don't be so sure. Bob's told me he fancies you. Of *course* he's gay.

Q: **Then why would you ask me?**

A: I wanted to see what you'd say. You've been pumping me about Valentino and Cooper and I don't know whom else. Or is it *who?*

Q: **I think it's who. Do you mind that I'm, as you say, pumping you?**

A: I don't mind being pumped, now and then. That's a metaphor, you understand.

Q: **Of course I understand. But I mean, Valentino and those are, or were, public figures. Bob isn't.**

A: And you didn't give his little secret away. I'm glad. You know a bit about discretion. (Here follows a conversational bridge about Bob's lesbian wife, initiated by Grant, who knows far more about the relationship than I do. . . .)

Q: **You once made a famous quote, "When I'm married, I want to be single, and when I'm single, I want to be married." First of all, is that a true quote?**

A: Yes, I said that.

Q: **And so you do feel like that? Now, I mean?**

A: Well, it's natural, isn't it? I mean, the other man's grass is always greener.

Q: **The quote indicates dissatisfaction.**

A: Not at all (annoyed). It's about restlessness, and that has nothing to do with being dissatisfied. I have every right to be satisfied. Doesn't prevent me getting bored, though. So many hours in the day. . . .

Q: **Do you miss moviemaking?**

A: 'Course I do.

Q: **Aren't you ever tempted to return? They keep asking you to.**

A: But I never will.

Q: **Is that vanity?**

A: Yes. I'm too old to do it.

Q: **You have a very virile image. . . .**

A: I'm too old for a closeup. I'm not too old to have fun.

Q: **I didn't mean to—**

A: (Curiously.) What has Bob told you about me?

Q: **Well, that you're charming, and how . . . he treasures your dinners together. Jealously, too, for he says it's always just you two.**

A: Did you think we were more than friends?

Q: **No.**

A: We're not, you know. Even if I *was* of a mind, he's too old (Bob was about 45 at the time).

Q: **What age do you like?**

A: What age have you got? (Smiles self-consciously.) You're 30, aren't you? Well past the age of consent. . . .

Q: **Thanks.**

A: Do you have a girlfriend? At present?

Q: **As they say, no.**

A: A boyfriend?

Q: **No.**

A: So you and Bob aren't . . . ?

Q: **He's a friend of a friend.**

A: You don't like him very much, do you? I'll bet you only used him to get to me. (Smiles indulgently.) Never mind. That's all right. I can't blame you.

Q: **I do like Bob. He's . . . a good banker (both laugh).**

A: Are you circumcised?

Q: **Yes.**

A: Because Bob says you're Jewish on your father's behalf.

Q: **Hmmm? Yes. Well, I am.**

A: Are you well-hung?

Q: **Mr. Grant. . . .**

A: Now, don't tell me you're embarrassed?

Q: **I guess I am. How come you want to know?**

A: We're *all* curious, aren't we?

Q: **Yes, I am. Hung. And curious. And you?**

A: Not in Gary Cooper's league—thank God. Can you imagine how impractical that would be? Especially if you liked oral sex!

Q: **And who doesn't?**

A: Ramon Novarro. You know, it's a funny thing about Mexican queers. The ones I've heard about like only one thing—getting it up the kazoo. Oral sex is taboo for them. Can't think why. Can you?

Q: **Maybe it's kind of a hygiene hang-up. I don't know.**

A: I can't imagine a man only liking to get screwed. (Mock-shudders.) Can you?

Q: **No. But it does take all kinds.**

A: Well, not during AIDS!

Q: **Of course not. I know safe-sex is important.**

A: Oh, this has turned dreary. Do you have more to drink?

Q: **I believe they have some Heineken in the fridge. Shall I check?**

A: Of course check. You're supposed to ply me with booze, and make me do your bidding, silly boy. That is, to get me to answer your questions. (Then, when I return from the fridge with two cans in hand.) You're not writing a book, are you? You know, you couldn't get it published, anyway.

It's like Rex Harrison said—something about the press watching out for you.

Q: **Did he say that to you?**

A: No, someone told me he gave an interview somewhere.

Q: **I've read that before. I think he said that the press will prevent gay or bisexual stars' scandals from seeing print.**

A: Poor old Rex found that out! (Alluding to Harrison's widely covered heterosexual peccadillos.)

Q: **Did you know Charles Laughton at all well?**

A: Why?

Q: **Because I greatly admire him. As an artist.**

A: Wasn't he overrated?

Q: *I* **don't think so. But** *did* **you know him?**

A: No.

Q: **So then you don't know his wife, Elsa Lanchester?**

A: Not socially, no. What are you getting at? Was *she*?

Q: **I was going to ask you.**

A: *He* was.

Q: **I know** *that.* **That's a fact. But I've heard conflicting reports about Elsa, though a few friends say she's bisexual, and other people say she's lesbian, yet others saying that she's completely asexual. The only person who's represented Lanchester as a heterosexual is Lanchester herself.**

A: Then she must not be heterosexual. If she's the only one going around saying so. Does she interest you?

Q: **Yes, because of two things. One, she's chosen to live in the shadow of a giant—I mean, when he was alive—and to maintain a facade of a marriage. And because I've always found her a scene-stealer, and an underrated talent, yet almost all her film roles are bit parts, and I wonder if that didn't start because she was always Mrs. Laughton to everybody.**

A: Good question. But who knows? Have you met her?

Q: **Yes (I had to catch myself, and not reveal that I had interviewed her). She's . . . a charming hostess.**

A: Did she serve you spirits? I hear she drinks a lot.

Q: **Really? No, she served one of those "international coffees"— they all taste alike to me, but I'm a tea drinker— and she had these persimmon cookies she'd made. They were very good, but a bit stale. I'd never heard of persimmon cookies.**

A: Count your blessings.

Q: **No, she was very nice. And we talked about Charles Laughton, until she tired of the subject.**

A: Why did you meet her?

Q: **Because I had the chance to, and didn't want to pass it up.**

A: You're not starstruck, are you?

Q: **I think everyone is, somewhat, and it's nice to be. I'd hate to be jaded about people . . . I'm thrilled about you. . . .**

A: (Touched.) Well, . . . that's very nice. Have you . . . seen a lot of my movies?

Q: **Everyone has. They're on TV regularly. You know, you did something smart, Mr. Grant—and maybe without meaning to. You got into dozens of movies with wonderful costars and directors. I mean, apart from you being in them too.**

A: I'm glad you enjoy them (stifles a little yawn).

Q: **I couldn't help noticing—and please stop me, if you don't want me to bring this up—that when I mentioned the author Kenneth Anger, your mouth went down at the corners . . . ?**

A: A natural reaction. (Sternly.) I suppose you've read his book?

Q: **Yes. You haven't?**

A: (Breezily.) I never read gossipy books about Hollywood. They're so boring. To *me*. Because I've been on the inside. I think the outsiders try too hard to get an inside view, and wind up revealing far more about themselves than anyone else.

Q: **Isn't it natural to be curious about the rich and famous—the admired and the worshipped?**

A: It is. But not these . . . obsessions.

Q: **Isn't great ambition an obsession?**

A: It results in something. For an actor, it results in entertainment. True, we're not a crucial profession, like doctors, or like attorneys *think* they are. But we provide a diversion and an outlet. That kind of thing isn't so important now, but it was when there was a depression on, or a world war. People knew the value of entertainment. Shall I tell you why? (Pausing.)

Q: **Please do.**

A: I sound like a preacher, don't I? My mother used to say, "If you want to preach, we'll rent you a hall."

Q: **Please go on. I know what you're saying—we have so much access now to entertainment. Do go on.**

A: It's you young people who don't appreciate it. Your whole lives have to be entertainment. You get bored so easily. That shouldn't happen until you're older, until you're done with a career. But now everything is gratification. And I'll tell you another thing: that's why you have AIDS.

Q: *What?*

A: It's not romance now, or spooning. It's sex, fast and hard and continuous. Don't you feel that's what's behind this?

Q: **I have no idea. The experts have no idea. It started in Africa, and from then on . . . who knows?**

A: Well, I don't like to sound like a prude. I'm anything but a prude, as my real friends will tell you. Bob is not a real friend, not a close one. You can discount anything he says. But what else caused this AIDS? It's this sexual revolution they kept writing about.

Q: **And encouraging?**

A: I think so.

Q: **I don't feel the American media encourages sex of any sort.**

A: What do you feel they encourage, then?

Q: **Consumption and reproduction. And more of each. One feeds the other.**

A: Are you a socialist?

Q: **Neither socialist nor communist—and you know how many dumb people think they're the same. But capitalism has to still put people before profits.**

A: Yes, that sounds reasonable. But let's not get to talking politics. You're not a Republican, are you?

Q: **No, and I agree that politics is a dull subject.**

A: They say it makes strange bedfellows, too! (Smiles, with an effort.)

Q: **I don't know where they got such an expression. It doesn't seem to make sense. Do you want another Heineken? By the way, do you know Rock Hudson?**

A: Someone told me he has AIDS.

Q: **I know. But they're saying that about every gay actor now.**

A: I know him. Don't tell me you do?

Q: **Okay, I won't tell you.**

A: What do you do, collect movie stars? . . . Did Bob introduce you?

Q: **No. I met him, again, through a friend—real estate, not banking—who knew one of his ex-lovers.**

A: What did you think of him? Or do you still keep in touch? Or should I ask?

Q: When in doubt, ask—that's my motto. I haven't seen him in a few years. You know how it goes. Well, I guess you don't. But . . . sometimes people cut you off.

A: Did he make a pass, and you rejected it?

Q: No, I did not reject a pass. . . .

A: What's Rock doing, these days? You fans always seem to know more about our goings and comings than we do.

Q: I don't know what he's doing. Nothing major. The reason I brought him up is that for years, I was fascinated by a photograph of you and Rock Hudson and Marlon Brando—whom I would love to meet!—and Gregory Peck. All four of you together, in one room, seated, as though for a meeting. I mean, what a quartet! Talk about the Fab Four. . . . Do you remember that photo?

A: No.

Q: You don't?!

A: Not offhand.

Q: . . . Well, I'm . . . surprised. My question to you was going to be what goes on inside your mind when you, Cary Grant, enter a room and pose for a photo with other superstars like Hudson, Brando, and Peck? You know, what kind of emotions do you feel? Envy, insecurity, jealousy, desire, or . . . ?

A: Desire?

Q: Well, all I know is, any movie fan looking at such a photo would desire like crazy to be invisible in that room with the four of you.

A: Why invisible?

Q: Because otherwise one would be scared to death—I mean, intimidated. So I wondered if it at all intimidated each of you, individually?

A: I wish I could remember. . . .

Q: You really can't?

A: (Testily.) Of course I can't!

Q: **I wish I'd brought a copy of the photo. I bought a used book once, just to cut out that photo from it.**

A: Your four favorite actors?

Q: **Not necessarily, but a true portrait of power.**

A: (Thoughtfully.) Powerful then. Not so much now.

Q: **Mmm. Did you ever work with a director you hated?**

A: Yes, all of them. At one moment or another. Directors are con artists, and they're your boss. So you like your boss, when he's playing up to you, and sometimes you hate him for ordering you about. Well, you're a stage actor—don't you hate your directors, sometimes?

Q: **I hate when they don't direct. The kind that don't give you input or feedback—the traffic-directors.**

A: That's a good way to put it. They herd the cattle. As Hitch might put it.

Q: **Was Hitchcock homophobic?**

A: Have you heard that?

Q: **Yes, I have. Was he?**

A: I don't know. But he once said that if he hadn't married Alma, he'd probably not have become heterosexual.

Q: **But one doesn't _become_ heterosexual.**

A: Married, then.

Q: **He hardly struck me as a man who revelled in marriage. Or anything indeed but food.**

A: No, Alma is no beauty.

Q: **Was Barbara Hutton beautiful when you married her?**

A: She wasn't a classical beauty. She had good features, a . . . handsome face.

Q: **I'll bet women hate it when they're called handsome instead of beautiful.**

A: You think so?

Q: **Well, handsome is not beautiful. I don't mean Ms. Hutton, but in general.**

A: Nowadays they call some men beautiful.

Q: **Yes, and I'll bet most men don't mind it. Unless they're insecure or overly macho.**

A: How secure are you?

Q: **Extremely. And you?**

A: Not very.

Q: **Well, that's honest. When I said "extremely," I meant in general. Not absolutely. May I ask what you're insecure about?**

A: No, because I'm too insecure to discuss it (smiles).

Q: **Do you keep in touch with Randolph Scott?**

A: He's a nice man. You like him, don't you?

Q: **He strikes me as a decent man. The sort that represents the good side of America.**

A: How interesting. Then who represents the bad side?

Q: **Well, that would lead us back into politics.**

A: Oh, let's avoid that, and have another beer. This is good, very good. Why aren't you drinking more?

Q: **I like wine or champagne, but not beer or the hard stuff. Just don't like the taste. Can I bring up another quote I read that was attributed to you?**

A: If you must. What a horribly good memory you have (drily).

Q: **You once, very honestly, said that you fully understood why all your wives had divorced you, that you were—in the quote—"horrible and loathesome." *Did* you say that?**

A: If you read it, I must have said it. I don't know . . . I don't know. I must have gotten out of the wrong side of bed that morning, if I did . . . (annoyed, while he quickly finishes the last available can of Heineken).

Q: **I won't bring up any more quotes.**

A: I'm afraid you won't be able, because I have to be going.

Before he left, Cary Grant said I should change the marigolds' water each day, to make them last, and to put in a "smidge" of sugar every other day. I listened raptly, though I was leaving town the following day and the owners were returning that night.

"Can I drop you anywhere?" he asked politely, and maybe a bit stiffly.

I wasn't about to miss the chance to ride with Cary Grant in his limo, so I asked—as a matter of form—where he was headed. "Up to Bel-Air," he answered. Foolish question.

"You can drop me at the gate to Bel-Air." There were two, and one was in Westwood, in front of UCLA, from whence I could get a taxi back to where I'd come from.

I threw on a new jacket, locked the door, and we headed for his limo. Whether it had waited there the whole time, or gone and come back, I didn't know. Grant didn't address the chauffeur except to mention the Bel-Air gate.

In the car, we were mostly silent. Grant pointed out some of the nicer homes, or restaurants he'd heard about. I pointed out the immaculate gardens and the flowering trees; we agreed that the purple jacaranda from Brazil was the most beautiful of trees, if very messy.

"Do you go everywhere in a limo?" I finally asked. I wanted to but didn't ask if he knew how to drive—if the answer was yes, it would sound like an insulting question.

"I like to walk, now and then. But I rely on transportation," he said idly.

A minute or so later, he pointed at a house on my side. "Isn't that rustic looking? I like that." It was a one-story house in brick, not really my taste, but I'd never say so. As he admired it, he leaned way over, and grazed my cheek with his. His was so very soft, almost not there—like a phantom cheek brushing mine. I stayed very, very still. "Well, I really like it," he said as if reading my thoughts.

Sitting back, he laughed softly. "I don't think you like brick houses," and he patted my left leg above the knee, then let his palm roam up my thigh and stay there, lightly. I was still looking where the brick house had been.

"I do like it," I said quietly.

"No, I can tell," he chuckled. *How* could he tell?

I smiled.

"How much longer will you be in town?"

"Unfortunately, till tomorrow. I have to go to Santa Barbara, and then up the coast."

"Oh, that's too bad," he said in the patented Cary Grant style, and when I turned to look through his side of the car, he had both his hands again.

"I'd stay over," I said, not mentioning the husband-wife doctors, "but my father has a bad cold, and asked me to come see him."

"Well, that is too bad." As he said it, I realized for the first time that my father, though 45 when I was born, was still younger than Cary Grant. "Well, you're doing the right thing," he said to his window. "Good boy."

Several seconds later, we were in Westwood. Suddenly, I felt quite sad. This was it. I didn't want to have to jump out after a quick good-bye, so I proffered my hand, and he took it, with an impartial smile. "It's been most wonderful and memorable to have met you," I said, trying not to gulp in embarrassment. "Thank you for coming over to see me."

He said nothing, but held my hand in both of his, and right before the car stopped, squeezed hard. He pressed his lips together in a sincere expression, and I smiled on top of my smile and turned to get out. Then I was out, and the limousine was gathering speed, up toward the Bel-Air hills.

I walked around Westwood a bit, not really seeing the cinemas or record shops or the students in all their unknowing youth.

An hour or so later, I realized I was hungry, and stopped in at McDonald's, then took a taxi back.

That evening, earlier than planned, the houseowners arrived home. They'd been to a medical convention and were full of news of a technical nature that they insisted on telling me, one interrupting the other. Had I bored Cary Grant at all, that afternoon? How easy it is to feign interest, and how different people's interests are. . . .

At 11 PM, we were all watching the news, or rather the wife and I were. The husband was in the armchair, snoozing lightly. The phone rang. The wife was tired, I well knew, so I got right up and answered.

It was a personal call, for me.

Some minutes later, I went back to the spacious living room. "Who was that?" she asked.

"Oh, it was Cary Grant."

She laughed tolerantly, then rose to go upstairs to bed.

I looked at the armchair with its second occupant of the day, and decided to turn in myself.

"And you are *absolutely* certain you won't try and market anything I say about Cary Grant?" Noel Coward raised his eyebrows and pursed his lips, resembling a squinting mandarin more than ever. Silently, I crossed my heart. He relented with a gradual smile. "If you do," he warned, wagging a well-worn finger, "you shall give me cardiac arrest and be sternly rebuked by your superiors, you naughty boy!"

Just how close Coward and Grant once were is anybody's guess, for even in 1972, in the twilight of his life, the Master wasn't telling. "There have been biographies," he sniffed. "None offers a portrait of the Cary Grant *I* have known." The two had grown apart markedly as their lifestyles and reputations diverged.

Since 1972, the Grant bios have multiplied, for celebrities "numerically drawn to Hollywood matrimony," as Coward phrased it, are automatically claimed by heterosexualdom and sympathetically, if often inaccurately, biographed for the delectation of housewives weaned on fairy tales of frogs and pretty maids who together yield up Prince Charmings.

"If you marry more than once, you excite interest," said Coward. "It's that elemental. People don't care about the career as much as what went on with assorted spouses.

"Unlike Cary, I had to earn my fame solely on merit. My *career* made me, and in the end I feel *I* am luckier. In nonmaterial terms, and quite apart from the superficial adulation of people whose idols change yearly or monthly, on whim.

"I am less famous, but more comfortable. I am *free*," he gestured expansively, taking in the space around us and indicating plenty more.

"My headlines never involved or encumbered other people. Neither contracts with them—which is marriage—nor contracts broken—which is divorce. They involved only my shows—*my* creations. But already I'm talking about myself, and you're more interested in charming Cary Grant." *Charming*, as if a first name, not just the most frequent adjective. "What, within the bounds of memory and reasonable good taste, do you wish to know, dear boy?"

"Well, I'm told stardom changed his way of life. Or its facade. How did it change *him*?"

When Coward finally answered, he was less animated than usual, as if pronouncing a grim truth. "He became *accepted*— through his stardom and a reversal of a circumstance which most people don't know or care about. The fact is, Cary Grant and I both come from extremely humble working-class backgrounds. What you in the States *might* call 'white trash.' Nobody imagines either of us was once veddy, veddy poor.

"But in this marvelous century, and in our profession, one can race up the social ladder via success, providing the success is grand enough. When this happens, people fail to realize, or pretend not to, that you weren't at the top rung all along.

"Now, I don't know if this made Cary consistently happy. But I imagine he stopped being quite so unhappy. He told me once how deeply and typically unhappy he used to be in England. How he hated it there, how destitute he always felt.

"Another thing stardom *should* have done for him was help him stop being miserly. Again, it's a matter of degree. Stardom doesn't solve problems, it only ameliorates them. I have never been as thrifty as Cary, though I am by no means recklessly extravagant. I've always believed in living well, and in hard times I had to make do without the necessities, but nevah without the *lux*-uries. Except of course during wartime. The war was the exception to everything.

"Above all, I think Cary Grant has an intense desire to be liked. At almost any cost. Then, as now. Professionally, it's probably cost him, in terms of art roles and an Academy Award. Yet who can fault such a successful career?"

I wondered aloud whether stars with commercial success don't envy—for, one often hears it—those with widely recognized artistic success?

"It's not that simple. Few real artists become so-called superstars. And Cary did his homework. He wasn't as lazy as some find it fashionable to believe. That seeming lack of effort you've seen on the screen—that elegant jauntiness—he rehearsed it with his life, nothing less. All his off-screen hours, he was practicing to be Cary Grant.

"He wasn't born that way. He worked on everything. The masculinity, as well. When he was very young, he was quite neutral. Not feminine, but not effortlessly masculine, either. He worked at it, probably practiced on his wives and the fond admirers who imagined him the better half of a happy couple. In

the end, he attained a low-keyed masculinity—by American standards. But it had become inherent."

"You don't mean to say you think his marriages made him
more butch?"

"No, my dear. Not 'butch', as you so provocatively put it.
Convincing. A man who has married more than once is no longer
boyish. The effort of it robs him of that quality."

"I think you're right. I'm thinking of gay actors I know about
who never married, and most still seem rather boyish."

"You *see* . . . Cary Grant is a gentleman in a business which
dotes upon brutish men. Yet he holds his own quite nicely in
terms of reassuring women. But you'll notice he isn't an active
sex symbol. He's rarely done love scenes, and his screen kisses
have been brief. In no way could one define him as that
Hollywood culinary absurdity, *beefcake*."

"I never thought him sexy, but rather, charming and good-
looking in a nonspectacular way. Sir Noel, do *you* find him sexually appealing?"

He rolled his eyes and cooed, "Even to*day*," then tapped his
forefinger against the side of his nose.

"You hit on something by saying he's reassuring. His manner
and longevity *are* comforting, aren't they?"

"They are. So is his class. Nobody would label Cary a snob.
But he does embody motion pictures' 'classiness', as Americans
would put it."

"May I ask if you ever wanted to be more like Cary Grant,
Sir Noel?"

"*No*, my dear boy. On the *contrary*. *He* always wanted to be
Noel Coward! Until he made it big in Hollywood. Then he realized his future was there, that he'd never become Sir Cary Grant,
and so he set about creating and rehearsing an entirely new character. For that particular place. You see, Hollywood is a state of
mindlessness."

Edith Head gave Cary Grant good wardrobe. Not coincidentally, he retired from Hollywood in the mid-'60s, when anti-
glamour was taking over and words like "style," "class," and "gentleman" had become box office poison as well as uncool, man.
Queried what Grant was like to dress, Head noted with her
trademark severity, "You could call him a perfectionist or
incredibly vain. You can take your pick.

"But he wasn't difficult. Big stars aren't. The difficult, insecure ones are the up-and-comers. Kids who don't know who they
are or what they're about, who don't trust the experts. Stars,
being established, are secure in their image. Unless they're trying to come up with a new image every decade, like Joan
Crawford did. Cary Grant found his, and stuck with it.

"He was very fussy about what he would and wouldn't do.
He had to look good, which wasn't difficult. Mostly, it meant
good tailoring. He knew what he should wear and shouldn't. He
was no hayseed, certainly not the denim type. He didn't care for
revealing clothes. Had a good body but didn't like to display it.
Of course, before the 1950s, men were never considered pin-ups,
so he had that in common with most actors then.

"Cary Grant wanted to have his cake and eat it too, and he
came closer than any star I've worked with. For example, he was
always well-dressed, but he cringed at the idea of best-dressed
lists or being called vain. To him, it was unmanly. It was my job
to make it appear as if he lounged about in well-cut suits, or
even got out of bed looking like that.

"As a man, Cary Grant is hard to get to know. People who've
repeatedly worked with him say he's unknowable. Katharine
Hepburn, who did some wonderful pictures with him, said
somewhere that Cary Grant didn't have that much of a personality to get to know. I doubt she meant it disrespectfully. But the
face he showed his colleagues was a simple and professional one.
Personally, who knows? I've heard he has complexes—who doesn't?"

I asked why Head thought that Grant—whom she habitually called by both names, like, say, Proctor & Gamble—had consented to appear in drag in *I Was a Male War Bride* (1949), a movie he reportedly later rued. "Darned if I know! I think Howard Hawks did a hard sell on him. Hawks was a man's man; they did some of their best work together. He probably felt Hawks would do it in a strictly comedic way, nothing gauche.

"But I strongly doubt Cary Grant would have done that picture if it had been directed by George Cukor . . . ," whose image was "a great women's director." Plus, Cukor was gay.

Cukor directed Grant (and Hepburn) in such stylish outings as *Sylvia Scarlett* (1935, with Kate in perfected drag), *Holiday* (1938) and *The Philadelphia Story* (1940). As with Noel Coward, over the years Grant became a virtual stranger to the contractually single Cukor, despite the latter's "discretion." "Sometimes husbands are more comfortable around other husbands," he observed quietly.

Cukor's tone while discussing Grant was notably strained. Perhaps by hurt or regret. "He began as an acrobat, you know. That's how he came to America, to work in the circus. Then he became a star, and not being married, that was unusual, but living with another handsome chap [Randolph Scott] made him a circus freak in the fan magazines' eyes.

"So he became a juggler, balancing fiction and reality. He became adept at juggling several wives and millions of women who thought he was their ideal, regardless how old he got or how many revelations about taking LSD or undergoing long-term psychiatry or abusing his wives or letting down his peers.

"Because the major revelation has yet to be made. The only one that can turn them against him. *That* particular revelation may not be made, even after his death. He's too revered, too much the institution, no longer just a man." More like Proctor &

Gamble?

Cukor exaggerated the press' reticence, if not their and the general public's indignation. It was inevitable that there be rumors about Grant's bisexuality. Printed, after decades in circulation, then more crudely voiced by Chevy Chase on TV.

After his death, Grant's sexuality could finally feature openly in articles and biographies, inevitably denied by conformists who knew little about him except his film turns and the general twists of his marital life—that he *had* a marital life. Never mind that the marriages reflected Irene Dunne's line in *The Awful Truth*: "I wouldn't go on living with you if you were dipped in platinum" (and none of his wives, save the widow, did go on).

Of dozens of women whose paths crossed Grant's, only the wives as a whole dared to oppose the publicly enshrined notion of Cary Grant as platinum-plated. The men sometimes carped, but not too loudly (ironically, Grant was never considered "a man's man"). Douglas Fairbanks Jr. admitted that Grant, less than a generous costar, deliberately stole scenes from him in *Gunga Din* (1939). After Grant's death, Fairbanks stated in his memoirs his conviction that Grant was the inspiration for Noel Coward's song "Mad About the Boy."

David Niven, who hotly refuted biographer Charles Higham's claims that his ex-roommate Errol Flynn was bisexual, readily conceded that Grant "and I were never really close, and definitely not on intimate terms, unlike him and some of the fellows I understand he fancied."

James Mason knew Grant in England, then supported him, as a villain, in the 1959 Hitchcock classic *North by Northwest*. He told a UK reporter, "If a man can be frigid, Cary Grant is frigid. . . . One gets the impression he's also frigid with women."

Fittingly, one of Grant's most enduring relationships—at one point romantic, as chronicled in Higham's posthumous *The Lonely*

Heart—was with another cold, insecure, and manipulative Hollywood fixture, Howard Hughes. Director Jean Negulesco felt, "They were two of the most mercenary men in Hollywood, not exactly enamored of humanity."

Ingrid Bergman informed Kenneth Williams, "Cary always envied Howard Hughes because of his money and invulnerability to public opinion. Hughes envied Cary's public image as a great lover, or at least a man irresistible to women." Grant's image as a perfect lover accrued after the marriages had piled up (though a few critics remarked that he still had no offspring . . .) and his callow youth had faded. He became less a screen ingenu or deft comedian than an unvarying star, a suave, solid, and incidentally middle-aged Lothario. Fan magazines touted him as the consummate man and lover, who improved with age and could always be trusted—a gentleman who would have no woman before her time.

To this propaganda, Zsa Zsa Gabor publicly responded, "They're trying to show he's a great lover, but they'll never prove it by me." Grant had allegedly spurned the amorous Hungarian, who said all she dared at the time via her dissenting opinion.

Hedda Hopper was one of Grant's few acknowledged foes, a rabid homophobe who called up and berated journalists who granted Cary the great-lover build-up. "He's nothing but a phony, and a very dangerous man for a girl to fall in love with!" she fumed. (Hopper's sometimes public meddling earned her a lawsuit after she wrote that she'd warned Elizabeth Taylor not to wed "queer" Michael Wilding. He sued and won, despite his bisexuality.)

Doris Day found that costarring with Cary Grant did not constitute an introduction. After *That Touch of Mink* (1962), she admitted, "He was distant. *Very* distant," then quickly praised his "gentlemanly" manners. Barbara Stanwyck was another tough-dame actress who never teamed with Grant. She told her pal

Joan Crawford, "The mouse is a man, or thinks he is." Likewise, Tallulah Bankhead told *her* pal Beatrice Lillie and a male friend-turned-biographer, "Charles Laughton used to say Gary Cooper was the best-hung man in Hollywood, and Cary Grant was his number 1 groupie.' Or was it his number 2 Lupe'?" The reference was to Cooper's very public lover Lupe Velez. Whether Coop and Grant were ever private lovers has long been a source of speculation and rumor, along with Cooper's reported bisexuality during his early years in tinseltown.

In his Grant biography, Higham quoted sources as diverse as Marlene Dietrich and George Burns on the star's nonheterosexuality, allowing that "Cary Grant is not spinning in his grave only because he was cremated." Its sexual frankness notwithstanding, the Higham tome sought more to shock than enlighten. Gay reviewer Vito Russo pointed out, "Writers of this kind of book have a vested interest in keeping the topic of homosexuality as controversial as possible and are loath to demystify it, lest it become just another mundane fact of life—which, in truth, it is. The everyday doesn't sell books."

Reviewer Wesley Harris compared Higham's *Lonely Heart* with another posthumous but less honest bio: "The stupidity, and the insult, is that these authors undertake to *explain* Grant's homosexuality! This makes sense only if biographers try to *explain* the heterosexuality of figures like Picasso, Clark Gable, or Hitler. Sexuality is a personality factor, but is not the result of it."

Elsa Lanchester knew Cary Grant socially. Both Brits lived in Hollywood from the '30s on. As previously noted, Charles Laughton starred with Cooper, Bankhead, and Grant in the 1932 nonhit *The Devil and the Deep*. Some two decades after Laughton's death, Lanchester created a minor bombshell when she revealed, in the introduction to a Laughton biography, the true sexuality of her late husband, whom she supposedly didn't know was gay until after their marriage.

"Back before the 1960s, when everybody started doing their own thing' and becoming more antisocial, I saw Grant at several parties a year. He had a fantastic smile. Pity he seldom used it. He wasn't a social creature, and my guess is he got to be paranoid at being looked at. Especially the older he got, when he was said to be so marvelous-looking for his age.

"I think that's why he retired, why he stopped going to very many parties. Vanity! Besides which, he had trouble relating to others. He's selfish. Hates standing in line, and because he is who he *was*," she grinned, "he thinks he shouldn't have to. And tight with a dollar! . . . Likes women to smile at him, but has little interest in what they have to say. Not a man of ideas, unlike Charles, who had great intellectual pretensions.

"I think Cary Grant is a fabrication. One of Hollywood's best—glossy, appealing, nearly age-proof, and almost entirely convincing. Unless you look too closely."

Rumanian Jean Negulesco helmed such classics as *How to Marry a Millionaire, Three Coins in the Fountain,* and *Boy on a Dolphin.* As a production assistant, he worked on what was also Cary Grant's first film, *This Is the Night* (1931). "That movie starred Lili Damita, who was French, and very matter-of-fact about her affairs with women. The moguls thought this most alarming, and married her off to Errol Flynn—it was a first marriage for both the 'Battling Flynns', as the press called them. On the set, it was a strange situation, because you had these two foreigners—Lili and Cary—casually flirting with members of their own sex! The crew didn't know what to make of it, or whether to take it seriously. Being a newcomer myself, it took me a while to notice their discomfiture.

"But someone must have tipped Cary off, because by the time we wrapped, he'd experienced a substantial personality change. He was guarded and no longer very spontaneous. He seemed more mature, but that boyishness—his fun and clowning, and, well, the *joy*—had mostly gone. Not just vanished, but banished. It's awful what Hollywood can do to a personality."

The awful truth. . . .

P.S. Although the practice was even more rare in 1904 England than it is there today, "Cary Grant" was circumcised.

RANDOLPH SCOTT

(1 8 9 8 – 1 9 8 7)

"**B**out the most famous thing about Randolph Scott these days is those rumors 'bout him and Cary Grant. 'Course, I wouldn't know 'bout any of that. I worked with fellers like Gene Autry and other genuine cowboy stars. It's kinda hard to believe 'bout Randy Scott, but Cary Grant came from England, so I don't know as much 'bout him. . . ." So said Western character actor Pat Buttram, known to TV viewers as *Green Acres'* Mr. Haney.

I'd corraled the garrulous actor lunching in a booth at his Studio City hangout, The Sportsmen's Lodge. He was comparing various Western stars, saving highest marks for Autry, his most frequent employer. (His comments on Eva Gabor and other *Green Acres* co-stars were hilarious but mostly unprintable.)

Despite Buttram's reference to "genuine cowboy stars," Randolph Scott was a major Western star who, unlike his contemporaries, typically headlined in A-list *color* Westerns. As time wore on and his face became more "leathery" from the sun, his preference for Westerns increased, and he limited himself to that genre—a genre that was virgin territory for Cary Grant, six years Scott's junior. In Hollywood, the inseparable—by tinseltown standards—pair was known as Damon and Pythias, after the hopelessly devoted classical Greek couple.

Scott made nearly 100 films between 1928 and 1961, but his other claim to fame was wealth. Unlike Archibald Leach, "the gentleman from Virginia" (buried in North Carolina) was born into affluence. In the mid-1980s, columnist Lee Graham reported that due to shrewd investments in oil wells, gas, and real estate, Scott was worth an estimated $100 million. If Bob Hope was the richest actor—eventually displaced as show biz's richest individual by openly gay mogul David Geffen—then Randolph Scott was the richest ex-actor.

No, Scott never came out as gay or bi (surprise). And his résumé included a brief marriage to a "forceful, tweedy" female DuPont—to use a Grant biographer's words—who was one of America's richest women, back when Randy and Cary were an item and living together by the sand and surf of Santa Monica. After the contractual union ran its course, she settled millions on him. In middle age, there were a lengthy marriage, a daughter, and a son. But Scott also kept a treasured scrapbook of his golden days (and nights) with Cary Grant in the 1930s.

(When Kenneth Anger published his 1984 sequel to *Hollywood Babylon*, one chapter mostly comprised handsome, sexy photos—but no legally risky descriptive text—of housemates Cary and Randy hanging out and relaxing together, with and without shirts, sharing a diving board, a breakfast table, etc. According to Grant's banker, Cary was shocked by the spread but "doesn't dare sue, for what could he sue about?—and it would only magnify a very obvious, even cozy truth" suppressed for decades.)

However the first tinseltown tattle linking the bronzed blond Scott with another male was after he got hired as dialogue coach for fast-rising star Gary Cooper. The Montanan was enthusiastically indebted to the Virginian, for although never as monosyllabic as his image, "Coop" was uncomfortable as a speaker or a reciter of several lines in a row. The charismatic, well-endowed, and initially beautiful Cooper was the subject of gossip in his early years (only), regarding the casting couch, favors received and given with such as Scott and William Haines, and also via a brief live-in relationship with a young homosexual millionaire.

Of course, more talk swirled about the homey and lasting relationship of emerging hunks Randolph Scott and import Cary Grant. To be sure, the men did go on arranged dates with studio females and made sure to invite notable and noted actresses (like the bisexual Dietrich) to lunch by their pool. In time, Scott made two films with Dietrich that also co-starred John Wayne, with whom Marlene had a reported affair. Asked by the press how she'd chosen between "getting to know" one handsome star over the other, she carefully replied:

"I socialized with Mr. Wayne while Randolph Scott was seeing someone else behind the scenes." Behind the camera? Perhaps. Behind closed doors—certainly.

Noel Coward, a reported early lover of Grant's and later a guest at Scott and Grant's beach house, refused to divulge what all Hollywood of the time knew but "protected." He noted cagily, "I would only admit or confirm what there was between them if they both admitted or confirmed it first." Both ex-stars were still alive, as was Coward's loyalty to the code of silence.

Howard Hughes may have been the first to urge the comely Scott toward Hollywood. The two Southerners, whose families apparently knew each other, remained friends over the years (though by all accounts Hughes became closer to Grant). For instance, when Hughes piloted his TWA's inaugural flight on February 15, 1946, his select VIP passenger list included Scott as well as Grant, also Tyrone Power, certain trophy wives, and a few female stars like Veronica Lake. Decades after, Lake told the British press, "Throughout our friendship, Howard never laid a hand, or a glove, on me. I don't know if he ever had sex with many people, but I kept hearing that with women Howard liked to be dominated, while with men he liked to be the dominator—to keep his ego intact in front of Hollywood actors, I guess."

To what degree, if any, did Randolph Scott's associations with Cooper, Hughes, and especially Grant help label him a "light leading man" in the film industry? Or the fact that he'd been a "male model," then a highly suspect business (for those who enjoyed suspecting inevitable human differences). Screenwriter Luci Ward wrote mostly Westerns, including such Scott vehicles as *Badman's Territory* (1946) and *Return of the Bad Men* (1948):

"They used to call him the poor man's Gary Cooper. Unfairly, I thought. There were parallels—attractive, taciturn, unwavering—but they were very different." Scott and Cary Grant were also sometimes referred to as men's men. Did Scott's sidelining himself into more and more Westerns stem from his trying to differentiate his career and image from the urbane Cary Grant's? Or from a desire to "prove" himself in that most traditionalist, yet man's man of genres?

Ward felt, "Scott had a modest opinion of his ability on screen. Westerns require the least amount of acting ability, but that Randy wound up doing nothing else could be laid at the doorstep of his personal insecurities or the fact that by then he looked too outdoorsy to be very believable in a parlor or drawing room."

Screenwriter Adele Buffington, who also penned Westerns,

including some with Ward (both were activists who helped found the Screen Writers Guild against high-handed and even illegal studio opposition), offered, "Randy aged prematurely. I'm not saying physically. His expression, the mouth, the eyes. First, there was life and sparkle, but as he went on, that dimmed, and he grew . . . distant. For all his money, he occasionally seemed a beaten or disappointed man.

"In his movies, he seemed increasingly remote, unreachable, until finally he removed himself from the scene." Friend and final costar Joel McCrea admitted, surprisingly, "Randy's sort of shy. He doesn't take much to kissing scenes. Westerns have fewer love scenes than most pictures, so that's fine by him." Post-film, Scott took to the more virulent type of country club life. Negative publicity accrued when he sought to join a local country club that at the time banned Jews, not to mention racial minorities. Scott's home bordered on the club, and he kept applying for admission until he was finally admitted under such conditions as agreeing never to act again and entering his profession on his application papers not as actor but "oil investor"!

(The Los Angeles Country Club—why not name it?—had turned down Bing Crosby and Bob Hope. Scott reputedly told the club's board that he was a better golfer than either of the rejected actors. "We know you love golf, but unfortunately you are an actor." He rejoined, "Oh, really? Have you seen my work?" Then he tried again. And again.)

During a telephone chat, James Coco informed me, "I heard Howard Hughes made Cary Grant a Republican."

"Really?" I wasn't sure if he was joking. "Out of what, knitting wool?" Later I asked, "What did Randolph Scott make Cary Grant?"

"Nothing," he replied. "He just made him."

When *Interview* magazine (it eventually dropped Andy Warhol's name from its own) approached Scott for an interview for a Western-themed issue, the first reaction editor Robert Hayes got was "no politics, no wives." Both topics were off-limits; insiders said Scott himself wasn't a bigot but had joined the club because he "liked its social status" and "preferred to mingle with nonactors." Scott also wanted approval over a projected Andy Warhol portrait of him—a middle-aged version—which would have graced the cover. It was the early 1980s, and Hayes inquired whether Scott could comment on an ex-actor becoming president? No. On whether actors should enter politics? No. On whether actors should "be allowed" to voice their political opinions? No.

I'd campaigned for the assignment, and when I got it and then Scott suddenly cancelled, I suggested a phone interview if necessary. "He suffers from deafness," said Hayes. We got it rescheduled, at the Beverly Hilton (not yet owned by ex-San Matean Merv Griffin), and I flew down from San Mateo for the interview—which never ran, along with most of the other Western features.

Actually, Randolph Scott's eyes did retain significant sparkle, and though he was much aged, there was a charm and boyish conviviality. It surged after we completed a shortish but specific list of assigned questions about his films and costars. I wanted to talk about Randolph Scott, not his mostly so-so movies, and I think he sensed and appreciated that.

Q: **May we talk about your friend and costar Cary Grant?**
A: Of course. I'm a fan of his too.
Q: **I'm sure he was a fan of yours.**
A: I don't doubt it.
Q: **I heard that in the mid-1930s he tried to decline doing a Jean Harlow movie, *Suzy*?**
A: (Laughs.) That *is* specific! But you said it. As you said—"a Jean Harlow movie." That's what it was. And a good one.

Q: Grant wanted his own vehicles?

A: Yes. You have to remember he was English, which made for rougher going in Hollywood. Cary wasn't yet assured of being or, rather, remaining a leading man. But I do remember that on *Suzy*, there was a lady scenarist (screenwriter) who promised to make his role more important.

Q: Is that where the imitator's "Suzy, Suzy, Suzy," comes from?

A: (Laughs.) It would have to be, though I don't think he was that repetitious.

Q: You were what they call all-American. Your looks, sound. Was it easier climbing the celluloid ladder for you than Cary Grant?

A: Hmm. Good question. It should have been. But we did okay. . . . 1930s. Went pretty high, pretty fast. It . . . we diverged after that, but Cary had some rather rude awakenings. I remember he was assigned to do a picture, *Kiss and Make Up* (1934). It should have been *three* words, you see? Makeup—he had to play a beautician in that. A Parisian one!

Q: Hard to imagine him sounding French.

A: It was all fantasy, though.

Q: It still is. Illusion on and off screen.

A: That's partly why I got out, in time. That kind of thing's okay for when you're young, but eventually. . . . (Pause.)

Q: We had to see your final film *Ride the High Country,* for one of my movie classes at UCSB (The University of California at Santa Barbara).

A: That's nice, I think. (Grins.)

Q: You do know that in Britain it was titled *Guns in the Afternoon*? (He laughs.) Why that title?

A: Ask Cary—he's English, or was.

Q: Can you see Cary Grant in a Western?

A: (Chuckles.) I'd have liked to.

Q: **Couldn't you have teamed up in one?**

A: Anything's possible. . . . He could have been my cousin from the mother country.

Q: **Kissing cousins. . . .**

A: Nowadays, anything's possible.

Q: **You both worked with Mae West. Who do you think enjoyed working with her more?**

A: I'll tell you who got a lot more mileage out of her pictures— he did. The two, they did helped his career quite a bit, though he was kind of a boy-about-town in them. By the time I worked with her, the luster had faded some from her star.

Q: **You were incredibly appealing, and quite shy, in that movie.**

A: Think so?

Q: **A crush, one would have.**

A: *You* did?

Q: **I did. Which I never did, much, on Cary Grant. And only when he was new to movies.**

A: Really? (Impressed tone.) Hmm. That's very nice.

Q: **Cary Grant was, and is, celebrated for being suave and elegant. For "charm." I hope you don't mind my—**

A: Of course not. He's all that and more.

Q: **I hope you don't mind my comparing you two. What would you describe as Randolph Scott's talent or stock in trade?**

A: I . . . what?

Q: **Your image?**

A: You know, I had no real, abiding talent. I suppose I was good-looking—not spectacular. I wasn't Errol Flynn or—

Q: **Thank goodness.**

A: Thank you! Buttering me up. . . . I suppose I had a certain presence.

Q: **Did you eschew heavy dramas for Westerns?**

A: Kind of. I like Westerns. I liked comedy too, but didn't think I was up to those actor's actor parts. The things Paul Muni did, or some of the heavier stuff like Freddie March did.

Q: **What was it like working with Cary Grant?**

A: Best friends. It was fun.

Q: **You complemented each other. You wouldn't have been up for the same roles.**

A: True. Anyhow, I wasn't very competitive.

Q: **Less than him, right? (No reply.) And less ego, I've heard.**

A: . . . He's entitled to some ego. Look who he became.

Q: **Who did he become?**

A: A legend.

Q: **But is anyone really Cary Grant?**

A: I getcha. . . . You know, I always liked the outdoors. I was always a pretty simple body. I was less of an actor—my Westerns—than just a working performer. More like a personality. . . . I'm not expressing it the way I should.

Q: **Do you mean that with you, what one saw was closer to the real man than with Cary Grant?**

A: Oh. You want to *dig.*

Q: **Scratch beneath the surface?**

A: I can only try and analyze myself. But . . . I've never said that much about myself. There isn't so much to say. I'd rather be out there with nature, in a warm climate, contented. I'm not very complex, I'm no mystery man.

Q: **Did you ever worry about the sun's effects on your skin in those days?**

A: (Laughs.) Not me! Cary did. I don't know if you mean the, uh, complexion, or the harm sunshine can do—the c-word (cancer).

Q: **Both. You say you're not a man of mystery, yet in your '30s heyday, your off-camera life was fascinating, and continues to tantalize. . . .**

A: (Pause.) I'm flattered. But I have nothing to add, really.

Q: **Do you recall which was Cary Grant's last movie?**

A: Yes. That Elvis Presley documentary (*Elvis: That's the Way It Is*, 1970).

Q: **Oh, that's right. (I knew Grant's final film as an actor was *Walk, Don't Run* in 1966.) He was a big fan of Presley's, right?**

A: He took to him right away.

Q: **Back when Elvis was "controversial"?**

A: Yes. I knew a whole bunch of folks who thought Presley was a dangerous new phenomenon.

Q: **"A communist plot to undermine America's youth"—I read that somewhere.**

A: Absolutely. Some strange theories out there. . . .

Q: **Even yet. What did you think of Elvis?**

A: . . . He's all right. Good-looking. Until later. I wasn't wild about his music. You couldn't say I'm a fan.

Q: **May I ask an odd question?**

A: You already have (chuckles).

Q: **Now, now. You did a movie with Forrest Tucker in it called *Rage at Dawn* (1955). Was it known at the time that he was . . . how does one say it?**

A: Very well-hung?

Q: **Yes. (No reply.) Was it known at all?**

A: Very much so. Things like that don't stay hidden.

Q: **Literally? (Both laugh.) Especially in Hollywood, where the business is show.**

A: I heard that he was, and that it was extremely impressive.

Q: **Did you see for yourself?**

A: (Chuckles.) We should compare notes some time.

Q: **Love to. Should we not talk about Cary Grant anymore?**

A: I don't mind. I'd rather talk about him, within evident limits, than myself. I'm not overly interesting (chuckles).

Q: **I wouldn't say that. The films I've seen you in, you sug-**

gested a lot beneath the attractive surface.

A: That's very pleasant to hear.

Q: Most of your films were Westerns, and I've not seen most, but people seem to have forgotten how big a Western star you were. That is, most of yours were in color and high-budgeted.

A: True. The majority (of other Westerns) were black and white.

Q: Westerns were typically in the B-movie category, and while John Wayne, Roy Rogers, Gene Autry, and such were usually in black-and-white ones, you weren't.

A: Neither was Gary Cooper.

Q: Most of his films weren't Westerns. Did you deliberately choose to do so many Westerns?

A: Yup. (Chuckles.) But . . . that's how it worked out, anyhow.

Q: Don't you think by sort of sidetracking into that genre, perhaps you unnecessarily limited yourself?

A: I might have. But they were color, like you said.

Q: You showed your flair for comedy in *Go West, Young Man*.

A: Thanks. (Pause.) I have nothing to add to that.

Q: That was 1936. You know what I noticed? Your upper arms were muscular. You obviously worked out, and most actors didn't.

A: (Laughs.) You noticed that? Then the effort paid off. You're right. Most guys, even actors, didn't work out with weights.

Q: Only those closer to their good looks. . . .

A: I getcha. It's a whole different ball game now.

Q: The peacock revolution.

A: Also the sexual revolution, and . . . whatever.

Q: Most actors, the sex symbols too, when one rarely got to see them minus a shirt, had great faces but were often very pale and not toned, or sometimes even flabby.

A: Well, I guess I wasn't too typical. I did work out, and I went in for sunshine. Too much sun.

Q: **The boy next door.**

A: I wouldn't say that. Background's too different for that.

Q: **Oh. You mean Southern and well-to-do?**

A: Well, yes. . . . What else about Cary?

Q: **It's been said that once his star solidified in Hollywood, he tried to become less English and cut the ties with England.**

A: . . . How does that go? "England. Where they separate the men from the boys—with a crowbar." (Laughs.)

Q: **It's always somewhere else, isn't it? But I know what you mean. In America, and no less in Hollywood, the stereotypical Englishman is upper-class and effete.**

A: A bunch of Oscar Wildes.

Q: **Who was neither English nor upper-class. Things are seldom as they seem. And perhaps Grant wanted to reinvent himself—a new country, a new beginning.**

A: He didn't want to be limited by all that. I can see his point.

Q: **But in trying to universalize oneself, doesn't a performer lose real parts of himself, or seem to?**

A: Or seem to. . . . I getcha.

Q: **It's interesting how some British actors remain so, like David Niven, while some, like Ray Milland—**

A: (Loud cough.) Not one of my favorite names.

Q: **Not his real one, either. Born Reginald Truscott-Jones.**

A: Not one of my favorite people, regardless.

Q: **Why?**

A: He disliked Cary and used to bad-mouth him.

Q: **Why? (No reply.) They even looked alike when they were young, except for the chin dimple.**

A: Very similar to a stranger or a viewer. But the resemblance was superficial, and only physical.

Q: **Did it bother Milland that Grant was the bigger star?**

A: . . . Could be. But Milland did win the Academy Award (for *The Lost Weekend*, 1945; Grant never won an Oscar).

Q: **Was it that people might think the two resembled each other sexually, and Milland resented that?**

A: I think by now we've spoken enough about Mr. Grant.

Q: *You're* **not a matrimaniac.**

A: A what?!

Q: **Have you heard that word? It's very apt for Hollywood. A matrimaniac is someone who's been married time and time again, for whichever reason. . . .**

A: Are we still, or are you, speaking about . . .?

Q: **You-know-who? Kay Francis was also said to be a matrimaniac, marrying men even though she had little use for them personally.**

A: Personally.

Q: **Sexually. Her costar Phil Silvers, to name one, said so. In print. Which was daring, then.**

A: I've heard that. What questions do you have about me?

Q: **You were a male model?**

A: I was a male model. Yes. (Chuckles.)

Q: **Even that was "daring" in those days.**

A: Everything was, in a way.

Q: **I read that in the 1930s, magazines wanted photos of you, but with "girls" in them too.**

A: Every photo had to tell a story.

Q: **Only one story. Do you think being a male model cast you in a lesser light, in Hollywood's eyes?**

A: . . . In some quarters. Sure. But my big break wasn't really how I looked. It was more how I sounded.

Q: **The Gary Cooper connection?**

A: Ha-ha! You've done your research. Yes. I spoke pretty good for a guy from Virginia.

Q: **What do you say to repeated talk—hardly ever in**

print—that on his way up, Gary Cooper engaged in some homosexual relationships?

A: I wouldn't even say relationships.

Q: **Casting couch?**

A: Casting couch. That's just . . . everybody's been propositioned. A hell of a lot of actors and actresses, or actresses and actors, did whatever was expedient. Depended how ambitious a body was. And what you felt.

Q: **Like lust?**

A: (Laughs.) Most producers inspired anything but lust.

Q: **I meant a big star giving a starlet, male or female, a boost in return for a sexual favor that's usually a pleasure for both men. (No reply.) It's been said about a lot of people—Clark Gable and—**

A: Yes, I've heard that. In his case, I'm sure it was just expedient.

Q: **Gary Cooper was reportedly very grateful for your helping improve his . . . diction.**

A: He was grateful.

Q: **Cooper lived for a time with a fairly openly gay millionaire.**

A: He wasn't a lot older than Gary, if he was older.

Q: **That's right. . . .**

A: Anyhow, he went back to Lupe Velez.

Q: **I imagine he was predominantly heterosexual. But so much of a man's public behavior is shaped by what is officially acceptable.**

A: I see what you mean. But I agree with you about Coop.

Q: **It's well-known in Hollywood about Ray Milland's homophobia. Yet the director perhaps most responsible for making him a star was Mitchell Leisen.**

A: Yeah (chuckles). They worked together often enough.

Q: **The stories say Milland was terrified of encountering**

Leisen in the Paramount fitting room (Leisen began as a costume designer).

A: Maybe he didn't want to be fitted. . . .

Q: **One story says Milland turned down a role in a period picture—set during the Borgias—because he feared Leisen might personally fit him for a codpiece.**

A: (Laughs.) That's ridiculous! Though I'd doubt that was why the guy said no.

Q: **Milland's fears seemed so extreme, one wonders what was really behind them.**

A: "The lady doth protest too much"?

Q: **You know Shakespeare.**

A: Not personally. Bit before my time.

Q: **Indubitably. I meant that behind most obsessive homophobes, or inside them, I should say, is a secret or latent homosexual or bisexual.**

A: That could be. Anyhow, so much for Milland. He might have been happier in that fitting room with (Paramount designer) Edith Head.

Q: **Because of her gender or . . .?**

A: *Or:* If he didn't want to be . . . propositioned.

Q: **I getcha. (Both laugh.) May I ask about a particular DuPont? One who was lesbian.**

A: . . . But not anyone in my private life.

Q: **Do you know which DuPont I'm referring to?**

A: Hmm. It's a colorful family. Rich but colorful.

Q: **Full of individualists, I've heard from people in Delaware.**

A: Do you mean Louisa? (Louisa d'Andelot Carpenter Jenny.)

Q: **Yes. A tall, blond woman ahead of her time. Chiefly remembered as the lover and companion of Libby Holman.**

A: But Libby had that husband—tobacco heir. Some folks figured she shot him. And she had a son, who died very young.

Q: **Holman was bisexual. At one time she was linked with Montgomery Clift, who was predominantly gay.**

A: I doubt she and Clift had a romantic relationship.

Q: **They seemed romantic about each other, but it may not have been sexual.**

A: That's what I sometimes say. Romance, sex, sex or romance. Not always the same thing.

Q: **In the Middle Ages they were supposedly quite separate.**

A: But Louisa. . . . She did have some achievements. If I have it right, she was the great-great-great-granddaughter of *the* Mr. DuPont, the founder. And she was kind of . . . known for liking to go around shirtless—or topless—in private.

Q: **An outdoorsy lass. She loved horses.**

A: You may not know she was the first lady master-of-hounds in this nation. And one of the first licensed lady pilots. She wasn't ugly, either.

Q: **No, quite good-looking. But she didn't want to be an actress, she wanted to produce—for the stage. I think that's how she met Libby Holman.**

A: I do remember that back around the time of the Crash (1929), Miss Holman was being escorted about Manhattan by Richard Halliday.

Q: **The story editor at Paramount? (Halliday later wed lesbian actress Mary Martin, a divorcee with a son—Larry Hagman.)**

A: That was the first time I *wondered* about Miss Holman.

Q: **Because of Halliday?**

A: She *had* to know. She was pretty sharp.

Q: **It was hinted in tabloids of the time that Holman sought the favors of attainable female performers like Jeanne Eagels and Josephine Baker.**

A: Things did make their way into the papers sometimes. *Some* papers. But you know, Louisa did marry at one point.

Q: Yes. A DuPont employee surnamed Jenny, to escape her father's house and please her mother. She adopted a daughter who lived with Louisa, Libby, and Libby's son Topper.

A: That does sound familiar. They were rather fascinating personalities.

Q: I know someone who was going to write a joint biography of Holman and Tallulah Bankhead. Then her editor died, and the publishers decided the project was "too risky."

A: As I heard tell, Libby and Tallulah were . . . you know.

Q: Lovers?

A: Yes.

Q: Did anybody not sleep with Tallulah Bankhead?

A: I didn't. If I dare say so myself (chuckles). You might keep that under your hat.

Q: What else would I do with it?

A: I've just remembered. Louisa's daughter was Sunny. Whether it was her nickname or . . . I don't know. But everyone called her Sunny, and Sunny's godfather was Clifton Webb. He should be well-known to you (chuckles).

Q: Well, he was a famous actor. Played Mr. Belvedere and all that.

A: You know just what I mean.

Q: One of Webb's good friends was Noel Coward, who was a very good friend of Cary Grant.

A: Meaning?

Q: Leading up to a question. Coward was a houseguest of yours and Cary's at your Santa Monica beachhouse.

A: That isn't a question. But it's true. And?

Q: And I sometimes wish I'd been alive in the 1930s. Where are these people today?

A: Hmm. Gone with the wind. Gone. . . . I suppose I have been pretty lucky, the people I've known, people who've passed through my life and that I was a part of theirs. Many were real nice folks. The rest were at least colorful.

Q: **As you were wealthy, you didn't have to act for a living. Did that dull the edge of your ambition?**

A: . . . Some. It was different for me than most actors.

Q: **Like Cary Grant? He grew up in poverty and reportedly has never learned to believe in his wealth.**

A: I'll talk about *myself*. (Sternly.) I was lucky. Of course I was. But show business seemed appealing, and the people in it exciting. I wanted to be involved in it, and when I no longer had an interest in making pictures, I stopped.

Q: **How many films did you make?**

A: Probably too many.

Q: **Any favorites?**

A: Oh, that kind of thing doesn't interest me. So I don't think it'll interest you.

Q: **That's all right. Was it known to you, doing so many Westerns and perhaps researching some of them, that Wild Bill Hickok was homosexual?**

A: I don't think this part's for *Interview*, is it?

Q: **No reason it shouldn't be. History's history. But it's true, Warhol and company aren't much for the pre-assembly-line past. *Hickok?***

A: Wild Bill . . . yes, I knew that. But not from research.

Q: **You just heard it somehow?**

A: I don't think Guy Madison knew it when he did all those TV and radio shows playing the fella. (Grins.)

Q: **Or Howard Keel in the same role in *Calamity Jane*, where Doris Day's heterosexual version of another gay historical figure misled and reassured most in the audience?**

A: But that's Hollywood's business.

Q: **Lies?**

A: Fiction. That's a better word.

Q: **Both apply, and yield the same result. Did you ever read up on gay characters—I mean real life—from the Old West? (Pause.) I forgot, there probably weren't any books which admitted their existence.**

A: I don't imagine. But a body could read between the lines. . . .

Q: **Like when a westerner was described as a "confirmed bachelor"?**

A: Yup. (Chuckles.) But no more Gary Cooper questions.

Q: **How about Noel Coward? Was he a very good friend of yours?**

A: He was a friend of Cary's and became my friend too.

Q: **Do you think the fact that he didn't do a contractual marriage was because: (a) he was British and worked there, or (b) he was theatre rather than movies, or (c) he wasn't only an actor?**

A: Hunh! I'll pick the easy one: (d) all of the above.

Q: **It's a good answer. But which one factor do you think most allowed him to last without a wife?**

A: Let me . . . ponder. Unusual topic, this, but I don't mind as much as. . . . I think the most important thing was that the gent wasn't an actor. First off, he was a writer, could always write for a living.

Q: **On the other hand, a surprising number of Hollywood leading men and successful actors never took wives. Do you think such men simply had more guts or integrity?**

A: What do you figure?

Q: **Yes. Obviously I'm talking about non-heterosexual men.**

A: If a man is for men, and it's in most walks of life, I can buy that. Why fool somebody into your own life for appearances' sake?

Q: **But as you know, many such marriages are pre-planned, in show business.**

A: We've all heard, yes.

Q: Was there pressure on you or Cary Grant to wed, in the '30s?

A: (Chuckles.) Believe it or not, there was a time when the studios didn't want their hot properties to marry. It could have diminished their marquee value with the fans. We all heard tell of certain actresses, the "It" girls, with clauses in their contracts that they couldn't become pregnant. So we *heard*. I never got to see or read such a contract.

Q: You wouldn't get to. But after you and Grant, or Cary, had been together some time, wasn't there pressure?

A: When said properties get on a bit in years, there is pressure, more pressure for a star who's foreign-born. There were plenty of foreign-born ones then.

Q: You personally didn't have much pressure?

A: Less than some.

Q: It's said Paramount eventually got you two to stop cohabiting.

A: Is that so. . . . I'd prefer a different line of questioning—do you mind? (But smiles.)

Q: Of course. Do you think Cary Grant wants to be knighted?

A: By the queen?

Q: By her.

A: (Chuckles.) I don't think "Sir Cary" sounds quite right, do you? But who knows?

Q: "Sir Archibald" sounds more authentic.

A: Too late for that now, I'd say.

Q: Do you two keep in touch?

A: We, uh, don't live on separate continents.

Q: I've heard more than once that Cary Grant was very close to Howard Hughes, yet Hughes discovered you, not him.

A: (Laughs.) I don't know there was ever anything to discover.

It wasn't a classic Hollywood scenario or anything like. Just that one time on a golf course, he commented on my looks and said I should get into the movies. I don't imagine he saw any outstanding talent in me.

Q: **I think he was more impressed by what he could see. He also promoted Jane Russell, who has said that despite their much-publicized association or "relationship," as the media prefer it, it was platonic.**

A: Do you know Miss Russell?

Q: **No, we have mutual friends in Montecito, a suburb of Santa Barbara, which is partly where I grew up. Was Howard Hughes bisexual?**

A: You should go straight to the source.

Q: **The source always proclaims he's straight, quote-unquote. Besides, this one is dead.**

A: Well, that's that. We'll never know.

Q: **Some of you already do. Besides, a person being deceased doesn't mean one will never know if they were heterosexual, homosexual, or both. You know what Noel Coward—Sir Noel—told me in Switzerland?**

A: You have a home there?

Q: **No, a cousin.**

A: Do you speak the language?

Q: **They have four official languages. I speak three, though Swiss German is very different from German German.**

A: Like English and American.

Q: **Like Sir Noel speaking English, compared to, say, Jesse Helms. You went to college in North Carolina?**

A: Yup. University of North Carolina.

Q: **Engineering? (Nods.) But you gave it up for Hollywood, where Gary Cooper was.**

A: (Laughs.) Yes, I did. Not necessarily for that reason.

Q: *Captain Kidd* **(1945) was an interesting movie. I like most** pirate movies—and the parrots, always. You do know your costars Charles Laughton and Henry Daniell had crushes on you?

A: (Laughs briefly.) Who says?

Q: Noel Coward did. Laughton told him.

A: Laughton was the real star of the picture.

Q: You were the hero. Mr. Mercy, correct?

A: Correct. Henry Daniell, eh? (Chuckles.)

Q: He was gay too, played the villain. Didn't you know?

A: (Grins.) I knew. And he *always* played the villain. Mr. Laughton could go either way . . . cinematically speaking.

Q: If memory serves, you had a serving boy, or valet, named *Cary*?

A: Yes. I remember the first name, not the last. Or was it Gary? Hmm. Anyhow, Cary, the character, was my valet. And after I got all wet, he attended to me. But what you can't know—I'm sure you want to know (grinning)—is that the logical thing would have been for him to towel me dry. (Pause.)

Q: To towel you off?

A: (Smiles.) That's right. But our director, Rowland Lee, thought otherwise. Censorship, potential problems—if Cary toweled me off. . . .

Q: And what went through your mind about Cary doing the job for you?

A: Something personal. But there it is. When there's censorship, the mind sometimes does some sexy wandering, trying to outthink the fellows with the dirty minds! (Grins.)

Q: I regret I've never seen the 1935 *She* with you in it. I have seen and much enjoyed the 1965 British remake.

A: Much better-looking actors anyway.

Q: No, you were stunning. Although the 1965 version had two gorgeous leads, Ursula Andress and John

Richardson. She's Swiss.

A: He's not terribly good of an actor, but he's one of the hand-somest men. The English accent's also very sexy.

Q: **Yes. Did Cary Grant sound more British way back when?**

A: (Laughs.) I don't remember.

Q: **It's been said that you looked 40-something for decades.**

A: Hopefully after I turned 40?

Q: **Of course. You played a very convincing young sailor in one of the Astaire-Rogers musicals in the mid-1930s (*Follow the Fleet,* 1936).**

A: Thanks. You liked *Ride the High Country?*

Q: **It's become a cult film, to some. Oh: redundant. It's a superior Western, beautiful scenery.**

A: Great scenery. How did I look?

Q: **Very good. As lean as ever. Do you ever overeat?**

A: Not usually.

Q: **Did I hear or read that Howard Hughes was a friend of your family?**

A: I'd rather talk about, but not dwell on, *Ride the High Country.*

Q: **It's since been recognized as outstanding in its genre, but at the time, MGM treated it as a programmer or a B-movie. Was that a shock or disappointment to you?**

A: Yes. But that's not why I withdrew (from movies).

Q: **Why did the studio dump it? Westerns were big then.**

A: (Clears throat.) I imagine it kind of had to do with me and Joel McCrea. Joel and me. We weren't young, and Hollywood may throw testimonials for the old-timers, but it doesn't much believe in them. Or accord them very much respect.

Q: **Well, the following year, *What Ever Happened to Baby Jane?* was a surprise hit though Warner Brothers hadn't accorded Davis or Crawford much belief or respect. I think they were referred to, in their 50s, as "broken-**

down old broads."

A: Our picture didn't have any extrinsic (sic) shock value, so it didn't do so good as theirs did. Or as well. (Grins widely.)

Q: **Were you looking forward to more leisure, and a country club lifestyle?**

A: ... Anyhow, it was time for a change. I could see everything was going young (on the screen), but mostly I lost interest.

Q: **Why were country clubs, right in Los Angeles, so bigoted, and also biased against actors?**

A: Old-fashioned, I reckon.

Q: **Old-fashioned toward actors, and hateful toward all minority groups. Who'd want to be a part of that milieu?**

A: Plenty of rich folks.

Q: **Published accounts make it sound like you had to renounce your acting past, as though you'd belonged to some undesirable political party or something, instead of having been a successful actor and star.**

A: It's just different requirements.

Q: **Is it true on your application papers you had to change your profession from "actor" to "oil investor"?**

A: (Chuckles.) That's kind of personal.

Q: **Apart from the renowned religious and racial bias of so many upper-crust country clubs, I'll bet they're mighty homophobic.**

A: Well, that's off-limits.

Q: **You mean being a gay country club member?**

A: (Smiles.) You're a rocket. Maybe if a body's bisexually inclined, they'll give him an associate membership.

Q: *If* **he's a nonthespian.**

A: Ouch. A bit harsh.

Q: **They are.**

A: Any other questions? It's drawing short.

Q: **What makes you laugh?**

A: . . . People's pretensions.

Q: **As in Hollywood or country clubs?**

A: Off-limits.

Q: **Who in movies do you particularly admire?**

A: Anybody that's pleased with what he's done.

Q: **The fact that you're one of the richest men in show business, perhaps the richest ex-actor, does that count more with you than the almost 100 films?**

A: Eh-heh (makes an embarrassed sound). It . . . sure gives me more security. (Chuckles.)

Q: **Do you think you or Cary Grant has—I was given this question—discovered the secret of perpetual youth?**

A: My goodness. Well, not I. Maybe Cary has. I just think it's better to forget you ever were . . . were one—a youth. Don't compare yourself now with yourself young. No good.

Q: **No good can come of that?**

A: Just regret. Even bitterness.

Q: **And if you're here now, it means you've survived.**

A: Well, there's a difference. A lot of it's luck. There's surviving in comfort and relative good health, and by comfort I mean no financial hardships. Or, at the other end, surviving and just hanging on in hardship or pain, even both. I wouldn't want that.

Q: **So has luck played the major part in your life?**

A: In my life? That's kind of personal. . . .

Q: **But you're a public figure.**

A: *Was.* . . . In my career, luck had most everything to do with it. I can't lay claim to too much of what came my way. The looks, I came with, the money, we had—of course, I augmented it, but that makes for a boring speech and we're just about out of time. You know, I was warned about you, and yet I've enjoyed it. It's been stimulating, in a nice way. A practical way. It's been nice comparing notes with you.

Q: Thank you, likewise. I'll definitely be viewing more of your movies, and enjoying them, I'm sure. I already have *Go West, Young Man* on videotape, but—

A: (Chuckles.) A Mae West fan?

Q: Who?

A: (Laughs.) That's what I like to hear. I don't need it to survive, but it's pleasing to hear. You know, it was all so long ago now. You weren't even near to being born. Most folks weren't. . . . (Shakes head in amazement.)

Q: Ah, but you movie stars are immortal.

A: (Snickers.) At least we were good-looking then. (Small shrug.) Sorry I can't oblige now. (Winks, then begins to rise.)

DAVID LEWIS

(1 9 0 3 – 1 9 8 7)

The second or third time we met, ex-producer David Lewis showed me a quote from the actress actually named Mrs. Patrick Campbell. "It doesn't matter what you do in the bedroom as long as you don't do it in the street and frighten the horses."

He pointed it out as his late lifemate James Whale's response to those who criticized him for living with another man.

Another time, at the West Hollywood public library on San Vicente Boulevard, he led me to a volume by the great British gay writer E.M. Forster and located a quote "relevant to Jimmy and myself, and others like us" in committed relationships:

"When two are gathered together majorities shall not triumph."

During our several interviews together over

the years, Lewis spoke little about himself and his not inconsiderable accomplishments. There were two reasons. The second was that Lewis was supposedly saving "all the juicy stuff" for his autobiography. The first was that I initially contacted him to talk about the cult figure and underrated director James Whale. Because Whale had been ignored since his suicide in 1957, Lewis, his biggest fan, was eager to re-illuminate the once-lionized director now mostly remembered as: (a) the director of *Frankenstein* (1931); (b) "that swimming pool suicide;" or c) one of tinseltown's "notorious" homosexuals (whose career may have been prematurely ended by Hollywood's notorious homophobia).

Q: Was James Whale (1889-1957) publicly shy? One's read little about or with him.

A: . . . One of the relatively few positive things the French have done, compared to the so many things they *say* they've done, is the *auteur* viewpoint they . . . launched or discovered in the 1950s. Before they made that into a movement, people didn't think so much about directors, and gave them even less credit. There were a few who sought out publicity, like DeMille and Hitchcock. Most didn't. And the public as well as many of the people in Hollywood thought of them as . . . ringmasters.

Q: Instead of as people who put their imprint on a given movie?

A: Who *could* put their imprint on it. Many directors punched in and punched out. Most of the pictures ever made. . . . But Jimmy was one of the directors who made a picture his own.

Q: How?

A: With Jimmy, every detail, he was there. Because he did begin as an artist. He did it all. Scenic design, costume

design, he acted—I did too, although there are more successful directors than producers who made the change after
being unsuccessful actors. Jimmy was a painter, a sketch
artist, he had an *eye*. He had a strong and distinctive artistic
vision. He loved the macabre, he had a dark sense of humor,
he liked the gothic, he had a taste that was a mixture of
English posh and Hollywood flash, stirred in with his personal tastes and individuality.

Q: **Was being gay a part of his artistic vision and unique-
ness?**

A: Without any question. I don't think a . . . commonplace
director would have done *The Bride of Frankenstein* (1935)
that way. . . . In some of the pictures, you can sense Jimmy's
indifference to the requisite love scenes; he saved his con-
centration and painstaking eye for the wit or the décor, the
plot, dialogue, the relationships between the men *or* the
women, the . . . place, the tone, and so on.

Q: **George Cukor was gay and perhaps helmed more classics
than any other director. Yet he's not always thought of as
an auteur.**

A: He was more of a company man. He had a good feel for the
printed word and for good stories. But he would accept an
assignment and do his best. Jimmy didn't take on just anything.

Q: **Right there, there's potential trouble with the studio.**

A: There was later, when Jimmy wasn't working at Universal.
He helped make Universal viable; at Universal he had
autonomy and control.

Q: **Cukor was less of an auteur than Whale; might this have
to do with his being less openly gay, less daring in his
private life and in his work?**

A: He lasted longer because he made more compromises. In his
work and possibly in his life at home. Either that, or he

never found one special man to share his life and home with.

Q: **Several film historians say Cukor made one idiosyncrat-ic film, *Sylvia Scarlett* (1935), but because it flopped badly (possibly due to its cross-dressing plot ploy, with Katharine Hepburn as a lad for whom Cary Grant has a "queer" feeling), he never again went out on an artistic limb.**

A: Cukor and Jimmy didn't get along. They were the same, but they were different.

Q: **It's sad that often gay men are the first to turn each other off, socially and professionally.**

A: Cukor was a closeted old poop.

Q: **He had a semi-feud with another gay Englishman, Sir Cecil Beaton, when they worked on *My Fair Lady* (1964).**

A: That might be because Cukor won his first (and only) Academy Award for that, and Beaton won two for it (not his first, either).

Q: **No, but their antagonism began before the film was com-pleted and the awards collected. Perhaps, again, it was a case of Cukor being uncomfortable around a Brit who was more open and free.**

A: Very possible. Cukor did his job well, but he was an old stuffed-shirt.

Q: **How do you feel about the claim that Whale's best films were his horror movies? (Also including *The Old Dark House*, 1932, and *The Invisible Man*, 1933.)**

A: They were among his best. No one ever made better horror than he did. Each is now a classic. But it would be doing Jimmy a disservice to remember him just for that. He made other pictures of lasting quality, and in the 1930s he was by no means thought of as a "horror director."

Q: **He lucked out by directing the London and Broadway**

stage hit, *Journey's End*, and then broke into film by helming the movie of it.

A: That took him to Hollywood. But so did his handsomely paid stint assisting Howard Hughes with *Hell's Angels* (for which Hughes got sole directorial credit).

Q: **They seem to have gotten along.**

A: They seem to have. . . . Hughes had unlimited money to spend, Jimmy was glad to help him spend it. Hughes worked slowly, redid everything, and Jimmy was, as I said, a stickler for details. The budget zoomed out of control, to something like $4 million. Unheard of. But Hughes had the money. However, later, when Jimmy was in charge of a picture, he usually brought it in on or under budget.

Q: **I believe both men—both non-heterosexual, though Hughes always tried to pass, and was bi, not gay—**

A: I have another young friend who uses a useful acronym for that. He says "b.l.g." (First smile.)

Q: **Sounds like a variation on bacon, lettuce, and tomato (b.l.t.).**

A: B.l.g. is "bi/lesbian/gay."

Q: **It's practical. When discussing the whole group. Anyway, Hughes was ultra-right-wing, somehow. Wasn't James Whale right-wing too?**

A: Not far right, but right wing. It's different with Jimmy. He came from a very large family. They were poor. He wanted . . . the high life. In England that meant the toffs, the aristos. Jimmy worked on his upper-class accent, he wanted so to be a gentleman. He loved this town because of the climate, because of the money one could make in it, and because with his highly polished accent he could pass for a born gentleman.

Q: **And so he identified with rich people's politics?**

A: He aped what they did. We didn't agree on it, believe me.

(Shakes head, smiling.) I was a Democrat, I was pro-liberal, I liked Roosevelt. To put it plain, Jimmy was a snob. But also, Jimmy was about 15 years older than me. He was a Victorian, and yet he wasn't.

Q: **I heard that on *Hell's Angels* he didn't get along with Jean Harlow. Why?**

A: Well, that made her a star. It was—what?—1930, and she may not have known it, but she was initiating that whole bleached-blonde trend among actresses that lasted through about the mid-1930s. Jimmy sensed she was trying to get by on her looks. Only.

Q: **He liked more personality-oriented actresses, right? Like . . . ?**

A: Bette Davis? Yes, he did. He liked character. He had a genius for casting. He created a number of stars—Karloff, Claude Rains, his good friend (slight frown) Colin Clive (aka Frankenstein). . . . Davis was in *Waterloo Bridge* (1931). She was at Universal then. They soon dropped her option; the boss' son thought she wasn't pretty or sexy enough. Jimmy liked her.

Q: **Universal's loss was Warner Brothers' gain.**

A: Yes, and I produced some of her more high-quality pictures. *Dark Victory* (1939) was one—her favorite of her pictures. I always liked her too. She was strikingly different from most actresses.

Q: **Don't you think gay men prefer actresses with personality?**

A: It's a generalization, but the average chap likes a woman for her body parts, and a gay man likes her for . . . as a person, for her personality.

Q: **For what makes her an individual. The later version of *Waterloo Bridge* (with Vivien Leigh and Robert Taylor) is much better known.**

A: Jimmy's *Waterloo* is never seen. I don't know what the snag is. But his was, objectively, much better. And a truer story;

it had to do with prostitution, but the later version, made during the (censorship) Code era, tried to camouflage her prostitution with dancing. And Bob Taylor was so wooden in it.

Q: **But the leading lady of the Whale *Waterloo* wasn't Bette Davis.**

A: It was Mae Clarke. A blonde. Jimmy cast her more than once. Now they remember her for the grapefruit in the face, courtesy of James Cagney. . . . Bette was thought too unusual to be a leading lady. If Universal hadn't dropped her contract, Jimmy probably would have starred her later.

Q: **Hardly anyone remembers Colin Clive, who died in his 30s of alcoholism.**

A: One didn't hear the word "alcoholism," to speak of. Clive had a drinking problem, but when he died, as when other people did, it was referred to in the papers as "due to intestinal and pulmonary ailments." Drinking and death from it were well-hidden. Times were different.

Q: **Not that different. Today there are all kinds of euphemisms for death from AIDS, whether it's the *New York Times* or *Variety*. Whale discovered Clive for *Journey's End*?**

A: For the play, and then insisted on him for the picture-play. And he used him as (the baron) Frankenstein in those two movies. . . . Clive didn't have a long career in film. Began in 1930, through Jimmy, closed about 1937.

Q: **I remember him in *Mad Love* with Peter Lorre. But he did a movie intriguingly titled *History Is Made at Night*. . . .**

A: (Grins.) He may have made history at night. He made it with men and women.

Q: **Yeah, I'd heard he was bi. Would that be, if he couldn't accept it, why he drank so much?**

A: I don't know. He was highly strung. Had a French wife—she was an actress, don't remember her name (Jeanne De Casalis).

She was older than he, and lesbian, possibly bisexual. She had affairs, but if he did, it didn't become as well-known.

Q: **You and Jimmy Whale met in 1929. He already knew Clive?**

A: Yes, from the stage, in London.

Q: **Do you think they ever had a romantic or sexual relationship?**

A: I think—and I prefer to think—that if they did, and I don't know, it would have been in England, when they were newer to each other. If it ever happened out here, it was very well-hidden. Jimmy did tell me he'd had carnal knowledge, and more than once, of young Larry Olivier. Jimmy gave him his first break, he cast him in *Journey's End*.

Q: **Not so remembered today, but it was a hugely successful play.**

A: Internationally so. It was a brilliant anti-war story, about (World War I). Jimmy had been in the war. He was taken prisoner by the Germans, and at the prisoner-of-war camp he became immersed in their little theatre group, and when the war ended, theatre was his passion. He wanted to make a career of it, and fate was smiling upon him, because he got to be in charge of *Journey's End*. No established stage director wanted it. It was an all-male cast, it was claustrophobic, and it was by a nonprofessional. The playwright was a rather mousey insurance man who lived with his mother. It was one of the biggest, most unexpected stage successes of the 1920s.

Q: **So Jimmy and Larry, eh?**

A: Young Mr. Olivier was *hungry* to become a star. He would have slept with anyone. But he enjoyed men. When he married, it was an actress (Jill Esmond) who was better known than he, and of good family.

Q: **Lesbian.**

A: (Nods.) She later left him for another woman. They moved

to Wimbledon, I think.

Q: They had a son—I mean Olivier and Esmond.

A: One, anyway. Tarquin. I've heard the father isn't close to him.

Q: So have I. He lives here, and when Olivier came to Hollywood to play a rabbi in Neil Diamond's *The Jazz Singer* (remake of the Al Jolson first-ever-talkie), the young woman who assisted him told me he wouldn't go visit his son in Malibu.

A: Seems he's much closer to his younger family (Olivier's off-spring by third wife Joan Plowright). Sad.

Q: Yes, sad and strange. And wrong. But the same with Bing Crosby and his first four sons (two of whom have committed suicide), versus his younger kids by the second wife.

A: . . . Another thing Jimmy liked about Colin Clive: he was descended from Clive of India. Very proud of that, was Colin. And James.

Q: An old imperialist line. Charming. Of course, one remembers young Clive as the title character in *Christopher Strong* (1933). It was directed by Dorothy Arzner and was the first starring role for Katharine Hepburn. She played an Amelia Earhart character.

A: (Grins.) Except . . . the character—never mind about Misses Earhart or Hepburn—falls in love with a man. . . .

Q: A *married* man, and thus she "has" to kill herself when she becomes pregnant by him. Idiotic plot.

A: Dreadfully conventional for the time. Despite the unortho-dox cast and director.

Q: Then as now, Hollywood gays—and lesbians—typically serve heterosexual entertainment and/or propaganda.

A: Jimmy sometimes tried to work around expectations. Carefully, though. In *The Old Dark House*, he cast an actress as the old patriarch, who was over 100; none of the actors he'd seen looked old enough, so he cast an actress—who had to wear chin whiskers—but in the credits she has a man's (first) name.

Q: *The Old Dark House* is a near-legendary film. Perhaps because it's almost never seen (until 1995 on cable TV).

A: Legal snags, copyright problems. It was (Charles) Laughton's first American picture. Jimmy had worked with him on stage (in the UK).

Q: So is Elsa, or is Elsa not?

A: I think so. Back in England, she was very bohemian. From a very bohemian family. . . . No question, she knew about Laughton when they teamed up. He was an ugly brute— nice man, but not someone to cross when he was angry—but he was clearly going places. He needed a wife, and my guess is they were a b.l.g. couple. Once they landed in this town, Elsa didn't seem so bohemian, and Charles had a "beard." Peculiar woman, but I can't blame her. She really took to being a film star's wife, she loved the wealth, the, um, lifestyle. But she always resented being tied to him professionally; she tried to make it on her own, but she couldn't. Not in any big way.

Q: Her talents were perhaps more modest than Laughton's, but due to sexism, her looks would have limited her more than his did. Even though she looked much better.

A: Who didn't? Laughton said he had a face like "an elephant's behind."

Q: And James Whale made a star out of Karloff. . . .

A: Yes, thanks to Bela Lugosi's stubbornness. He got first choice of the Frankenstein monster (having made a hit as *Dracula*), but felt insulted to be offered a character who had no lines.

Q: Boris had a secret, didn't he?

A: There have been rumors. More of the Englishmen have rumors of a sexual nature than—

Q: **No, I meant his ethnicity. Karloff was born William Pratt.**

A: Many friends called him Billy.

Q: **What he hid was being part-Indian, as in *India*. As did Merle Oberon, whose mother was Indian; in England, she passed her mother off as her maid, and in Hollywood pretended she was all-Anglo, by way of Australia— Tasmania, I believe.**

A: Karloff had a darker coloring that came out more in his old age. He was undeniably exotic.

Q: **But to account for it, as it couldn't be hidden, he pretended to be part-Russian rather than part-Indian. For, Russia's in Europe, and India's in Asia, and that's how people thought.**

A: Although Indians are Caucasians, aren't they?

Q: **Yes, regardless of skin tone. But the skin tone was what led to the caste system.**

A: Everywhere, people make too much of differences. I've traveled mostly in Europe, and even if two Europeans look similar, to those two people there's a world of difference because of something like varying languages or religious sects or nationalities.

Q: **Whatever is different causes one of the two to think he's better than the other, instead of just . . . different. You were born Levy, and became Lewis. . . .**

A: Most Jewish people entering the arts did that then.

Q: **Usually to counter discrimination, right?**

A: Yes. Not to change or hide so much, to pursue your career without . . . further hindrances.

Q: **Though ironically in one of the fields with a large Jewish influence.**

A: A very large Jewish influence. But a business selling to the masses. . . .

Q: **A business braided with image and public relations. James Whale also brought Claude Rains to America. Can you elaborate?**

A: Can *I* elaborate?! (Grins.) *The Invisible Man.* From H.G. Wells, so it was a big-time project. Universal, predictably, wanted Karloff. Jimmy insisted on Claude Rains because of his voice. You see, you didn't *see* this invisible protagonist—who finishes by becoming the villain—until the end. So the *voice* was everything, and Jimmy held out, and he brought over unknown Mr. Rains, and the picture was a great triumph, and it launched Claude Rains's Hollywood career.

Q: **Whale had wonderful taste. He also liked using that fabulous shrieker, Una O'Connor, in his horror films.**

A: Yes, an Irish original. A maiden lady, I believe (grins). Hard to tell about the ladies. . . . Everyone remembers Dwight Frye as the lunatic (Renfield) in *Dracula.* But right after that, Jimmy used him as Igor in *Frankenstein,* and then he used him again. Frye was an appealing young man, nice-looking, but he got typecast as loonies and fiends, and his career and life . . . it all ended *before* (prematurely). Frye idolized Jimmy. For all I know, they had a little thing, who knows? Frye was AC/DC. Jimmy liked working with the same people, he was loyal to people; he was able to be loyal because he picked actors of quality and versatility.

Of course he loved English actors particularly. Voices were very important to Jimmy, and the English *trained* their voices. . . . I know he was thrilled when Mrs. Pat(rick Campbell) worked for him (*One More River,* 1934).

Q: **What was she best known for?**

A: The stage. A legend of the stage. In 1912 she created the role of Eliza Dolittle in Shaw's *Pygmalion.* She was rather naive about the cinema. She entered it late, for money really. It was all new to her, and one day she came to Jimmy and said, "I've just seen a *film*, and I would like to look like a woman called *Garbo.*" To put it politely, Mrs. Pat was middle-aged.

They couldn't even make her look like Garbo's *mother*, and after she saw the rushes she became more realistic. She told Jimmy, "I look like a little chest of drawers."

Q: **That's marvelous. That quote of hers, about not frightening the horses—what does it mean to you?**

A: . . . To Jimmy it meant that what one did privately, at home, should be of no consequence to one's career. But in the picture business, they thought everything was everyone's business—what one did in one's bedroom, and who you lived with. But that's . . . another time.

Q: **I understand. Was (John) Gielgud James Whale's idol in the 1920s?**

A: Yes. Fellow actors, but Gielgud was already the star, the voice, the talent. And the gentleman. Jimmy thought he was aces. I once asked if he knew John, or now Sir John, was sexually uncommon? Jimmy said Larry Olivier told him. Then he laughed and said no one had had to tell him about Olivier. He said because Larry was trying more desperately to hide it.

Q: **One Englishman who couldn't hide "it" was the unique Ernest Thesiger, best remembered as Dr. Pretorius in *Bride of Frankenstein.***

A: I did not like him. A snob. An unpleasant snob. Jimmy liked him—he was from some old aristocratic tribe. Jimmy was impressed. Not me. Thesiger was the sort of toff that thought all Americans were "working-class," meaning lower-class. Very stuffy. Treated me like an unwanted guest in my—Jimmy's and my—own house. I was civil to him for Jimmy's sake. Barely.

Q: Dr. Pretorius was clearly meant as a homosexual character.

A: He was. Though not *sexual*, I'm sure.

Q: And this was after the Code which decreed no depiction of non-heterosexual characters.

A: Not everyone recognized Pretorius as gay or . . . b.l.g. (Grins.) Those who did, they might not have said so, otherwise the next person might say, "Is *that* on your mind?" It would be like accusing someone of having a dirty mind. Then too, Pretorius is a villain, so if he has traces or suggestions of the sexually unorthodox, that's fine, because he's clearly an evil character.

Q: And he's destroyed before fadeout. In fact, *Bride's* ending is easily read as homophobic. The monster who is rejected by his intended bride says "We belong dead" about himself and the female monster who refuses to couple with him, and about the single—and as the script says, "queer"—doctor.

A: I haven't seen it in some time, but it comes back, yes. Also, despite Frankenstein (Clive) being equally responsible for making the monster, he's allowed to live. He has a wife. . . .

Q: Is it true Thesiger would sit on the *Bride* set and do needlepoint?

A: It is. He also wore pearls—strands of valuable old pearls. Said they would "die" unless they stayed in contact with warm human flesh. I doubt his flesh was very warm, he always looked like a marble effigy to me.

Q: Or a gargoyle on a gothic cathedral.

A: To show you how credulous people were at that time, Thesiger in real life, as an actor and a man, never got the "treatment" from the press. That is, the hints and insinuations that he might be . . . queer. Some stars got the treatment when they offended a columnist or if they avoided the press. And of course if they stayed bachelors. But what transpired was that Thesiger had been in the Great War (WWI). He was actually in the trenches—knitting, said Jimmy; I doubt I ever had a sustained conversation with Thesiger. I think he was wounded . . . and if what he said to Jimmy was true, he'd had a marriage.

Q: **To a woman.**

A: Of some sort. God knows which. The upshot of this is, when the papers did write about him, these were the two things they didn't forget to put in—his war record and his marriage. Ergo, he was as normal as the next reader. And a hero, to boot.

Q: **Any military service seems to render a man, any man, immune to suspicion.**

A: It was very much a part of Jimmy's publicity—when he got any publicity. The war hero, the prisoner of war. It would come right after the part where they'd say he hadn't married or was a bachelor.

Q: **Some of his publicity said he'd been engaged to Doris Zinkeisen (a designer of costumes and sets whose murals are part of the *Queen Mary*). Was that genuine?**

A: They were good friends all along. Both artists, both admired each other's work. If he'd felt compelled to marry someone for outer reasons—professional, social—she would have been a convenient, practical match. As a director, he didn't have to. In Hollywood he was less compelled to adapt his . . . to be the norm than he would have been in England. Hollywood gave Englishmen more leeway.

Q: **Even while suspecting them all the more? (He nods.) Claude Rains, who was heterosexual, said toward the end of his career that even though he married several times, he was asked if he "liked" women more often than various American actors who wed once or never.**

A: . . . I liked him. Moody but, to use our slang, a good joe.

Q: You know, there were several sequels to both *Frankenstein* and *The Invisible Man*. After James Whale's career was cut short, couldn't he have helmed some of those sequels? I assume they'd have wanted him, at least in that capacity.

A: They wanted him, and they didn't want him. What *he* didn't want was hack work. He was picky. He *was* picky. He was an autocrat. And he had no fondness for sequels. He did do two. Universal finally coaxed him into *The Bride of Frankenstein* by letting him have his vision and his way. And because he made a name for himself with a war drama (*Journey's End*), he directed a sequel (*The Road Back*, 1937) to *All Quiet on the Western Front*, which was the most successful war movie ever made. He preferred work that was original. He wanted to put his imprimatur on a motion picture.

Q: Interesting that he seemed to have little problem working around the more conservative censorship Code, but ran afoul of the tinseltown code against being gay off the screen. Specifically, living in the same house with the man he loved.

A: (Long pause.) Hollywood's for the birds.

Q: It's only a gilded cage. . . .

A: (Smiles wearily.) That's a whole other . . . thing. (Pause.) I know one of those *Invisible Man* sequels brought in an invisible woman. But I remember—because Jimmy brought it to my attention—one sequel, *Invisible Agent*, that had a censorship problem. It had Jon Hall. He was invisible, but even invisible people get dirty, I suppose, so he got under the shower. The problem was that the bathroom door was ajar, and in the next room there was a woman, a visible woman. Now, she couldn't possibly see this invisible man taking a shower, but the scene was cut. All because the door was open, and you couldn't—by the censors—have a contiguous space, the two rooms, containing a woman and a naked but invisible man who wasn't her husband!

Q: **Astounding that people put up with such nonsense.**

A: There was so much of that. . . . One picture, it might have been entitled *I Married an Angel*, the censors objected to either the title or the chap marrying an angel. They held that it was offensive or obscene, sacrilegious, I don't know, to have a man screw an angel. . . . They fretted more over invisible and nonexistent beings than flesh-and-blood human beings. But people will have their myths. . . .

Q: **Not if those myths hurt other people, they shouldn't. And won't—not indefinitely. There does come a breaking point. May I say that *if*—if, indeed—James Whale's career was ended by homophobia, and it wasn't that he took his life due to health problems, then I think he was wrong to commit suicide. That's giving in to the bigots.**

A: Better to live. . . . Usually.

Q: **So long as one isn't in chronic pain. That has to be an individual decision. But why give up, or in? There's always plenty to live for. At absolute minimum, there's the next meal.**

A: (Smiles.) I wasn't with him by then. He'd found someone else. In France (frowns). It was never as close as *us*. The question I do not answer is how it might have been, and would he have gone on, had the two of us still been togeth-er. I won't answer that.

Q: **There wouldn't be any point in speculating, would there?**

A: None. You know it was hidden for about ten years. That it was a suicide. They withheld the suicide note—notes. I mean note. I'm sorry, it's . . . difficult. . . . I'm not for suicide either, and I hate getting old, I'm sure as much as Jimmy did.

Q: Well, what more than appalls me is when a member of a persecuted minority gives in. I know a young man, he was gay and handsome, and people wouldn't have guessed he was gay; I knew him slightly, through someone else. His father was a plumber, and in 1972 when we were the first set of 18-year-olds to vote, I voted for McGovern and Jeff voted for Nixon, which surprised me, but he said he did because his father wanted him to. Later, the father threw him out when he found Jeff was not only gay, but permanently gay. Jeff went to live with his grandmother. Still felt guilty about his *father's* shortcomings, blamed himself and not the father or the homophobia. Point is, due to guilt and unhappiness—and not enough anger at the enemy—in his mid-20s, he fatally shot himself.

Left a suicide note that the grandmother withheld. It said life was too difficult going through it in guilt and hatred from others. . . .

A: (Shaking head.) He *shouldn't* have. So very, very young. All his life ahead of him. . . . Jimmy was in his late 60s.

Q: I think of Jeff when I hear homophobic evangelists like Jerry Falwell saying that gay people are more dangerous than ever because now, when they catch AIDS, they'll have nothing to lose, and they'll be potential murderers of their opponents. The dangerous ones, and the murderers, are the hate-mongering, ultra-right homophobes. The bullies and gay-bashers, the fanatics with guns.

A: It's too bad that Falwell isn't correct. . . .

Q: Well, murder's never an answer to anything, but neither is inactivity or self-hate and certainly not suicide.

A: Better murder than suicide.

Q: I don't disagree with you. If, for instance, Whale was put to an end by Harry Cohn, as has been rumored, then his putting an end to "Genghis Cohn," as he was called, might have done something toward ending or ameliorating Hollywood homophobia. It certainly would do more and have more impact than just . . . another suicide.

A: I know. People just . . . didn't do that then.

Q: Today anything's possible. And when a bad situation is prolonged, it's more likely. . . . What did Jimmy Whale think of Oscar Wilde and that whole sorry episode in English history?

A: One time, he joked that he'd like to do a picture biography of Wilde. Of course, he knew it was less than unlikely. No one touched Wilde until the 1960s. . . . Jimmy did quote Wilde now and then. If I can remember . . . oh, yes, one thing was, "The youth of America is their oldest tradition." Because the movie people were increasingly pitching towards younger audiences. Then there was a quote about immorality being what other people disapprove of or can't do themselves—better phrased than that, needless to say.

   And once, when Elsa (Lanchester) asked, during a dinner conversation, whether Jimmy was "high church" or "low church," and Jimmy would never have said "low" anything, he quoted Wilde. He said, "Truth in matters of religion is simply the opinion that has survived." Charles was most impressed—he smiled at Jimmy and winked at me.

James Whale's last movie was precisely titled *They Dare Not Love* (1941). Despite a wide range of popular films—among them the acclaimed 1936 *Show Boat* and the costume adventure *The Man in the Iron Mask* (1939)—his star dimmed drastically by 1940, due to a mixture of bad luck, homophobia from more than one studio (and bigoted stars like Wallace Beery, George Brent, and Louis Hayward), and Whale's own intransigence. I'd sought out David Lewis to discuss what happened, plus the director's *oeuvre*, especially the non-horror films.

After 16 years without directing a movie, mostly spent in well-heeled idleness in the L.A. suburb of Pacific Palisades, James Whale took his own life. He did it meticulously, with that same eye to detail, and with consideration for those left behind. Health problems did play a role, but not the sole one, as Hollywood apologists would have it. Most insiders admit his decline commenced and his restlessness, even hypochondria, increased after he was banned from the movies. In the 1980s, heterosexual director-producer Robert Aldrich was quoted:

"Jimmy Whale was the first guy who was blackballed because he refused to stay in the closet. Mitchell Leisen and all those other guys played it straight, and they were onboard, but Whale said, 'Fuck it, I'm a great director and I don't have to put up with this bullshit'—and he *was* a great director, not just a company director. And he was unemployed after that—never worked again."

(Further details about Whale's life, career, and long demise can be had in biographies by Mark Gatiss and James Curtis, and no doubt in future works.)

David Lewis ceased producing films the year of James Whale's death, 1957, and survived him by three decades. Out of tinseltown's sight, Lewis was out of tinseltown's mind. His impressive credits weren't stated until his death at 83 in March, 1987. Newspaper obits duly listed *Camille*, *Riffraff* with Jean Harlow and Spencer Tracy, *Arch of Triumph* with Bergman and Boyer, and four Bette Davis vehicles. Also *King's Row* with Ronald Reagan and Lewis's last, *Raintree County* with Montgomery Clift and Elizabeth Taylor.

Of over two dozen L.A. and show business newspapers, only

one mentioned Lewis's relationship with James Whale, with whom he spent about a quarter-century. But almost all noted that Lewis was survived by a brother and a passel of nieces and nephews.

I met David Lewis in 1978. He was living in West Hollywood, not yet an independent township. "I read in the paper that West Hollywood is 'partly gay-populated,'" he later recounted with a sardonic smile. "A few weeks ago the same paper called it 'gay-dominated.'" I noted, and he nodded, that every town on earth is "partly gay-populated." Lewis inhabited a small, overheated apartment on Hilldale Avenue, the same short street as a former magazine editor of mine who departed Manhattan upon her retirement.

I went to discuss James Whale at the behest of another magazine editor and out of my own curiosity about Whale and their relationship. The crotchety Lewis relaxed his manner considerably at the sound of Whale's name. When I did inquire about Lewis's career, he literally waved the subject aside: "I was a producer when producers got very little credit." Indeed, for a long while they weren't called producers, but production associates.

We spoke again the following year, throughout the 1980s when I was in town, and after I moved to Beverly Hills in 1986. In time, David opened up somewhat about himself. But I found out via his obituary that he'd spent a period in the '60s trying to package productions in Rome, Paris, and London. From another source I learned that Whale had left his estate partly to Lewis and to a French boyfriend whom Whale brought back to L.A.; David moved out in the mid-1950s, but according to several sources lost interest in "the rat race" after Jimmy's suicide.

Like most unions (it had been one of Hollywood's best known but least publicized), Lewis and Whale's had its trials and tribulations and occasional intruders. But it was clearly, as David said, the deepest and primary relationship of both men's lives. In the 1940s, Lewis was referred to by Joan Crawford as "the prince of Whale's." Crawford's closest friends included William Haines and *his* lifemate Jimmy Shields, and Cesar Romero. In the 1960s Crawford over-cautiously admitted in an interview:

"The studio chieftains were tyrants. . . . Our whole studio system was a very well-compensated form of white slavery. . . . Louis B. Mayer and Harry Cohn were in some ways the most vindictive . . . they hated any star who'd failed to get *(contractually)* married." Mayer and Cohn had died in the 1950s. At Cohn's crowded funeral, Red Skelton quipped, "It proves what they always say—Give the public what they want and they'll come out for it."

(As for the man aka Louis B. *Merde*, Ralph Bellamy declared, "Mayer was a Jewish Hitler, a fascist. Had no feeling for any minority, including his own. No feeling for people, period. When he found out that MGM contract player Lew Ayres [the pre-Richard Chamberlain Dr. Kildare] was a conscientious objector, he was furious. He informed everyone that 'Lew Ayres has some kind of a phobia about killing people.' And he killed Lew's career.")

Two years after Whale directed—and at least got credit for— *They Dare Not Love*, Columbia's "Genghis Cohn" helped terminate another brilliant gay Hollywood career, that of Dorothy Arzner. Halfway through shooting, he fired the mannish director who, like Whale, was used to and insisted on controlling a project. Both Whale and Arzner were replaced by house director Charles Vidor. However, unlike the male Whale, Arzner did not receive credit for her last film, *First Comes Courage* (1943).

As already stated, post-Whale, Lewis gave up making movies, but retained some interest in the business. A friend explained, "He led a very quiet existence. He was a voracious reader and loved crossword puzzles. He watched a lot of public

TV and occasionally liked to go out to see a movie. . . . He wasn't one of those people who pined for the old days. He had a wealth of information about those old days, but was interested in the work of today's people."

Former child actor Russ Randall owned the building that Lewis lived in for the last decades of his life: "He gradually slowed down and just became a very old man. And he didn't like it one bit. I remember sending him a card on his eightieth birthday, and it made him furious."

I was not David Lewis's only younger visitor, and he admitted that he liked the "rejuvenating company" of young people. Lewis followed the latest fashion trends and watched the TV news regularly, and was heartened by the burgeoning gay rights movement. He had it in him to pen or cowrite a sensational and honest autobiography about both his marriage with Whale and gay Hollywood of the allegedly golden era. He could have named deceased names and highlighted his and Jimmy's relationship *vis-à-vis* b.l.g. Hollywood stars and homophobes (e.g., Jack Warner asked Lewis not to invite Whale to sneak previews of Warner pictures).

Instead, *The Creative Producer,* which appeared in 1993 via a tiny publisher and is exceedingly difficult to obtain, could have been titled *The Closeted Producer*. It was devoid of most anything "juicy," and omitted Lewis's private life, save to allow that he and Whale lived together. While a producer at Warner, Lewis was asked point-blank by an executive—on behalf of Jack Warner— "Do you *have* to live with Jimmy Whale?" David answered, "I don't have to, but I want to."

Wrote Pat McWilliams in the newsletter "Hollywood Now and Then," "A thoroughly dishonest book, and—worse—dull. What should have been interesting and insightful is dull and flat. The list of projects and venomous associates grows tedious and is unrelieved by contrast with Lewis's all too private life. One would not know Lewis was homosexual, nor born into a Jewish family, nor that he and director James Whale were any more than pals." Lewis also made sure to comment how "lovely" various actresses were but wrote how unimpressed he supposedly was by the good looks of Errol Flynn and other actors he knew.

He did reveal that director Rouben Mamoulian had wanted him to enact (bisexual) Lord Byron in *Becky Sharp*—the first Technicolor film, in 1935—but that an antagonist lied to Mamoulian, saying that since leaving acting, Lewis had become "fat and unattractive." The book clarified Lewis's talents— "Warner knew that I could cast, that I could cut, and in cases of emergency, actually direct for a day or two"—as well as his lack of aggressive energy and the no-lack of fellow producers, executives, and moguls who imposed a glass ceiling on Lewis's ascent.

David had hinted at more than mutual flirtation with young Gary Cooper and with Buddy Rogers, fellow gym-mates in 1929 and the early 1930s. When I asked him to elaborate, he put a finger to his lips and said he was "saving" the material for his memoirs. True, his book was edited posthumously by a young, self-avowed heterosexual, but few if any insiders felt Lewis's material had been tampered with. One said, "David knew the book would get published *after* his death, and as an old, retired man, even, he had nothing to lose. And had he not been so cowardly, he had a lot to gain, namely a bigger publisher and audience, and the gratitude of a younger generation." The book came and went almost as unnoticed as Lewis's passing.

In his final years, David's health deteriorated fast. He became frail and had difficulty breathing, due to emphysema. Also bronchial problems, then an injured back after falling while attempting to tie his shoelaces. An independent type who preferred to rely minimally on his devoted housekeeper, David would check himself out of hospitals against doctors' orders, and return by cab to his own home and self-contained way of life.

The ex-producer's friends were eventually few, and included nobody currently working in motion pictures. But in death he returned to the fray, in the celebrity heaven of Forest Lawn. After being cremated, David Lewis's remains were placed in a niche in the mausoleum that also houses the remains of Irving Thalberg and Jean Harlow. And, across the hall, James Whale.

Q: **You were a pilot?**

A : Yes. I served in World War II.

Q: **I hadn't known. . . . What's ironic is that gay men served, like you, James Whale, and Ernest Thesiger in the previous war, and it almost comes as a surprise. But then you have militant heterosexuals like John Wayne and Ronald Reagan who, even though they were eligible, did *not* serve in the Second World War. Unlike you. . . .**

A: Some chaps toot their own horns more than others.

Q: **Despite, or because of, having less to toot. . . . I've heard it said that Dorothy Arzner stopped directing movies because of poor health. On the other hand, this is how things are phrased—in a way to hide Hollywood homophobia: that Kay Francis *voluntarily* gave up her acting career, that William Haines became—as if by choice—an interior decorator, etc. What do you say?**

A: I think Hollywood made Dorothy sick. It was worse for her than Jimmy, patently worse. A *woman* . . . from day one, she got the runaround.

Q: **She had to deal with both homophobia and sexism?**

A: . . . Everyone said Mayer bad-mouthed her all over town. But if she'd directed a hit for him, he'd have held his tongue. It all comes down to money. Metro hired her to do a Joan Crawford, *The Bride Wore Red.* It lost a lot of money, so Mayer figured he had grounds to put the evil eye on her.

Q: **And if she'd been a male director?**

A: The studios would hold on to most of their male directors—
the sexually orthodox ones. A few flops or failures, that was
expected. It didn't cause Mayer or Warner or Cohn to turn
around and bad-mouth a chap.

Q: **I'm told George Cukor, who seemingly never "offended"
Mayer, was contemptuous of less "discreet"—that is, less
closeted—directors like Whale and Arthur Lubin. . . .**

A: Cukor disapproves of most everything and everybody. But
he's loveless. Most of the time, he'd *pay* for sex. Pay-for-play.
He was loveless.

Q: **So much for "discretion." Which usually means invisibility. Some people say James Whale was flamboyant,
others say no.**

A: Some people think anybody like that, or this, is flamboyant.
They don't think you can be different—(grins) b.l.g.—without being flamboyant.

Q: **They go by stereotype, not by what they see. Or remember. I'm going to read you two quotes from James
Whale, if I may. "All the world's made of plaster of
Paris," and "I'm pouring the gold through my hair and
enjoying every minute of it."**

A: (Grins happily.) Jimmy was entranced by Hollywood. He
loved the artifice of it, and all the money to be made here.
He could scarcely believe what he'd fallen into.

Q: **Of course time brought disillusionment, didn't it?**

A: I think what most disillusioned him was at Universal, after
the Laemmles had to sell it to a pair of gentile businessmen,
Cowdin and Rogers—or they were the head of the consor-
tium; anyway they ran it. They began by trying to monitor
Jimmy, in spite of the outstanding and efficient job he
always did. He brought Universal *up*—it was a B-studio, and
it had only two A-directors, Jimmy and John Stahl, of
whom Jimmy was easily the more important.

Then . . . well, Jimmy was adamantly opposed to the Nazis. As anyone today would expect. But in the mid and the late '1930s, it wasn't necessarily so. Even in Hollywood. There was more than a little appeasement of the Nazis— Germany was an important overseas market, and Hollywood, its studios, they never liked to make waves. So when Jimmy was doing *The Road Back*, a war picture, Rogers in particular got involved. His concern was that it not be seen as anti-Nazi. Then the local . . . the German consul, or whoever, got in the act and threatened anyone who was showing the Nazis in a bad light, and the Universal businessmen were ready to kiss that Nazi's ass, and Jimmy was beside himself. Then they took the picture away from him. He protested, to no avail, and Universal retaliated by giving him inferior projects.

Q: **He moved to Warner, where you were, right?**

A: For a time he was at Warner. He was at MGM. He was unhappy at Universal, but tied to them contractually, and when he tried to plan his future at another studio—not even so much for money or prestige, but to do quality work and have more control over his work—the system sabotaged him. Rogers or Cowdin contacted the bigger studios and pleaded that they not hire Jimmy because without him they couldn't compete with the bigger studios. There was collusion. Jimmy's wishes didn't matter. He was obliged to stay at Universal. Universal wanted him so desperately, yet they treated him shabbily. They gave him lousier scripts to direct, and when they inevitably failed to become box-office successes, that gave Universal, and all of Hollywood, ammunition to attack Jimmy and write him off.

Q: **It's also said that during his last various films, he grew indifferent. That eye for detail was . . . half-closed.**

A: (Indignantly.) Of *course* it was! I'm not mad at you, I'm mad at them. Of course he was indifferent, and why *should* he pay attention to details if the story, the whole picture, was a piece of junk? No one can transform a fifth-rate script into anything more than, at best, a second-rate picture. And Jimmy was being dragged down by one dud after another, and for no better reason than protesting the studio's appeasement of the Nazi government in Germany, and undeniably because Jimmy was a homosexual and we lived together. And his future at other studios was blocked.

Then, when America finally got into the war, I went to war, and we were apart, and Jimmy got more depressed, and his health, and . . . it snowballed. And . . . but when he was taken off that last picture, *that* did it. As far as he was concerned. As far as Hollywood was concerned.

Q: **It's tragic. He should have fought back.**

A: The war . . . that seemed more important, lasting it out. And Jimmy was financially comfortable . . . so disillusioned with Hollywood, he wasn't certain whether he wanted to return to directing. He did have friends from the old country, to help pass the time.

Q: **But you missed each other.**

A: Of course.

Q: **I know you generally avoid it, but please let's talk a little about David Lewis's distinguished career.**

A: (Smiles indulgently.) Today everyone thinks you went west, you came to Hollywood. It started for me, as for most people past or present, with connections. *Then* on merit. But I was in New York, and in 1929 I was an associate story editor for Paramount there. Some of us were unfulfilled actors—a few were b.l.g., we'd tried, but weren't the more commercial sort of actor, although I can say I had a slight, a temporary health problem that cut my acting life short.

You've said the name of Mary Martin and the chap who

became her second husband (Richard Halliday), her lasting husband—

Q: **Arranged marriages, or "marriages of convenience," often last longer, at least in show biz.**

A: Of course, because there's a lot of money at stake. These extravagant sums of money are a great motive for most people.

Q: **And a great excuse. Please go on. You and Richard Halliday . . . ?**

A: He was a little . . . *too* (flicks wrist) . . . to be an actor. He was in the story department too, and then he rose, and . . . marrying her and all that. But we did . . . we had an affair. No one had their sights trained on us, we weren't celebrities, we could get away with it—no one knew. All right. This tells you nothing about my "distinguished career," which I don't wish to ramble on about. Just ask me what you want to know.

Q: **You were at Paramount, then RKO, then you went big-time, to MGM?**

A: Paramount was big-time too. But Metro had Irving Thalberg, and to work for him was quite a feather in one's cap. When I went to work for him, he lowered my pay. It was a test, in a way. But then he "passed" me, and gave me a $10,000 bonus. That was like a dead uncle leaving you $100,000 in his will today. It was exciting to work with him, he had a . . . *fire* for making movies, a passion. And he was better than most bigwigs, in several ways.

Irving was more . . . sophisticated. More tolerant. Like most any of the bigwigs, he was Republican. But not as homophobic. Mayer was rabidly anti-gay. Irving had a more European curiosity. When *Maedchen in Uniform* (1931) was so successful throughout Europe a year or two before the Nazis came in (they were *elected* . . .) in Germany (the

Nazis then burned all the *Maedchen* prints they could seize),
Thalberg asked (screenwriter) Salka Viertel if she couldn't
put some of *that* into the story she was doing for Garbo.

Q: **Which was *Queen Christina* (1933), right?**

A: Thanks to Irving Thalberg it did have a few lesbian touches.

Q: **Which it wouldn't have had in late 1934, due to the cen-
sorious religious right-wingers?**

A: No, it wouldn't. And if Mamoulian had had his way, either.
He was of the old Armenian school, he had no time for that.
He did remove some of the . . . sapphistry in Viertel's story.

Q: **Salka Viertel, an ex-actress from Europe, was rumored
to be more than close to Garbo.**

A: Salka was b.l.g.—she did it all. Whether with Garbo, I don't
know. But she happily put in the lesbian touches in *Queen
Christina*.

Q: **I would hope so, as the real Christina, who was the
monarch—not the queen—of Sweden, was lesbian. . . .
And Garbo?**

A: A dyke. I'm sorry. Probably the most glamorous dyke who
ever lived.

Q: **Her affair with John Gilbert, her co-star . . . ?**

A: There may have been an affair. Who's to say yes, who's to say
no? But the Hollywood flacks just had to see them holding
hands once, and next day you'd have news stories heralding
their engagement.

Q: **To this day, the studios and publicists want people to
think the leading man and leading, uh, lady aren't just
acting "in love."**

A: I think they went to even more desperate lengths then. As
an example, when Metro did a silent picture of *Anna
Karenina*, they called it *Love* . . . so they could publicize
"Greta Garbo and John Gilbert in *Love*." In countries that
didn't speak English, it was called *Anna Karenina*.

Whatever did or didn't happen, the flacks just ran with it, blew it out of all proportion. It may have been, or it may have been a friendship—Garbo, being Garbo, had several platonic male friends, not all of them . . . b.l.g. (grins). Same thing happened with Hepburn and Tracy—whatever it was, the publicists made much *more* of it.

Q: **And yet people undervalue friendship. Asked if someone is a lover, they'll often say, "Oh, no, we're just friends." Though the lover—whatever the orientation—may last two months, and the friendship may last 20 years.**

A: Or a lifetime.

Q: **A lifetime is always the ideal—for a friend or a partner.**

A: A mate for life.

Q: **Yes (both smile). You produced *Camille* (1936), the Garbo classic helmed by George Cukor and co-starring Robert Taylor.**

A: Taylor certainly *looked* the part. He wasn't that self-conscious then . . . battling himself. . . . *B.l.g.*

Q: **Did you know Garbo well?**

A: Better than some. She liked me, I think, because we both were shy. She didn't like boisterous men. She knew me well enough to praise the beauty of other ladies in my presence; she seldom praised a man's looks. Sometimes she praised his clothes. . . .

Q: **Man-tailoring, eh? There's a well-known gentlemen's tailor in Hong Kong, in the Mandarin Hotel, called Robert Taylor. Let's get back to Thalberg. Why did Mayer dislike him so?**

A: Wonderful question! He disliked him—putting it mildly—because he needed him. He disliked him because he wasn't under Mayer's thumb. Because he was more sophisticated, more liberal. Now, Thalberg was very anti-union, he was anti-communist, but he didn't despise the Democrats as Mayer did. Mayer was . . . pathological.

Q: **A fanatic. Didn't he try to get MGM employees to vote his way?**

A: Shameless man. Yes, he used any means at his disposal. Never mind about him. Irving Thalberg. The other Metro executives were Republicans, almost all—else, they didn't last very long. Irving's lawyer was a shrimp named Eddie Loeb. Rabid sort, angry little man. When he found out I was a Democrat, he went straight to Irving and said, "You know you have a Democratic snake here?" He wanted me fired. But Irving said, "The man's entitled to his own opinion," and that was the end of that.

Q: **But after Thalberg died, Mayer consolidated his power, and you, among others—on either side of the camera— left or had to leave. . . .**

A: That's not news. (Sighs.)

Q: **Thalberg died in his mid 30s (in 1936).**

A: Are you wondering about Irving? B.l.g.? I know a few people have written that he was . . . AC/DC or what I think's more probable, he didn't get around to trying it, but wanted to. He was definitely intrigued by men and women who *were*. . . . I do have one parting anecdote that illustrates two aspects of him, because he was one to pit people who worked for him against each other. (Studio manager Eddie Mannix later said, "Thalberg was a sweet guy but he could piss ice water.")

One day, I was driving Irving home. We often socialized, and he'd sometimes have me escort his sister. So in the car, Irving asks, "Do you like Al Lewin?" Lewin was his fair-haired boy. I fibbed and said, "Yes."

"He doesn't like you," Irving answers, letting it sink in. Then he pats my arm and smiles. He says, "It's only an old wife's jealousy of a new young mistress."

Q: **Hmm. It's too bad he died young.**

A: Too bad the old turd died so old.

Q: **There's a saying in Spanish: Bad weeds never die. After the war, you helped set up a major production company, did some big-time movies, but . . . ?**

A: They cost too much. Everything was in a state of flux, the business was . . . the studios were about to be divested of their distribution arms—the theatre chains—and motion pictures were changing, also the teenaged market was coming up, and . . . never mind television, that was a monster yet to come.

Q: **And you did return to MGM—after Mayer's reign you were there producing films like *Raintree County*.**

A: The year Jimmy died. (Long pause.) Let's get back to the present day.

Q: **I see a stack of books on that side table. Read any good books lately?**

A: I start books, but sometimes I can't finish them. I saw this Australian picture, it was directed by a young . . . a young woman. . . . *My Brilliant Career*—I nearly said My Distinguished Career (grins). Bit on the dull side, but . . . pleasant. Compared to so much of the junk one. . . . Then a young friend says it's a true story. I didn't know that. And the heroine, who gives up the handsome suitor, she was a dyke, in the true story.

Q: **But not in the movie version. What else is new?**

A: So I found the true story. But it's even more dull than the picture was, and nothing lesbian so far. . . . (Shrugs.) You having any better luck in the reading department?

Q: **I just started a book of excerpts from the Dhammapada, one of the Buddhist holy books. The quote that's jumped out and stayed with me is: "Those who conquer others are powerful; those who conquer themselves are strong."**

A: (Nods.) Words to live by.

Q: Words to try to live by. And, speaking of gay directors, I know Colin Higgins. He was a screenwriter *(Harold and Maude)*, then he got into directing *(Nine to Five* and others) as well.

A: I've heard of him. I know he's gay.

Q: Well, a publishing friend in New York told me that in her forthcoming book, Shirley MacLaine—of all people, and that's all I'll say—depicts him as heterosexual!

A: I thought he was out of . . . the closet.

Q: How officially out he is, I'm not sure. But anyway, MacLaine is *inning* him.

A: A friend of a friend said that he's ill.

Q: Unfortunately, he is. We visit every month or two. He still says he'd like to write a screenplay based on two chapters from *Conversations With My Elders*. (Higgins died at 47 in 1988—AIDS—and requested that donations be made to the L.A. Gay and Lesbian Community Services Center.)

A: . . . I wish him well.

Q: We all do.

A: Makes one feel one shouldn't complain . . . quite so much about aging.

Q: Because it beats the alternative, eh?

A: And . . . as I see it, in this world you've got two choices: you can live the life you like, or you can like the life you live. Some people don't even do the second. . . .

WILLIAM HAINES

(1 9 0 0 – 1 9 7 3)

Columnist Richard Gully used to be Jack
Warner's "right-hand man." In 1995 he wrote in his
column in *Beverly Hills (213)*, "Boze Hadleigh's
book *Hollywood Babble On* is a treasure trove of
anecdotes and observations about Hollywood,
which are both clever and amusing. I quote them
continually. In it is a comment by Joan Crawford
that I find especially interesting:

"'The unfortunate truth is, in this town men
and women do compete. . . . The happiest marriage I've seen in Hollywood is Billy Haines and
Jimmy Shields.'

"At one time Bill Haines was an MGM star
who later became a prominent interior decorator.
He decorated Ann and Jack Warner's palatial
home. Over the years Bill became very rich, but
as he grew older he lived more quietly. This led
people to say that when his charming boyfriend,

Jimmy Shields, gets Bill's money he will really make whoopee. Ultimately Bill died and Jimmy got the money, but there was no merry-making.

"On the contrary, Jimmy withdrew into a period of intense mourning. Without Bill he was so miserable that six months after his death he committed suicide. Joan Crawford was right."

(Interestingly, Gully's column is titled "The Best of Times," also the title of a live-for-today song from *La Cage aux Folles* by openly gay composer-lyricist Jerry Herman. Without Jerry's knowledge, the song was appropriated by the Republican Party for use at their notoriously homophobic 1992 convention. As for the Warner estate, it is now in the hands of openly gay billionaire David Geffen, who bought it for $47.5 million, the top price ever paid for a private home in the United States.)

Sadly, Billy Haines is now missing from many, even most, reference books about the movies—partly because his heyday was the silent era (in more ways than one). When he does show up, it's usually not as a former star but as tinseltown's leading interior designer. And authors who should know better typically elide the reason for Haines's transition from actor to decorator; that Hollywood homophobia destroyed his career is seldom deemed worthy of mention.

More recently, in books by this author and others, Haines pops up in the long-suppressed story of why director George Cukor was really fired from *Gone with the Wind*, well into production. Back when Haines was a Roaring '20s pudgy-but-boyish star at Metro, Clark Gable was a struggling, ambitious newcomer (his first two wives were older women who helped him; he didn't marry for love or beauty until he was a star). Haines fancied the sexy male starlet and discreetly flirted with him at parties and entertainment functions.

Rumor had it that Gable may have been a heterosexual gigolo when he started out earning a living, or trying to, via show business. And that he wasn't above—when money demanded or a big break proffered itself—being serviced by orally-minded gay actors or men of means. Whether Haines paid Gable in coin or a boost is unknown, but worship at the budding MGM actor's shrine the MGM star did, later telling a few confidants like MGM director George Cukor. Of course in the sound era Gable's star eclipsed Haines's; for one thing, Haines—just a year older than Gable, who died in 1960—had become too mature to keep playing the eternal college boy.

The difference is that Gable was allowed to keep his screen career after killing a woman in an automobile accident in 1933; Louis B. Mayer covered up for him. While Haines, caught with another man in his cot at the YMCA in the same year, had his screen career killed by Mayer, who covered up any publicity but fired Haines and saw it to that no other studio would hire him, not even as a supporting actor. Haines lost his stardom and any future hope of work in film. However, his wasn't the only career destroyed; Haines had a thing for men in uniform, and sometimes met them at Pershing Square in downtown L.A. This particular sailor, reportedly ten years his junior, accompanied him to the nearby "Y" where Haines had a room on the seventh floor. There, the house detective and members of the so-called vice squad—more concerned or threatened by consensual adult same-sex sex than by heterosexual prostitution or violence against women—burst in, handcuffed both men, and ended both their careers. . . .

Ironically and coincidentally, Haines's final movie, released in 1934, was titled *The Marines Are Coming.*

It was a 1926 movie via the newly merged Metro-Goldwyn-Mayer that made Billy Haines a star—*Tell It to the Marines.* Born January 1, 1900, Haines attended a military school in Virginia and later informed *Coronet,* "I didn't care for some aspects of such a regimented, strict life, but I liked the company. I was always a smart aleck, and the other boys sort of liked me." In the late 1920s he apprised *Motion Picture*, "You have to remember, I'm a Virginian," when asked why he hadn't yet matrimonied.

In 1914 Billy ran away and began life on his own, never fully explaining why he left home (or perhaps was made to leave). He told one periodical, "I wanted my freedom." Few 14-year-olds want it that early and with that much responsibility. Over the next years he worked at jobs in a powder plant and a rubber factory, as an assistant bookkeeper, and as an office boy on Wall Street, where a casting director for Samuel Goldwyn noticed him and entered him in a New Faces contest, which he and Eleanor Boardman won. Each was put under contract and sent to Hollywood.

Haines's screen bow in 1922 was in *Brothers Under the Skin*. His film persona was the smart aleck who treats the young lady honorably and wins her heart and hand by the last reel. His movies did well at the box office, and he was one of the '20s' leading male personifications of carefree youth. As a major asset to MGM (he starred in the studio's first talkie), he was able to boost newcomers' careers—not only Gable, who kept on Haines's good side until the star was no more, but platonic pal Joan Crawford.

Via arranged studio "dates" and working together, Haines and Crawford became chums—he nicknamed her "Cranberry," for she hated her screen name (chosen for her by a magazine reader in a studio-sponsored contest). The dancer-turned-actress born Lucille LeSueur felt that "Crawford" sounded too much like "crayfish" (Mayer had vetoed LeSueur because to him it sounded like "sewer," but then, he initially opposed Greta Gustafsson's new surname of Garbo because to such a mind it sounded like "garbage.") Ambitious, Crawford proposed to the star, who declined.

Haines already had a partner for life, his stand-in Jimmy

Shields, whom everyone agreed was better looking than Billy. The two lived together—which annoyed Mayer no end—and around 1930 bought an antique shop together. Their home was a showcase, and customers began asking for decorating advice, which Billy was glad to give for free. After Hollywood terminated him, there was no guarantee that Haines—and Shields, for despite the nonpublicity they were professional partners as well—would succeed as an interior decorator. That he did was largely thanks to the business of such loyal pals as Marion Davies, Carole Lombard, and Crawford, who then recommended him to their friends.

But in 1936 the men had to weather another homophobic storm—described in detail in *Hollywood Babylon II*. Basically, it was due to the friendly couple giving a neighbor boy of six money to buy some candy or ice cream (or to get lost). Haines and Shields were staying at their beach house at El Porto. The boys' parents asked where he'd obtained the six cents, and that night the father and fellow white trash attacked the two men and their car. The homophobic bullies were gowned in white sheets with eyeholes, for they were members of the White Legion, the Southern California equivalent of the Ku Klux Klan. The cretins even kicked the couple's white poodle, the diminutive Lord Peter Whimsy (sic). (It was rumored that Haines's subsequent aversion to white sheets led him to create the first color-coordinated designer bedsheets for his clients.) Battered and bleeding, the men left town in their egg-and-tomato-splattered auto.

The haters tried to make a legal case of what they imagined to be or hoped was a molestation incident. The parents took their son to the police station to testify, but the case was dismissed, lacking evidence. Some friends in L.A. urged the pair to sue, but the two men preferred to drop the matter entirely, and never returned to that beachside community again.

Thanks to genuine taste, personal popularity, and good

business-sense, the men prospered over the decades. The Haines office and showroom on Sunset Boulevard (in what is now West Hollywood) was a "must" for anyone with big bucks who aspired to tasteful interiors. It was later the headquarters for designer Don Loper (now best remembered from an *I Love Lucy* fashion show episode) and is currently the site of the star-studded Le Dôme restaurant.

Now, as for Gable and Haines, various writers have disagreed about how often "it" happened. As Kenneth Anger said, Billy was "not lip-lazy." Writing of the '20s and '30s, he explained, "Haines loved his boyfriend Jimmy . . . but like most gay men—like most *men*—he liked to play around from time to time." Anger believes Haines serviced Gable "a few" or "several" times; some writers believe it happened but once. The frequency isn't important, really, and wouldn't alter Gable's predominant heterosexuality.

(In 1987 the *New York Post* ran three short articles about revelations in my *Conversations With My Elders*. One was titled "Would You Believe Clark Gay-ble?!" and was based on the story of Gable being serviced by Haines. As ever, the media fixates on all-gay or all-het; had the sexual interlude or interludes at all affected Gable's sexuality, the more realistic headline would have been "Would You Believe Clark Bi-ble?!")

So what happened is, Haines and Cukor stayed good friends and became decorator and client. Cukor's house on Cordell Drive was said to be the finest in Hollywood, and in 1937 Cukor threw an even more than usually memorable party to celebrate the completion of Haines's decorating his home. Less than two years later, Cukor was suddenly fired from *Gone with the Wind*. The typically foggy "creative differences" were cited as an excuse, and later film historians declared it was because Cukor, a noted "women's director" (code for a gay director, yet he guided more actors through Oscar-winning performances than he did actresses),

COUPLES: *William Haines* / 349

had tried to favor Vivien Leigh and Olivia de Havilland over Gable! (Englishman Leslie Howard was never said to utter any such complaint.)

Box office-wise, Gable was aka "the king" of Hollywood. (Third wife Carole Lombard once stated, "If Clark had one inch less, he'd be the queen of Hollywood' instead of the king"—no wonder he was often so cranky; it makes one stop and think about the more obsessively homophobic evangelists and politicians . . . and by all accounts, Bill Haines was the *bigger* of the two men. . . .) Yet his insecurity caused him to resent being directed by Cukor, who knew what Haines knew. Eventually, Gable blew his top and insisted to producer David O. Selznick that he fire "that fag."

Which Selznick did, replacing Cukor with Gable's equally homophobic drinking buddy Victor Fleming. For most of his life, Cukor hid the real reason, out of embarrassment, generally evading discussion of the incident and underplaying his disappointment and fear when it looked like perhaps his career would also be sacrificed to Hollywood homophobia.

It was Cukor biographer Carlos Clarens who first told me the story of the *GWTW* firing. And it was Carlos who in 1972 arranged for me to interview William Haines at his and Shields's beautiful estate on North Rockingham in Brentwood (a few blocks from Shirley Temple's house and also near the *Mommie Dearest* house—decorated by Haines—where Joan Crawford ruled from 1929 to 1959). First, I had to pass a few tests. Mr. Haines asked Carlos to view my driver's license, to prove I was 18. Then I was asked to meet Haines at some friend's house in Pacific Palisades. It was a barbecue, and besides the three of us (not Jimmy, who was visiting an ailing actress friend at the Motion Picture Country House and Hospital in Woodland Hills), there were five or six other guests, including a young woman and Estelle Winwood, who was close to 90 and would live to 101 (and was a future interviewee for a British book of mine).

I was forewarned not to ask "call me Bill" any questions. It was social, and if I made the grade, I'd get to interview the celebrity who was very social but not often prone to do interviews, especially about his first career. Carlos advised me, "It's going to be on tape. See, Billy does want to speak for the record, but nothing that can do him or Jimmy any damage . . . and he wants me to help with some questions and also he'll do it if he can keep the tapes for seven years." I knew nothing was to be published within Haines's *or* Shields's lifetime, but I'd thought Carlos was going to sit in—at least on the first session, if there were more than one—and keep the tapes himself; he was a film scholar, and maybe in time we'd cowrite a book. I didn't realize the tapes (three of them, it turned out) would be kept from me until I was all of 25.

But of course I agreed, and Carlos—he did contribute some questions, on paper—absented himself. Alas, I didn't get to see the famed home in Brentwood, for we met the same week at the same house in Pacific Palisades (the owners were in Europe, I found out). Jimmy Shields, smiling and still boyish like his mate, looked in on us twice. The time flew, we were both pleased, but it was the first and last session. Billy Haines—during the interview he said, "Call me Billy"—died of cancer just before 1974, the year I began (while at UCSB) freelancing for a myriad of periodicals.

Jimmy Shields sent the tapes to Carlos Clarens, who sent them to me in Santa Barbara after Jimmy died. (For some reason, instead of mailing all three at once, he sent two and then the other, but the third one never reached me.)

In 1974 Jimmy Shields took his own life. The suicide note said, "It's no good without Billy." Haines and his other half (not his "boyfriend" . . .) had been together since the early 1920s. Despite the golden era of the silver screen.

Q: Is it true that when Mayer gave you a choice between your career and Jimmy, you asked him whether he would choose between *his* career and Mrs. Mayer?

A: (Smiles.) Not exactly. But he would have picked his career. . . . He asked me to stop living with Jimmy, and then I asked him how he would feel if someone asked him to stop living with his wife.

Q: And did he hesitate?

A: (Smiles.) I think he was shocked. My reason for asking that was to show that that's how much Jimmy meant to me.

Q: It's inaccurate, isn't it, when books say that your acting career was a casualty of talkies?

A: Times were changing rapidly. Some foreign-born stars were hurt, on account of their accents. The things you read about men stars with high-pitched voices losing work, I don't know of one case where that happened.

Q: They say it about John Gilbert, but also about men like Ramon Novarro and you. . . .

A: They *would*. But it's not true. Sound didn't hurt me. I had an accent, on account of my background, but we had voice teachers at the studio. They were always busy dusting us off. Anything rural-sounding was the first to go. But most of the accents they worked the hardest to erase were the Brooklyn accents. Some actresses, it took years!

Q: So many movie stars in the 1930s sounded semi-English.

A: The studios wanted respectability. . . . *Class* (with an English accent).

Q: One of my teachers used to say about class, you either have it, or you belong in one.

A: I'll borrow that. That's where silence was golden—in silent movies it didn't matter what you sounded like.

Q: Joan Crawford wrote a book in the early 1960s, and she

said your and Jimmy Shields's marriage was the best in Hollywood.

A: Joan is a good friend.

Q: **Is it true she proposed to you?**

A: She . . . brought up the subject. I was getting closer to being coerced into a marriage. By the studio. What was fairly commonplace then (in the 1920s) was a husband and a wife who each had the same inclinations (eyebrows rise).

Q: **Both gay.**

A: So I explained that to Joan, and later, when the studio thought I could wait no longer, the publicity had me opposite Pola Negri.

Q: **Lesbian?**

A: Yes. But so very privately. In public, it was always men. When Valentino died, *then* she said she was engaged to him. Pola was very willing, she loved the attention. Some of the ladies who liked other ladies wanted as little to do with that (fake publicity) as possible.

Q: **Such as Garbo? (He nods.) I hear that you not only helped Joan Crawford at work but socially?**

A: I helped her, but so did Eddie Goulding. He was a (gay) director, and I worked with him too. I think at first we felt sorry for Joan. Not everyone accepted her. She was brash and she wanted to make it big, but she had a strong accent and people looked down on her socially. Some made up stories about her past (even prostitution and appearing in a "stag film" that never turned up). I liked her. She was fun, she listened, she liked me and my friends. She would often date my friends, knowing they liked her for herself and not as . . . an experience.

Q: **You also went out with her?**

A: We'd be at the studio by day doing . . . *Sally, Irene and Mary* (1925) with Eddie, then at night we'd go out dancing, and later I'd return home to Jimmy.

Q: Crawford's first two husbands were from socially elevated families. Do you think the marriages were for advancement in Hollywood?

A: She did love the men, but Cranberry has said as much to me. I remember she used to call Douglas (Fairbanks Jr., her first husband) "Dodie," and he called her "Jodie." Joan was older than he was, and she paid for their (Brentwood) house. I had already introduced Joan into social settings that might have been closed to her, but as Mrs. Fairbanks she entered a new cycle of being accepted. However it still took a long spell for (Joan's stepmother-in-law) Mary Pickford to take Cranberry to her bosom.

Q: Joan wanted to get into Pickfair?

A: And how! Mary made her wait. . . .

Q: Is it true you introduced her to her second husband, Franchot Tone?

A: No, false. But I did tell him not to talk nasty about Joan in my presence. At a party. At Tallulah's house or Bette Davis's—they were all convinced he and Bette were like *that* (having an affair). I think they were doing some film together (*Dangerous*, 1935, which won Davis her first Oscar). Seems like everyone cheated on everyone when they were doing a film and had love scenes.

Q: An actor and an actress?

A: That's the combination that dared to do it.

Q: An actor who liked men had to go beyond the acting community for satisfaction?

A: Because of anonymity. If the studio got wind of an actor and actress committing adultery, they'd disapprove, but they would see that it didn't get into the papers. If it did, it would be in a blind item.

Q: But if an actor was even known as gay, then what?

A: Then his future was open to discussion. Or the whim of whoever ran the studio. . . . There were blind items about me, and about me and Jimmy. Too many blind items, and the studio would panic.

Q: **Is it true you later had to introduce Jimmy as your "secretary"?**

A: It sounds funny now, but in those days most secretaries—and the really important ones, the executive secretaries—they were men.

Q: **Yes. But I meant having to disguise his relationship to you.**

A: Words . . . that was important. Not to ordinary, everyday people, but the Hollywood watchdogs. I remember after I was out of the movies, a guest told us at a party how the censor had gone and decreed that in the new Frankenstein picture, the monster couldn't use the word "mate." That would imply marriage, which certainly implies sex. So somebody at the studio said they'd say "companion" instead. Then they watered it down some more, and said "friend," but the studio decided to call the whole movie *The* Bride *of Frankenstein*, so that brought marriage and sex right back into the picture, monster and all!

Q: **What do you think brought on that extra-repressive censorship?**

A: The Depression, of course. When people started escaping from Hitler's Germany and coming to Hollywood about that time, they told us how it all began there after the war (WWI), with their own depression. Times were so tough, and people want scapegoats at times like that.

Q: **And they listen to the crackpots more at such times.**

A: The same in Italy. Mussolini got in when they were real poor. So times were tough, and during the Depression leading men had to be more tough. My type was going out the window. Not only I was too old, but the college boy was too soft and pampered for the '30s. Very few men went to college in the '20s. Fewer went in the '30s. Audiences wanted real tough guys.

Q: **Dramas and musical fantasies. Gangster movies were popular, weren't they? And actors—or personalities—like Clark Gable?**

A: (Smiles briefly.) So when sound came in, plenty more things changed than just adding voices. I was in the movies a total of about 12 years, but the cycles went more quickly then. So by the early 1930s my cycle was ending.

Q: **Is that why when your arrest occurred—which shouldn't have occurred—the studio didn't bail you out?**

A: They blacklisted me, is what they did. Mayer, who was lower than a kneeling bedbug.

Q: **People keep saying that about ten years later, the same thing occurred to another gay star at MGM, but they bailed him out because his movies were still making money for them.**

A: This . . . actor, he had—he has (a warning finger)—the same initials as one of the celebrations of the end of the war (as in V.J. Day). He'd risen up fairly recently, and it was World War II, when most of the men stars were away at war. So the studio had a number of reasons to keep the guy in clover, making honey for 'em.

Q: **I have a rumor that perhaps you can confirm.**

A: If it's a Metro rumor, possibly I can.

Q: **It is. They say Lionel Barrymore fancied the lads, and one of them was Clark Gable (he frowns slightly). I believe Gable, very early on, was often referred to as Barrymore's *protégé* (which means "protected one" in French). It's said Barrymore secured Gable his first screen test. . . .**

A: Very possible.

Q: **And it's said that Gable allowed Barrymore to . . .**

sample his wares. Or ware.

A: (Huge grin.) *Quite* possible.

Q: **Is it true Gable wore dentures?**

A: That is true and no doubt verifiable from some dentist's records. Unless the studio got hold of those too. Gable had all his teeth pulled, and a movie set made.

Q: **Vivien Leigh complained that during their *Gone with the Wind* kissing scenes, the dentures gave him terrible breath.**

A: Miss Leigh was a great actress.

Q: **With movies, it's what you *see* that counts.**

A: That is *all* that counts, my boy.

Q: **You know, since Gable was, to some extent, involved the way he was with men, what made him so anti-gay later on?**

A: You *are* young. . . . That can be a portion of the man's self-cover, if he's so adamant against it. But Gable got in with an unkind set of men who liked to drink a lot and bitch a lot. And they liked to hunt and to tell dirty stories, mostly about women.

Q: **Is it true Gable was against hiring women writers because then he couldn't tell his dirty stories in front of them?**

A: He got around that, one time I heard tell of, by giving his blessing to a lady scriptwriter who told dirty stories herself. I don't know how much of a *lady* she was. . . .

Q: **Were Gable's pals—all conservative, I've heard—mostly non-actors?**

A: You mean like himself? (Smiles.) I don't know if he had any actor friends. I think he thought acting was "sissy."

Q: **For every actor except himself?**

A: His set was directors, writers, and hunters. Oh, and they liked cars. A lot.

Q: Some cars are substitute phallic symbols.

A: Well, the Jaguar is. . . . Gable and his cronies hated everyone, not just men who hankered for men.

Q: Anti-Semitic? (He nods.) Who else?

A: Well, the whole East Asia set. He hated "Chinks" and "Japs" and "Gooks." When Pearl Harbor came along, he was practically the first to sign up. Went around saying he wanted to kill Japs.

Q: Is this story true? When Pearl Harbor was attacked, Joan Crawford was on the set, knitting (he laughs). And somebody ran in, yelling, "The Japanese have destroyed Pearl Harbor!" and Joan supposedly said, "Oh, dear. Who was she?"

A: (Laughs.) The knitting's true as could be, and Joan probably didn't even look up to ask the question, *if* she asked it. That's very clever—I should ask her if she said it.

Q: Then, after the war, Gable was involved in the witch hunts?

A: He was of that faction. Name on committees, in there with DeMille and . . . Wayne, Ward Bond, . . . Ginger Rogers and mother, Robert Taylor, Adolph Menjou, let's see . . . Charles Coburn, Robert Montgomery (father of liberal and pro-gay Elizabeth Montgomery of *Bewitched*), Gary Cooper. . . .

Q: And our ex-actor governor (Ronald Reagan)? (He nods.) And certain directors and writers, and most studio heads. Didn't Gable come between you and Carole Lombard?

A: Carole and I were very good friends. All through—it's just . . . you *can* not see someone as often as before and still stay friends.

Q: She was the one who helped launch you as a decorator?

A: I did her house for her. Color, lots of it, and to match her personality, to highlight her. I knew people would see what I did with her house, and if they liked it, we were *on*.

Q: And you didn't charge her. (Bows his head.) You were
     very close, but in 1939 she married Gable, and he didn't
     like her gay friends. . . .

A: When she married him—after they'd known each other for
     some time—she let him pattern her life. They moved and it
     was . . . dogs and hunting, loads of outdoorsiness, and
     Clark's hairy friends.

Q: What about Irving Thalberg?

A: We were friends. I'd go out with them, sometimes a four-
     some with some girl he asked along. But I'd gone out with
     Norma (Shearer, the MGM star whom Thalberg married)
     when she was single. She used to see particular actors she
     liked, but . . . not in public. In public, I'd go out with her . . .
     mid-1920s, that time.

Q: Didn't Thalberg try and help you and other actors who
     were punished by Mayer for being gay?

A: He . . . interceded—of course while he was alive . . . so sad,
     so terrible his passing for everyone, except Mayer and his
     personal skunks—he tried to help. I did have some very
     good and loyal friends, Irving was one of them. But (pub-
     licity chief) Howard Strickling and Mayer got busy trying
     to clamp down on *us*, about the same time ('33) the other
     skunks were pushing through the tougher new (censorship)
     Code (which took effect in July, 1934). Irving was having
     health problems, he and Norma went on a long vacation,
     and some of the dastardly work got done while he was gone.

     When he was there, and in good health, he could help to
     counter-effect some of that. There were these blind items
     I've referred to, and not just about me, about Novarro, . . .
     Nils Asther, I think, others, not just at Metro, but each stu-
     dio. And this was *before* 1933 and the arrest, and I was called
     on the carpet. I had to account to Strickling, to a few oth-
     ers, and to the grand poobah—Mayer. Irving did speak up

on my behalf, and so did Marion Davies. She had some say-so because of her link to (her married lover) William Randolph Hearst, who was . . . associated with Mayer. So their intercession—Irving and Marion—may have saved me from an earlier . . . end to all that.

Q: **Someone who used to go to Hearst parties at San Simeon said that Hearst—it was his policy—and Marion Davies used never to invite unmarried heterosexual couples or lovers—even if they were single and available—to week-end at Hearst Castle!**

A: I never heard it voiced, but I saw it practiced. The men and the women had to be "legal," or drive back the same day.

Q: **Hypocrisy, thy name is Hollywood.**

A: It's that all right, and a taste level that. . . . Alva Johnson said that a press agent in the movie capital who worried about taste was as miscast as a soldier who hates violence.

Q: **So Hearst Castle, on a weekend, was one place where a gay pair of lovers might have more fun than a "straight" pair who wasn't married.**

A: Old W.R. never saw the jest in that.

Q: **On the other hand, a gay pair, or a lesbian pair, never had the choice to make it legal or, quote-unquote, respectable.**

A: (Sighs while smiling.) I don't talk freely about my long, long past cinema career. It was about a dozen years, and no one remembers it now. But I am gratified that you're interested, and about what happened. I mentally let go of those bad episodes long ago—as much as I could. More for Jimmy's sake.

Q: **You both had to live through a lot of awful times and—**

A: Crap. But we had each other, and we have each other.

Q: **You were lucky to survive. Some didn't.**

A: There were situations similar to ours, and an unknown quantity of actors didn't survive the scandals and the firings.

Then, in the McCarthy period, more of the same. Most of it political, but not all. And suicides. People Jimmy and I knew. Or people not permitted to earn a living. There has been more than one blacklist in this business—the rewards are great here, but so are the pitfalls and the punishments.

Q: **Couldn't you have screamed bloody murder? Or done something?**

A: In those times, if one screamed, one was silenced. You either didn't hear the scream—others wouldn't hear it, like the tree falling in the forest—or you were shut out. Contained. Segregated. Just made into a pariah. There were scandals among the straight set, high and low, in front of the camera and in the executive offices . . . and I could have spilled the beans. But who would print it? Who would put it on radio? Even if they had, I'd then have been frozen out of the picture business, and most other businesses besides.

   The fact is, if I'd been on my own, who knows? Things did enter my head . . . I felt like taking reprisals. But I didn't dare do anything rash. Not just for me—and I had good contacts, good friends, I *hoped* I could continue to earn a living without leaving California. But you see, I had Jimmy. Anything rash would probably have backfired on me and, more importantly, on him. When you're not on your own, you have to consider the other person. You have to be responsible to him too.

Q: **But it was all so unfair—so illegal, so unconstitutional, etc.**

A: My boy, the laws, the . . . even the Constitution, it only means what the not-so-honorable gentlemen in charge want it to mean.

Q: **Is it true there was a gay brothel that male stars used to visit?**

A: There were *brothels*. There was one for men . . . got closed down, with Mayer's conniving.

Q: **Was it more difficult for a gay star than a lesbian star?**

A: I'd say there was more fun for the men. But it was more dangerous, professionally. I've never known about any brothel for the sapphic set. They always catered to men, just men. . . . We *all* went on studio "dates." But I think, in their 20s, there was more of an urgency for an actress to find a husband. They could stall by saying that having a career didn't leave enough time for romance or searching out a husband, and the studio skunks liked that reasoning better than having an actress of easy virtue on their hands.

Q: **One who slept with more than one male?**

A: Or one, if she wasn't married to him.

Q: **What about bisexuality?**

A: Don't you have any small questions? (Smiles.) If you're getting at, has William Haines tried women, yes. A few times, and I acquitted myself honorably. I was able to perform, but it wasn't something I ever craved, and I can understand why sometimes the . . . heterosexual is impotent. He may or may not be doing what he craves. Or with a woman that he craves. Homosexuals are never impotent—two doctors have made that known to me.

Q: **Is that because gay men are doing what they like, sexually?**

A: There you go. If a man *wants* another man, then he's doing what he desires and craves to do, whether it's allowed or not, and he'll perform out of sexual desire, not duty or pressure or. . . what he's been ordered to do.

Q: **Whereas a gay man with a woman. . . .**

A: Is doing what he thinks he should do.

Q: *If* **he buys the line that there's only one way, which there isn't.**

A: He might be able to function with her, depending how she looks, depending what he's thinking of—if his mind can really take hold of another man he craves, or some . . . act or image he craves, then he can do it. You asked about lesbian stars. Well, in regards to lesbians—never mind the star part—they, like other women, don't have to show proof of desire, if they're doing it with a man. A man, any man, if he's with a woman, has to *show* proof . . . do you catch on?

Q: **One can't fake an erection.**

A: You're learning fast. (Laughs.) You ask who has it easier? No one has it easy, not really.

Q: **Perhaps not, but the sexual minority group has it the toughest.**

A: This, I know. . . . It comes back—Thalberg. Let's finish this sordid episode about . . . with Mayer. I was sent to jail, but Mayer saw to it, and not for *my* sake—for *business*—that I didn't have to go to court. That would have made the papers. And to fire me, within the law, he invoked the "morals clause" in an actor's contract with the studio—

Q: **Which it's amazing no one has legally challenged as unconstitutional, don't you think?**

A: It doesn't amaze me because the person or people who came up with that clause knew to a *hair* what they were doing. If anyone speaks against that clause, people will want to know why—"What has he done?" No one wants to be seen to be outside of the morals of society.

Q: **But *words* have to be questioned. What does "morals" mean? *Whose?* And they have to be revised and updated— this isn't the Old or New Testament time when a woman could be stoned to death for cheating on her husband, while the husband who cheated just got a pat on the back.**

A: Or a second wife? (Grins.)

Q: **But someone has to challenge such nonsense, legally or otherwise.**

A: If a man challenged it, and he wasn't pregnant and he wasn't married—so he couldn't be accused of adultery—then people would ask why he was challenging it. . . .

Q: **And, as long as his career was being ended, he would say he was being fired and blacklisted simply because he was gay—and actors do act; gay actors do portray heterosexuals—and that that isn't right, fair, or legal.**

A: You forgot constitutional.

Q: **So if the studio's going to get away with ruining his career—*and* his future prospects—the least he should get out of them is a financial settlement. Preferably generous.**

A: No one ever did that. No one was open. Who's to say some private blackmail didn't take place, but. . . .

Q: **If it had been done publicly, that could have helped those who followed.**

A: (Shrugs.) No one did that.

Q: **So one just slinks away, tail between their legs . . . ? I mean *today*. If this happened today, don't you think it should be different?**

A: It *should* be . . . and maybe someday it will. You know what I think? I think when an actor gets *inside* the business, it gets inside of him. The pretense and the rules—wrong though they may be—he accepts them, and it becomes part of his own code.

Q: **Even if it hurts him, and all those like him?**

A: (Shrugs, bigger.) That's Hollywood.

Q: **That's lousy.**

A: (Cheerily.) Let's decorate!

Q: **Hmm?**

A: I've spent far more time, and more happy times, doing interiors than doing pictures. Go ahead. . . .

Q: **Ah. Joan Crawford.**

A: She wanted to improve herself. She wanted culture and

beauty. I did her home in Empire and white moderne. She
liked a formal look. Carole was less formal, and she liked
color. Everyone's different, and that was part of the challenge—to create a setting that reflected and enhanced the . . .
propriétaire (giggles). This may interest you more, but Joan
dated scads of gay men when she wasn't married. I think she
may have dated more of them than the sort that wanted to
take her to bed.

Q: **Don't you think a lot of heterosexual men would *not*
want to take her to bed?**

A: You mean . . . she's a little frightening to some men?

Q: **The ones who think women are the softer sex.**

A: (Laughs.) I'll have to think twice before letting her in on
that one. . . . She's always been tight with Cesar Romero—
nice guy—and whenever a handsome new star came along
and Cranberry wasn't maritally engaged, she'd try and date
him. To show her interest in the up-and-comers and to be
seen with a handsome, important face.

Q: **Like who?**

A: . . . George Nader. *That* was a dish! And his best buddy, Rock
Hudson. She said she thought that Rock thought she was too
old for him to be seen with. George had better manners.
(Hudson reportedly left most of his estate to Nader and
Nader's mate; according to *People, Confidential* outed George
in the '50s in Rock's place—both were contracted to
Universal—thus ruining his American career; he then
enjoyed screen success in Germany. . . .)

Q: **Why would a Hudson or a Nader agree to go out with
Joan Crawford?**

A: Why else? *Publicity!*

Q: **I keep forgetting: in Hollywood, that's almost everything. I suppose some heterosexual actors with no sexual interest in her would also go out with her . . . to be
seen?**

A: You're catching on, my boy (pats my knee).

Q: **And, uh, with all these platonic dates, was Joan doing anything for fun, or . . . ?**

A: All my friends love a good time. Joan had her private diversions—sometimes they were already married. (Finger to lips.)

Q: **. . . Here's a quote. You said, "When Mayer gave me a choice between my career and Jimmy, I didn't hesitate. I don't have to hide and lie any longer. Having my freedom means more to me than becoming a myth." (He smiles widely.) That's a wonderful quote, and it is a brave attitude.**

A: I wouldn't have given up Jimmy. But even if I'd been on my own, it wouldn't have been worth it. How many decades of staying one jump ahead of trouble, or trying to cover up day and night, night and day . . . and for what? So some perfect stranger can inform me that they saw one of my films on television the other day?

Q: **It takes a toll.**

A: Every day of your life, it takes a toll. Thanks, but no thanks.

Q: **There's another side to it. In your work now, you get to express yourself—**

A: And my clients.

Q: **Your clients, through your eyes and your taste. But as an actor, all you played were roles that . . . were alien to you.**

A: There wasn't any choice, then. In a way, it was a challenge, almost fun, to see if I could carry off the masquerade. When I did, it sort of enlarged my ego—and made me laugh.

Q: **You say that was "almost fun," but I'll bet interior decorating *is* fun.**

A: It really is. Every new job is all new. A *fun* challenge. Are you interested in the field?

Q: I like décor and styles, but I think I like architecture more.

A: Do you like mathematics?

Q: Not much. I'm not bad at it, but to work with it daily. . . . Ugh!

A: How about acting?

Q: You obviously won't mind my saying that I think movies were more interesting in the old days. I see so little one would want to play today. It would just be for money. Not much fun.

A: In the long run, it's what you enjoy that matters. Do that.

Q: Thank you. . . . Is it true you were almost engaged to Thalberg's sister?

A: (Laughs.) Good night! Who said that? Not at all. But I was, it was my understanding that I was, her unofficial escort. Irving had some other escorts for her. . . . Oh! I altogether forgot, and this is very important about Irving Thalberg. After the . . . the 1933 arrest, he could easily have turned his back on me. Jimmy and I had a party—I was, we were, celebrating the success of our new venture. Irving and Norma attended. And what Irving and Norma did, all of Hollywood knew about. It was like a royal blessing.

Q: A question: how did Mayer get to cover up so many things?

A: Company town. Corrupt cops, corrupt D.A.'s or assistant D.A.'s, people in high places, informants, the newspapers, of course—the press was the easiest to control, and the biggest columnists owed everything to their cooperation and conniving with Mayer and all the other studio skunks.

Q: No wonder people could be frozen out so easily. Were you ever called a male flapper?

A: (Smiles.) I was called lots of things . . . "oldest living college boy." "The big lug"—being over six feet. A "pretty-boy"—I never thought I was so pretty!

Q: You've aged very well.

A: Aren't you a dear. . . . I had a friend, passed away recently, who said George (Cukor) used to call Clark "dear" on the set. I can't feature it. George might've called some other actors "dear," but not that weasel. George knew which side his bread was buttered on.

Q: **Actors are sometimes represented as dumber than they are, but is this true? Gable was introduced to William Faulkner (who was doing a screenplay), and he didn't know who Faulkner was?**

A: That, my dear, is entirely possible. An eyewitness to their meeting said that they shook hands, then Clark asked, "What do you do, Mr. Faulkner?" Faulkner said, "I write. And what do *you* do, Mr. Gable?"

Q: **Fabulous.**

A: Most actors don't read. Except scripts.

Q: **What other actors hired you to redecorate their homes? Your big three were Lombard, Crawford, and Davies.**

A: Cranberry also invested in our business, when we had to hire. But, yes, there were . . . there was the Mocambo, Jack and Ann Warner, Claudette Colbert, Lionel Barrymore, George Cukor, the list goes on . . . the Annenbergs' house near Palm Springs, and thanks to that, Ambassador Annenberg's residence in England. It doesn't end, and we get to work as much as we want.

Q: **As a decorator, you're familiar with closets. . . .**

A: And *you* (pointing forefinger) want to know . . . a little—I hope—about the more recent sort of closet, is that right?

Q: **It's not recent, but that name for it is. What surprises me is that so many areas, including the ones people assume to have gays in them, are and stay closeted. *Fashion* designers . . . I *mean*!**

A: Money. (Rubs fingers and thumb.) That's why. Greed,

insecurity, but some people don't want to chance losing *a* customer. I know interior designers—decorators—who are homosexual, but they pretend not. In order not to lose, possibly lose, that sort of client. But with us—well, because it is *us*, we're a *couple*—it's harder to pretend, if we even wanted to. On top of which, my life story, and my travails, are fairly well-known.

Q: **It's as if gays don't allow themselves any profession to be open in.**

A: It's not that they're so brainless they think clients will be shocked to meet a gay fashion designer or interior decorator. It's the greed—that they think a client might be offended to meet someone homosexual, so to prevent losing any clients, they pretend the opposite.

Q: **Never thinking they might lose gay clients that way?**

A: No.

Q: **And do they really fool anyone?**

A: A gay actor can . . . whether a gay designer does (shrugs)? There is a . . . couturier who's been in America some time (from France—name: Mainbocher). When he designs for a particular actress, she pretends he's straight.

Q: **What, she's embarrassed on his behalf?**

A: He does go along with it, he likes that image. It means success to him. But the reason *she* does it is her own camouflage. She's not straight, either (Mary Martin).

Q: **One closeted individual closets another . . . ?**

A: In show business, some of the worst (smiles) "closeters"—of other people—are those who are themselves in the closet.

Q: **. . . As in misery loves company?**

A: They're not so miserable. Just paranoid. Some gays don't want to publicly admit they know anyone who's homosexual. Pandora's box—you know that story?

Q: **I've grown up reading all kinds of mythology, from**

ancient Egyptian, Greek, Judeo-Christian through to Viking, Aztec, you name it. But I understand what you're saying. These people don't even want the topic to come up. I guess they're that terrified.

Q: It's why most would never play a homosexual role.

Q: **Too close to home?**

A: If the subject was brought up in an interview, they might blush or get nervous or . . . lactate. One exception: Barbara Stanwyck did play a sapphic lady (in *Walk on the Wild Side*, 1961), and I think she was the first in Hollywood to do that. Everyone was agog.

Q: **And then she did *The Big Valley*.**

A: She was made for Westerns. With *Stella Dallas*, watching it now, half of me wants to cry and half of me wants to titter.

Q: **But do you think knowing that a performer is different in reality from the character portrayed should affect a viewer's perception of the performance, if it's well-done?**

A: It shouldn't. It does, sometimes. But finally I have to laugh at the hypocrisy. So much for Stanwyck and those ladies. Her deportment in private—at parties and places—always reminded me of a young man in need of finishing school.

Q: **When Cukor was fired from *Gone with the Wind*, did you imagine that that might be the end of his career in film?**

A: We held our breaths. Part of the time. No one knew which way it would go. But as Jimmy said, the man's not an actor, they can't discard him so easily. There wouldn't be the same excuse as for an actor; it is a half-valid excuse. . . .

Q: **It's half-assed. Please go on.**

A: I knew one thing. George can get very upset when he's upset. And George can be litigious. He'd gone to court in the earlier part of the '30s when he felt he wasn't getting his due, and long after the *(GWTW)* debacle, he told me he'd have gone to court if they'd tried to freeze him out. I think Metro

gave him *The Women* (1939) as a consolation prize, and that
was a plum.

Q: **And he's had this long, glittering career. Maybe it's the
ones prepared to scream, when they have to, who survive. . . .**

A: (Shrugs.) He's a survivor, is George, and when need be, he's
a screamer.

Q: **Someone recently said that the reason Tyrone Power got
rather bloated-looking toward the end was drugs or med-
ication. Was he an unhappy man?**

A: *That* was a "pretty-boy." If he was unhappy about it when
he was young, then he was a fool. Looks like that are to be
enjoyed. He did get more and more shopworn, worn down
by care. Why he got puffy, I have no idea. My guess is food.
He was some dish, but he was making himself into a tureen.

Q: **He and Cesar Romero were lovers? (Nods.) One guy
married more than once, had kids more than once, the
other didn't—and didn't. Why, other than one was a star
and one was a—**

A: "Featured player." That's what they used to say. Why?
(Shrugs, smiles.) Why is one guy different from the next
one? Why are some persons more compulsive? . . . I didn't
finish the thread of a thought, earlier. I was telling you that
in her 20s many an actress was nagged toward finding a husband. In their 20s, the actors, not so much. The studios didn't
want an actor marrying too young—business reasons. But
in his 30s, that's when the skunks narrowed in on any
unmarried actors, and gave them the works. Then they forgot about the actresses and zeroed in on us actors and
nagged us full-time. I'm well out of that rat's nest! (Laughs.)

Q: **Cary Grant is another compulsive type, wouldn't you
say?**

A: Phoney-baloney. *Boring.* Cheap—his only decorator is Hap

Hazard. . . . Frank Sinatra used to call him "Mother Cary" on the set of one of their movies—they must have done *one*.

Q: **Is he bigoted?**

A: Not spectacularly, that it shows, but . . . I've . . . learned a few things. (Elizabeth Taylor was turned down by Sinatra when she asked him to participate in Hollywood's first major AIDS fund-raiser.)

Q: **Do you agree with this quote? "Fashion is what one wears oneself. What is unfashionable is what other people wear."**

A: Good night! (Laughs.) Half my clients could have said that! Who said it?

Q: **Oscar Wilde.**

A: The old darling! Half my clients would say that about other people's interiors (shakes head).

Q: **Why do you think a few men get into fashion design and others into interior design? How different are they from each other?**

A: Oh, I couldn't have gone into fashion design. It's all personal taste, I'd have to say. And I'm not bragging. I just would have been bored silly, working with women's clothes. I like beautiful objects and the blending and contrasting of colors, but . . . I'll say this anyway, I happen to think it's true: I think most of the men who design clothes for women are designing what *they'd* like to wear . . . but whether they'd want to be women, I don't know.

Q: **You've done Danny Kaye's house?**

A: Boy, you nearly gave me a coronary, the way you started to phrase that! (Laughs.) I did decorate his and Sylvia Fine Kaye's house. They have good taste. He's the one who loves to say, "I have a Fine head on my shoulders!"

Q: **I know Danny Kaye played Hans Christian Andersen as a heterosexual, which he wasn't, in the movie musical.**

My mother called Samuel Goldwyn to get permission to show it at Campbell Hall at UCSB. What about Kaye himself?

A: (Pause.) You asked . . . so I'll just say what I think, that he's the most repressed innate homosexual I ever met. Do not ask me if he's been with this one or that one, I have no idea if he's ever done it. But it's *there*, in *him*.

Q: **Other people will often take it upon themselves to say, "Oh, he's not gay," or, "He couldn't be gay." How could they know that?**

A: They might . . . if they're with him 24 hours a day—and if they can read his thoughts and fantasies.

Q: **Or the wife of a man who's gay or bisexual will totally insist that he's not. . . .**

A: Public relations. Sometimes *pubic* relations. . . . She either lies, or she tells a half-truth: possibly he does do it with her. But not just with her. . . .

Q: **I think women who marry men who aren't heterosexual worry that if the public knows, then they'll wonder about the wife. . . .**

A: Or they feel, even if he's gone to his reward or his just desserts, that they're keeping up his reputation by denying everything. Chances are, if you leave anyone behind—anyone besides my Jimmy—they are going to deny, deny, deny. All innocent-like. (Grins.) But everyone's an actor, and when you're an entertainer, you have to be an actor in that other way, if it applies: you have to act, and act like you believe it—*all* the time, in public—as if you're not gay.

Q: **And it is easy to fool the public, isn't it?**

A: It is. They *want* to be fooled. But you have to keep fooling them . . . it's tiresome. You have to act in your career, and *for* your career.

Q: **Even non-actors. What do you think of Liberace?**

A: Because he's gay or he's an eyesore? Did you catch him in hot pants last year? Everywhere I turned, there he was, same photo, over and over. (The most widely run wire-service transmission ever to come out of Las Vegas was a 1971 photo of Liberace in hot pants at Caesars (sic) Palace.) The man has taste-minus.

Q: **His taste in home décor is pretty amazing too.**

A: You call that décor? I call it Early Everything.

Q: **He's never asked you to decorate for him.**

A: I'd have to start with a bulldozer, dear.

Q: **Someone that obvious, why doesn't he come out of the closet?**

A: I guess he's too fucking busy. And too busy fucking. Some of the last ones who would ever come out *are* the most obvious ones.

Q: **Sometimes extreme wealth is a camouflage—as with Howard Hughes?**

A: He had another camouflage—all the actresses he put under contract or was seen with. I think he was sexually . . . varied.

Q: **One hard-to-picture alleged romance was with Katharine Hepburn. . . .**

A: (Chuckles.) A few times that I know about, Hughes had all-male parties. Which some columnist would report as a "stag party." Cary Grant was at one or two of those. . . . But Howard and Kate? They may have gone out—which was all the press needed. But I do know Howard would often fly to the location of George's (Cukor) *Sylvia Scarlett* to see Cary. In Malibu, I think. Whether Howard used Kate as a "beard," or she used him, I haven't a clue. But he went there to be with Cary. Brian Aherne was also in that picture, and he said so too. Brian likes women. Maybe it was a quota situation, and they needed to hire *one* heterosexual. . . .

Q: **Do you agree with this? Someone refuses to say that a certain actor is gay because it might "harm" him. Yet that's the attitude that perpetuates the vicious circle. What do you think?**

A: It is a vicious circle, and if no one challenges the belief that something's bad or harmful, then it stays that way. But with gays, I couldn't expect the others—the heterosexuals—to change or think any different, or even begin to, unless we do. It's up to us. They take their cues from us, from how we feel about ourselves, and what we're willing to put up with.

Q: **It's changing already.**

A: But how fast it goes, that depends on us.

Q: **On breaking the vicious circle.**

A: One of our more famous houseguests recently said to us—I don't know why he said it to *us*—"A closet is a vertical coffin." Where he got it, or if he came up with it himself, I don't know. Sounds good, though.

Q: **Who said that to you?**

A: (Chuckles.) Oh, he's an old Hollywood friend: *Anonymous.*

Q: **So he knows whereof he speaks.**

A: He knows. His closet's a big one, rich and well-appointed. But I wouldn't want to live there, and neither would Jimmy.

EPILOGUE

After publication of my collection of quotes, *Hollywood Babble On*, I received a nonfan letter asking why I was "so obsessed with homosexual stars."

I was unable to answer her, as there was no return address. Had I chosen to do so, I could have mentioned some of the following points:

- When I did a book about *Hispanic Hollywood*, the first on another long-overlooked subject, no one wrote to ask why I was "so obsessed" with Hispanic or Latin stars. I wonder why. . . .
- *Hollywood Babble On* comprises some 1,500 quotes, each uttered by one star about another star. So if she didn't like a quote noting that Tyrone Power was bisexual—he was indeed bi or gay, not heterosexual, despite some people's obsession with heterosexuality—don't blame me. Blame the star who

knew him personally.

- Since that book, out of eight chapters, has *one* about stars who were/are b.l.g. (David Lewis's useful acronym for bi/lesbian/gay), the person focusing on the non-heterosexual stars wasn't this editor, but the discomfitted reader. . . .

- I can understand that the average Ms. Bookbuyer or Moviegoer might be disappointed if her favorite male icon turns out to be gay. (As for being disappointed if the guy is bi, that can only be due to homophobia.) But don't get mad at the truth. Or if you do, expect a little of it to come back your way:

    I gifted an Englishwoman friend with a copy of *Conversations With My Elders*, and her primary response after reading it was *such* disappointment—via the Sal Mineo chapter—that James Dean had been bisexual. My response to her was a smiling shrug. What I felt like saying was, "First of all, he's dead. But even if he weren't, do you think you'd ever have had a chance with him? If and when he went to bed with 'the opposite sex', it would have been with someone of Hollywood physical standards. . . ."

- Most people corresponding to the sexual norm may equate gay invisibility—practiced by the media and by closeted gays—with the mistaken notion that there are very few gay people, or that one can always "tell" them. But show business happens to be one of the fields with a higher percentage than usual of gay people, especially men. So why act indignant when it turns out more than one or two stars were gay? The word for that is bigotry.

    Off the top of my head, I could recite a list of ten "golden age" stars who were gay, or ten today who are. If I did, some people would say I was "obsessed" or exaggerating. Yet if I recited a list of 25 past stars who were heterosexual, or 25 today who are, that would elicit either no reaction, no challenge (some stars hide their non-heterosexuality *very* well), or even smugness.

- Why does it threaten some people that everyone isn't alike? Diversity is the most obvious fact of nature, including human nature. Some people insist on asking, about the minority, why they're that way, what "causes" the difference? Studies have been needlessly done to determine what causes left-handedness. Whatever causes some humans to be left-handed is what causes the others to be right-handed; it's called nature.

    And what insecurity or obsessive need for control causes so many members of majority groups to feel the need for 100 percent? Heterosexuals are a reported—if one doesn't count bisexuality—90 percent, yet the more phobic ones never seem happy unless under the delusion that at least 99 percent of people are like them. It's rather like the male chauvinist who, back when India and the UK had female prime ministers, threw up his hands and muttered, "The women are taking over the world." Two nations out of more than 150, and females were supposedly eclipsing the male of the species! (Like they could do any worse a job than the patriarchy has. . . .)

- A reviewer of one of my gay-themed books wrote something that this nonfan might have: that it's "a gay fantasy" that all stars are secretly gay. What baloney! On the contrary, it's a "straight" fantasy that in all show biz, only the likes of Liberace or Boy George (and possibly Richard Simmons—or is he just extremely cheerful?) are gay. Do a book about six or ten gay stars, and the threatened type of reader or reviewer feels like you're declaring that all Hollywood is gay, all the world's gay. Never mind that they'll turn around and pretend that only the most obvious stereotypes are gay or lesbian. Of course, that the average heterosexual is even able to believe that she or he has never met somebody homosexual or bisexual is finally due to the cooperative invisibility of the vast majority of non-heterosexuals. However, that is changing.

Someday—sooner or later—very few fantasists will be able to deny the truth: that there is *nobody*, not one individual on this planet, who doesn't have a gay or lesbian relative, friend, coworker, and/or role model or favorite Hollywood star.

INDEX